Values and Norms in Sport

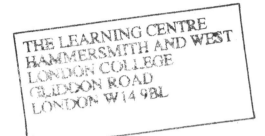

Johan Steenbergen/Paul De Knop/Agnes Elling (eds.)

Values and Norms
in Sport

Critical Reflections on the Position and Meanings of Sport in Society

Meyer & Meyer Sport

British Library Cataloguing in Publication Data
A catalogue record for this book is available from the British Library

Values and Norms in Sport
Johan Steenbergen/Paul De Knop/Agnes Elling (eds.)
ISBN 978-1-84126-057-0

© 2001 by Meyer & Meyer Sport (UK) Ltd.
Aachen, Adelaide, Auckland, Budapest, Cape Town, Graz, Indianapolis,
Maidenhead, New York, Olten (CH), Singapore, Toronto
Member of the World
Sport Publishers' Association (WSPA)
www.w-s-p-a.org
Printed and bound by: CPI Wöhrmann Print Service
ISBN: 978-1-84126-057-0
E-Mail: verlag@m-m-sports.com
www.m-m-sports.com

CONTENTS

CONTRIBUTORS

Dr. **Anton Anthonissen** is a social-cultural scholar and researcher, at Utrecht School of Governance (Utrecht University), focusing on the management of (sport) organisations. He explores managerial actions in voluntary sports associations, the structure of the Dutch sports sector and issues of gender and ethnicity in leadership. His current research focuses on relationship and responsibility in processes of multi-culturalism in (sports) organisations.

Paul Baar studied Sport, Human Movement & Health at the Department of Educational Sciences at Utrecht University, with a special interest for youth sport withdrawal. Since his graduation in 1991, he is a lecturer at this department and gives courses on (sport)pedagogical themes and research methodology.

Annemarie ten Boom is policy advisor at the Dutch Sport Federation and Olympic Committee, NOC*NSF, and coordinated the research programme Values and Norms in Sport (II). She also developed the Dutch policy against sexual harassment in sport and coordinates various research projects, for instance sport clubs monitoring

Dr. **Gert Biesta** is senior lecturer in the School of Education of the University of Exeter, UK, and editor-in-chief of 'Studies in Philosophy and Education'. His research interests include the role of communication in education, moral and political education.

Dr. **Jan Boessenkool** is an organizational anthropologist and an experienced researcher in the area of sport (Utrecht School of Governance, Utrecht University). He is also involved in international sport research (e.g., in South Africa). His research focuses mainly on the organization and management of sport clubs and the relations of sport clubs with other stakeholders like sport federations and (local) government.

Albert Buisman is senior lecturer in the Department of Educational Sciences, at Utrecht University. His research interests include youth sports, values and norms in sport and fair play in sport. He published several articles and books on youth sport, fair play and sport pedagogy. He was chair of the first 'Values and Norms research programme' (1993-1998).

Evelien Dirks graduated from the Free University Amsterdam in 2000 (developmental psychology). Interests include developmental psychology, psychopathology, emotional development, moral development and problem behavior.

Agnes Elling is currently working as a researcher and writing her thesis at the department of Leisure Studies at Tilburg University. She is secretary of the 'Values and Norms research programme'. She has been involved in several sport sociological research projects, with a main interest in critical analysis regarding gender and ethnicity.

Ivo van Hilvoorde studied Human movement sciences and worked two years as a researcher on the topic of sport and health at the Free University in Amsterdam. At this moment he is finishing his dissertation on the development of the disciplinary identity of academic pedagogy in the Netherlands (Utrecht University). He is also teacher at the Academy of Physical Education (in Amsterdam and Zwolle).

Prof. Dr. **Paul De Knop** is full professor at the Free University in Brussel and extraordinary professor of 'Social, policy-oriented and didactical aspects of sport and physical education in the Netherlands' at Tilburg University (Leisure Studies). He is chair of the 'Values and Norms research programme' (II).His research areas include sport sociology and sports management.

Dr. **Annelies Knoppers** is a sociologist and researcher in the area of gender and (sport) organizations in the Utrecht School of Governance (Utrecht University). She has conducted research in the USA and the Netherlands that explores the coaching as an occupation, the culture coaches create, the images soccer players have of coaches and of men's and women's football and the meanings given to gender and ethnicity by the sport media.

Dr. **Kristine De Martelaer** is doctor in Physical Education and licentiate in leisure agogics. She currently teaches at the Free University in Brussel and at the University of Gent, and conducts research in the fields of sport pedagogy, physical education, sport and youth culture.

Dr. **Jacques van Rossum** is lecturer/researcher at The Faculty of Human Movement Sciences (Free University, Amsterdam). His research areas include motor learning and talent development of youngsters in sport, physical education and dance.

Esther Rutten graduated from Leiden University in 2001 (special education). Her interests include developmental psychology, psychopathology, and moral development and delinquency.

Prof. Dr. **Carlo Schuengel** is programme director on 'Challenges to childrearing relationships' at the Free University Amsterdam. His research interests concern attachment, predominantly within the clinical domain.

Dr. **Geert Jan Stams** is a lecturer and researcher at the University of Leiden (Center for Child and Family Studies). His main research interests are attachment, and moral development and education.

Johan Steenbergen worked as researcher and lecturer at the Faculty of Human Movement Sciences, Free University Amsterdam and at the departement of Leisure Studies at Tilburg University. Currently he works as teacher at the Academy of Physical Education and Sport in Zwolle. He has published several articles and books in the field of the philosophy of sport with a particular emphasis on conceptual questions and ethical issues.

Dr. **Marc Theeboom** is doctor in Physical Education and licentiate in leisure agogics. He is lecturer at the Free University of Brussels and gives several courses concerning agogical aspects related to sport and movement. His research interests concerns youth sport in general and social vulnerable youth in particular.

Ricus Timmers works as a sport policy maker for the local government of Eindhoven. The previous 18 years he worked as a researcher at Tilburg University and two years as researcher for Amnesty International. His research interests concerns the Modern Olympic Games and the Olympic Movement.

Jeroen Vermeulen has taught sociolinquistics at the department of General Linquistics at Utrecht University. Currently he is working at the Utrecht School of Governance of the same university. His research interests are institutional communication and identity formation in organizational settings.

Prof. Dr. **Paul Verweel** is professor of organisation and policy from a multi-cultural perspective at the Utrecht School of Governance (Utrecht University). His areas of expertise include diversity in organisations, mergers, strategic management, organisational culture and dynamics, and the construction of meaning. He is a member of various national and local advisory boards of sports organisations.

Dr. **Wiel Veugelers** is a senior lecturer and researcher at the Graduate School of Teaching and Learning of the University of Amsterdam. He has published on moral education, school-home partnership and youth cultures, in particular on playing soccer and on hooliganism.

FOREWORD

Valuing sport: within and beyond the present and the particular

I am particularly pleased to write these foreword notes for "Values and Norms in Sport" having presented at one of the earlier conferences when the researchers were promoting the importance of value-related considerations in sports. I was then impressed, and still remain so, at the way in which these academics had set about making their research work for the betterment of sporting practice and had not merely contented themselves with developing theoretical research for those within the ivory towers. This volume is then the fruit of their labours. It cultivates a significantly broad range of issues critical to the normative health of sports in Netherlands and Flanders.

It is a sociological commonplace to observe that sport is a global phenomenon. Merely to record its apparently ubiquitous nature is to fail to recognise the load that it now bears. While this load is multi-faceted – who could deny the import of commodified sport in global economy – what is explored in these covers is the ethical dimension in its broadest conception. Sport, as many commentators have noted, is the new religion. It has superseded Christianity in many cultural theorist's eyes as *the* social practice *par excellence* that initiates persons into rules and norms of virtuous and vicious behaviours which orientate us more broadly in the world. The language of sport and its rich metaphors of "rule-following" and "rule-breaking", of "spoiling" and "upholding the spirit of an activity", of "playing the game", of "keeping one's eye on the ball" attune players, fans and critical objectors to the manner in which sport refuses to be confined to the dimensions of the pitch. Instead overflows onto the front pages of newspapers, it spills out onto the dinner table, runs through pubs and cafés and, sometimes with deadly consequencess into the streets of our frightened cities and towns.

I do not wish to replicate here the introductory comments regarding each essay below, but wish to draw attention to a few of the noteworthy features of the book. First, it is true that sport, precisely because it is a human endeavour, may transform our expressive energies into the ugly almost as easily as the sublime. The authors in this volume are all critically aware of sports' rich potential to uplift and degrade the human spirit. The essays open up and interrogate the full panoply of sports' many manifestations from childhood play to Olympic competitions. Moreover, they situate in these many forms or instantiations of sports, issues ranging from fair play and the ethics of sports, gender and sexuality, social integration and inclusion, professionalism and organisational values, and moral/value-development in and through sport. The range of issues addressed in one volume is impressive in breadth.

Secondly, it is a chief value of the book that it is multi-disciplinary in character. The distinction drawn between philosophical and empirical research into issues of normative significance is not universal. The cake can be cut up in many ways. Here, the authors approach the range of values and norms in sport both by philosophical analysis and by social theory and empirical social science. This renders the text a valuable multi-disciplinary resource for those interested in contemporary issues in sport practice and sport scholarship. Thirdly, the authors in the book, though they are driven by ideological and theoretical agendas that are by no means homogenous, all appear to recognise sports double character. It is at one and the same time and real cultural practice as well as an ideal-type; a cultural form that exists as a series of rules in a book. This duality brings with it an unavoidable ambiguity. We think at one and the same time of sports-as-they-are at the same time as sports-as-they-could-be. The authors have a keen sense (though it is not made explicit in every chapter) of sports intrinsic and extrinsic values. They recognise properly that in contemporary societies sports is frequently a tool of social or economic policy. For sport exclusively to be relegated to the agenda of politics or commerce is of course to abuse it. Sport enshrines certain values within its idealised structures; equality of opportunity to contest a goal, perfectionism, excellence, discipline and so on. The list is familiar, indeed so familiar to be platitudinous. One has indeed to be a rich sceptic to deny the pervasiveness of sports' platitudinous metaphors. Though one might do well to observe that a platitude attains it status, and preserves it, largely in virtue of its veracity.

Finally, although it speaks to the values and norms of Dutch and Flemish contexts, the book surely reaches out beyond those boundaries. If it did not, of course, the globalization thesis would be a grand lie. No modern state can survive hermetically sealed off from the rest of the world. Internationalisation is not only the name of the game in economics (if you will pardon the gratuitous metaphor) but also in sport and sports scholarship too. The volume is Janus faced: it looks closely and critically at particularly Dutch and Flemish contexts yet it looks too to connect these in the light of dis/similarities in the development of sport globally. In this light, I welcome Values and Norms in Sport to the emerging philosophical and empirical literature on ethics and sports and commend its editors on the ambitious scope of their endeavours.

Dr. Mike McNamee
Leisure and Sport Research Unit
Cheltenham and Gloucester College of Higher Education, England
President of the International Association of Philosophy of Sport (IAPS)

PART ONE

THE MEANING OF SPORT FOR SOCIETY

1 VALUES AND NORMS IN SPORT

**Annelies Knoppers, Annemarie ten Boom,
Albert Buisman, Agnes Elling & Paul De Knop**

Introduction

Values and norms manifest themselves implicitly and explicitly in different ways at individual, structural and cultural levels. For example, athletes may behave according to stated and assumed norms (individual level); these values and norms are often embedded in the way sport is organized (structure) and the type of culture that is created. Values and norms are not static givens but are constructed and given meaning by individuals based on their experience, emotions, power and privilege. Not all values and norms carry equal weight; there are dominant and marginalized values and norms. Power and privilege play a significant role in the hegemony of certain values and norms. The tension between dominant and marginalized values and norms means that values and norms are dynamic, that is, often in a state of flux. They are continually supported, resisted and reconstructed. These dynamics and the diversity of values and norms are often made visible by empirical research and theory development.

Explicit and implicit values and norms function as guidelines for practice, as subject for debates and for the creation of policies. Some of these guidelines change almost overnight, like the change to sexualized uniforms in women's volleyball. Other changes are part of ongoing struggles, because many people resist change. There was for example, much resistance against the participation of girls and women in football in the Netherlands since football was and still is primarily valued as a male activity. Or, for example, there was a great deal of discussion about changing the age limit when boys and girls can begin to play football. The norm was eight years old but currently there are 20,000 Dutch five-year-olds that play football. The diversity of values attributed to playing football became visible in the discussion about the age limit. On the one hand, there are the values pertaining to what many people think is 'good' for a child, such as a playful attitude, a need to be involved in activities of his or her own choosing and a need to feel safe and secure. On the other hand the discussion about the age limit is also shaped by values attributed to involvement in competitive sport such as the development of a competitive attitude, a will to win, self discipline and task orientation. Some people think that five-year-olds are not ready for competitive sport. The National Youth Sport Coaches Association (NYSCA) in the USA for example, has a non-competitive developmental program for five – six year olds and a relatively low-key sport introduction program for seven to eight year olds (NYSCA, 1999). Others do not want an age limit because they think that children are never too young to learn. The Ajax football school in the Netherlands for example, trains boys between six to eight year old in a way that clearly focuses on competitive football.

The change in societal values and norms that is visible in education, public health and sport, is a major political topic in the Netherlands, Belgium and many western-European countries. Sport not only reflects and reinforces dominant societal norms, it also challenges them. For example, the participation of ethnic minority groups in sport may be valued as a means to stimulate societal integration. Simultaneously, relative over-representation by specific ethnic minorities in some sports, such as basketball, boxing, and certain athletic events, and their relative under-representation in positions of leadership and in sports such as cycling, volleyball, and swimming, may reinforce stereotypes about their physicality and mentality. Similarly, 'Sport for all' may be an explicit value addressed in many policy statements, yet giving the physically challenged a full-fledged place in sport may require questioning the high value that is put on performance outcome in sport for the physically abled.

This tensions between explicitly stating what is socially desirable and implicit values, and between what are seen as 'traditional values' and 'new' values, led the Dutch National Sport and Olympic Association, (NOC*NSF), and a number of universities (Free University of Amsterdam, University of Utrecht and the Free University of Brussels) to launch a research program in 1993 entitled "Values and Norms in

Sport (WNS I)".[1] In 1998 a follow up program (WNS II) was begun. This book reflects the results of both WNS I and II.

The discussion in the Netherlands and the Flemish-speaking community in Belgium regarding the values and norms in current sports was launched in 1991 by a document on Sports Policy by d'Ancona, who was Dutch Minister of Welfare, Health and Cultural Affairs at that time. She proposed a public discussion about the quality of sport practice and about the changing nature of sport. Why did the government suddenly pay so much attention to the quality of sport and why was it prepared to fund a large part of a research project such as WNS I (and later WNS II)? Although there is no straightforward answer there were several factors that played a key role:

1. The increasing social importance ascribed to sport may have made the study of sport practices important. This conclusion was confirmed by the results of a literature study and eighty interviews with experts from various sections of society, such as sport, politics, the business sector and government (Kearney, 1992). We note here that the voices of athletes were not included in this report. Many of the research studies conducted under the auspices of WNS I and II attempted to fill this gap and ensure that their voices were heard as well.
2. A major shift in possibilities for sport involvement may have played a major role in the increase in governmental interest. Competitive sport was no longer the most frequent form of sport participation (Crum, 1991). Other forms of sport and recreation, such as fitness and adventure sports, had also developed into full-fledged (and often alternate) forms of sport.
3. Changes in the needs and expectations of members of sports clubs may also have stimulated the scholarly study of sport (Anthonissen and Boessenkool, 1998). The 'traditional' sports offered by clubs, and the way of organizing them, often failed to meet the different needs of its members. Sport managers needed to learn to be more client-oriented and to manage diversity (Knoppers, 2000). This shift towards recognizing and accepting a diversity of values and norms was often interpreted in a

---

[1] The first part of this program ended with a symposium on June 5, 1998 and the publication of a book summarizing and discussing the results (Steenbergen, Buisman, De Knop & Lucassen, 1998). The same group of universities plus the Catholic University of Brabant initiated the subsequent program (WNS II) which ended the summer of 2001.

negative way. Board members of sports clubs, for example, often attributed the decreasing involvement of club members in their club to this diversity and paid little attention to positive aspects of diversity.

4. The change in the traditional sport population (white younger men) also drew the attention of governmental officials and scholars to sport. The increase in the participation and visibility of girls and women, ethnic minorities, the elderly, the physically challenged, gays, and lesbians in sport did not mean that these social groups no longer encountered marginalization, and that their (possibly different) norms and values were incorporated into club and governmental sport policies (Elling & De Knop, 1999; Knoppers & Bouman, 1996, 1998). In addition, members of these groups rarely held positions of leadership.

5. A few widely publicized incidents in youth sport might have played a role in the increasing interest politicians have in sport. The (late) discovery by medical staff that a girl who was part of the Dutch gymnastic team had been seriously injured, raised the question of who was responsible for top youth sport (Buisman, 1993). In addition, in the mid-nineties there was much commotion in the Netherlands about the sexual harassment of several (top) female judokas. The government reacted by funding a prevention project that focused on improprieties in relationships between trainer and athlete and on the negative aspects of dependency relationships that may occur between coach and athletes in youth sport (Gaell & Ten Boom, 2000).

6. Lastly, another factor that played a role in the increase in interest in the scholarly study of sport from a social science perspective, was research that had been conducted by several researchers on values and norms in youth sport, and on the conceptualization of values of and in (competitive) sport (Buisman, 1987; De Knop, 1989; Steenbergen, De Vos & Tamboer, 1992).

These factors played a large role in highlighting the need for a research program that focused on values and norms in sport. A pivotal event occurred in July 1993 at a national congress on 'Fair Play' in Valkenswaard. Many participants expressed a need for conceptual clarification and empirical studies of values and norms. The program "Values and Norms in Sport" (WNS-program) was therefore begun to meet this need.

A perspective was needed however, to situate the content of this program. What kinds of values were to be studied and from which theoretical perspectives? Tamboer (1994) made an important distinction between the 'transfer' and 'clarification' of values that shaped both WNS I & II. He argued that there is a great danger that a few people (for example, experts or sports officials) decide what 'fair play' is and that 'traditional values and norms' must be restored and taught. He called this 'transfer of values'. Instead, Tamboer said, justice should be done to different views concerning fair play in a multicultural society. One party cannot impose its views on values on the other party. He introduced the idea of 'clarification of values', in which a multiplicity of views is accepted and by which people are held accountable and responsible for their own actions. 'Good' sport is therefore the (always changing) result of what is defined as "good" by all those who are involved in sport (Tamboer, 1994). This concept of 'clarification of values' became the root of the entire WNS-research program and enabled it to embrace a variety of projects using a diversity of theoretical perspectives.

1.1 Defining the concept of values and norms

Frequently values are defined in terms of perceptions of what is socially desirable. They are and become the underlying, often implicit, assumptions by which individual and social goals are chosen. We evaluate our own and others' behaviors in terms of these values. People will usually expend great energy to achieve those features of social life that they deem important and worthwhile. For example, Rokeach (1973) named 18 values that serve as goals such as peace, beauty, equality, brotherhood (sic), freedom and happiness and 18 instrumental values such as ambition, courage, honesty, independence and obedience. The disadvantage of this 'universal' non-contextual value approach is that everyone will be in favor of these values in principle, while in practice on the level of actions – there may be differences of opinion about the meaning of a specific value or norm.

Consequently, the WNS programs used another notion of values. Values were seen as meanings or interpretations of the human existence, that is, social constructions that are viewed as guidelines for actions. A norm was considered as a realization of a value, that is, a guideline for action (Van der Ven, 1985). Values and their accompanying norms are explicitly and implicitly visible in the teaching of athletes, in the development and implementation of policies, in the way people express themselves, their interactions and how they give meaning to their sport involvement and in the construction of organizations. Thus, as was indicated at the beginning of this chapter, these values are visible at three levels: individual, structural and cultural/symbolic. This approach to defining values means that values can be seen as positive and as negative. The WNS research program did, therefore, not have to be legitimized by a negative view such as the loss of values and norms since it would have been difficult to determine which value has been "lost".

An underlying assumption was therefore that values can be interpreted or given meaning in various ways. "Individualism" for example, can mean that people have the opportunity to meet their own needs and to be assertive in their social context; 'individualism' may also be interpreted as social isolation. An assumption underlying WNS I and WNS II therefore was that a study of values has to be conceptually balanced, and has to include that what is considered positive and negative.

1.2 The objectives of the research programs

The general objectives of the program were:
- To provide elements for a (more) coherent policy with respect to values and norms in sport.
- To obtain empirical evidence that could be used in debates about values and norms in sport and that could be translated into practice.
- To make suggestions for incorporating discussions about values and norms in sport education and training programs for leaders.
- To develop theoretical notions of values and to explore their consequences for sport policies.
- To use triangulation to integrate the results of conceptual and empirical research methods.

The central research question of the program was the following:

> What values and norms do those involved in the world of
> sport (actors) implicitly and explicitly construct to give
> meaning to sport and their experiences in sport, and to what
> extent do these reinforce and/ challenge dominant societal
> values and norms?

All the projects in the research program dealt with the interaction
between (conflicting) values and norms within sport and societal
practices. The projects included questions such as: What 'values' or
meanings do individuals, collectively and individually, give to sport?
How do sport organizations deal with differences in expectations for and
meanings given to participation by athletes from different social groups?
How do sports clubs that are more oriented towards 'traditional' values,
react to changes in societal values and norms that seem to threaten the
existence of the clubs? What are the norms used to assess 'quality' in
sport clubs and what types of athletes are attracted by these norms?
When do athletes consider their sport experience as 'valuable'? Which
norms and values are reflected in the sport media's representation of
gender and race/ethnicity and how are these related to the construction of
gender and race/ethnicity in society? Possible answers to these questions
and others will be discussed in the chapters of this book

1.3 Theoretical perspectives of the program

The initial conceptual framework of the program was situated in one
theoretical perspective 'the double character of sport' (Steenbergen, De
Vos & Tamboer, 1992; see chapter 2 of this book). Initially this
conceptual framework was assumed to provide a foundation for the
exploration of all the themes/values contained within the various
research projects. The double character of sport refers to a perspective in
which a distinction is made between values and norms in sport and about
sport. 'Traditional' competitive sports are seen as 'the heart' of modern
sport. Certain 'intrinsic' values and norms are ascribed to these sports,
such as achievement, competition, performance and fair play . These
values give this 'heart' a unique nature. Yet because sport is also part of

society, sport is continually confronted with and influenced by changing societal values and norms (extrinsic to sport). This perspective sees sport as a unique voluntary activity that has its goal in the activity itself. At the same time, sport is also viewed as a historically and socially constructed activity that primarily reflects dominant societal values and norms, such as the pursuit of excellence. It can be used as an instrument to achieve certain extrinsic values and goals (such as 'health' or 'the integration of ethnic minorities').

This perspective about the double character of sport was initially chosen to provide the conceptual framework for all the projects in WNS I & II. As the research program got underway, however, it became evident that this perspective was not adequate in answering all the various types of questions asked by the researchers. The results of research conducted with athletes, sport managers and coaches showed that these sport participants gave meaning to sport in ways that could not be placed within the double character of sport perspective. Thus other approaches were needed. Consequently, critical/cultural studies, structuration and symbolic interactionist perspectives informed various projects.

The critical/cultural studies perspective sees sport as a cultural practice where many (societal) meanings are reinforced and challenged; one or two meanings or discourses become dominant and hegemonic, that is, they become self evident. This dominance is linked to power that can be located in specific social groups. In sport this power tends to be held by white middle to upper class heterosexual men. This does not mean that those who are not members of this group do not assign meanings; they do, but their meanings, if different from the dominant meanings, are often marginalized.

The structuration and symbolic interaction perspectives regard athletes, officials, managers and researchers as actors, acting within a specific context to reinforce or challenge (dominant) meanings of sport practices. The symbolic interaction approach is often used to detail the experiences of sport participants, coaches and managers with the use of phenomenology while structuration theory tends to be used to explore agency and constraints in a specific context (actor in context).

Although these various theoretical perspectives were used throughout the book, the way in which they were used depended on the academic discipline of each researcher: critical pedagogy, social psychology, anthropology, sociology and communication studies.

1.4 Organizational Framework of the Research program

The WNS program was initiated and managed by a steering committee that was responsible for the general organization and for stimulating reflection on intersections among the results of the projects.[2] A general advisory board enabled a high quality of scholarship and developed program policies. It included representatives from the (Dutch) Department of Health, Welfare and Well-being (VWS), the Belgium sport federation (BLOSO), the national Olympic sport federation (NOC*NSF) and the various universities. A promotional and public relations committee developed strategies for disseminating results. Thematic events were held to increase the visibility of the program and to translate theory and results into practice. The Department of VWS and the Foundation of the National Sport lottery (Toto/lotto) funded the program. Non-financial contributions were made by NOC*NSF and the participating universities. Additional grants were given by sport organizations and federations for projects that focused on specific sports.

---

[2] Five people were responsible for the daily management of WNS I: drs. Albert Buisman (chair, University of Utrecht), dr. Jan Tamboer (Free University of Amsterdam), Prof. dr. Paul De Knop (Free University of Brussels), drs. Jo Lucassen (NOC*NSF) and drs. Agnes Elling (secretary – University of Utrecht). Three persons were responsible for the daily management of WNS II: Prof.dr. Paul De Knop (chair, Free University of Brussels/Tilburg University), drs. Agnes Elling (secretary, Tilburg University) and drs. Annemarie ten Boom (NOC*NSF representative).

1.5 The values and norms research program (WNS I & II): Research projects

In total, WNS I & II included 18 research projects. Their themes were clustered around four main topics: societal meanings given to sport, values ascribed to sport (participation), values embedded in organizational structures, and, values emphasized youth sports (see the different themes within the box(es)).

---

1 Societal meanings given to sport

1.1 The double character of sport
This project consisted of conceptual analyses of notions such as 'sport', 'game', 'fair play', 'competition', and 'integration'. How can 'sport' be conceptualized and in which ways can values and norms in sport be systematized or categorized?

1.2 The social significance of sport for society
Two studies focused on the connection between the meanings given to integration and socialization in sport.

1.3 Integration of immigrants into sport
This study investigated how the integration of immigrant youth groups into sport is realized, how the values attributed to integration are perceived, and, to what extent meanings given to integration differ.

1.4 Sport and health
This project analyzed concepts and methods and categorized discourses used to describe the relationship between sport and health-related issues such as fitness, injuries and doping.

2 Values ascribed to sport participation

2.1 Fair play in sport
This research project examined how the notion of 'fair play' is defined in programs designed to promote it, the underlying perspectives and how those definitions are implemented in various countries.

2.2 The Olympic philosophy: values and norms associated with Olympic sport in the Netherlands
A survey was conducted to determine how Dutch people give meaning to Olympism. How do contemporary processes such as globalization, professionalization, media and commercialization influence such opinions?

2.3 Gender and ethnicity in the sport media
This study examined how the sport media (newspapers and television) construct sport, gender and ethnicity. The project consisted of three separate but related studies of the sport media: content analysis (quantitative and qualitative), an investigation of the production process, and an analysis of the way readers/viewers use the media to construct discourses about gender and ethnicity.

3 Values embedded in sport structures and organizations

3.1 Quality of sports policy
This study analyzed the content of policy documents to investigate the manner in which they give explicit and implicit meanings to sport and to values and norms in sport.

3.2 Vitality of sports clubs
This study investigated the dominant values of sports clubs and their managers and the extent to which these values mirror current social developments.

3.3 Managing and organizing diversity in sport clubs
To which values and norms do managers of sports clubs explicitly or implicitly adhere and which value orientations can lead to a revitalization of existing club structures?

3.4 Communication processes among sport organizations
This study examined the critical success factors that determine the 'fit' between communication about organizational needs and resulting organizational support.

3.5 Gender, coaches and sport.
This research project explored and discussed the dominant meanings that coaches give to gender in sport.

4 Values in youth sport

4.1 Perceptions of children in sport
This research study investigated the perceptions of young children about 'play', 'game' and 'sport.'

4.2 The child-orientation of organized youth sport
This study used the experiences of children in swimming to explore how (organized) youth sport can be enriched through a more child-oriented approach.

4.3 Martial arts and young people
This study attempted to determine the contribution of martial arts to pedagogy. Interviews with young practitioners and their trainers were used to examine how young people experience the martial arts and to what values and norms do trainers adhere in their training programs?

4.4 Top-level sport and talent development
This project attempted to explore contextual factors that may play a role in the development of talented athletes.

4.5 The pedagogical task of the sports club.
This investigation used a moral reasoning approach to explore which pedagogical tasks and meanings can be assigned and attributed to sports clubs. Observations and (group) interviews were used to gather data about interactions among leaders, managers, and parents and children/young people.

1.6 The significance of the research program

As we indicated in the introduction to this chapter, studies that clarify the values held by sport participants, administrators, sport managers and coaches are sorely needed to explore the extent to which general assumptions made about sport and its role in society, can be supported. In the closing chapter we will explore the extent to which the research program of WNS succeeded in articulating and clarifying these values.

One of the strengths of this research program is the diversity of its research projects. They were diverse in the underlying assumptions about sport and society, in their conceptualization of values to be studied, in the various research methods that were used, in the research sample/population and in the conclusions. They ranged from research conducted from a functional perspective to that which is critical (cultural studies) and that that focused on interactions (actor in context). This diversity ensured that the research program was rich in its dimensionality and in that way, unique, since most research about values and norms in sport is conducted from only one perspective. The concluding chapter will include a reflection on the various results and an attempt to explore their cumulative meanings.

It is also possible to view the significance of this program from a practical viewpoint. The research program enabled many researchers and practitioners in sport to discuss values and norms in sport more concretely and to distinguish among meanings given to values by individuals, values embedded in structures and values that are an implicit part of the sport culture. Several researchers contributed to the debate about values and norms related to sports via the media. For example, media coverage was given to the effects boxing and doping have on health and to the discussion about the participation of girls and women in sport. Several researchers wrote pamphlets and booklets in which they 'translated' their results for practitioners; others constructed educational programs to be used in youth sport and for the development of fair play. Other researchers maintained a more detached relationship to the areas of their investigation because they felt that administrators, policy makers and sport participants were primarily responsible for implementing the results of the project.

Lastly, the significance of this research program also lies in its ability to add to the discussion about values attributed to and emphasized in sport. We hope that this discussion will receive a new impulse with the publication of this book.

1.7 An outline of the book

In this book, which consists of four different segments, most of the above mentioned WNS research projects are presented.

The first part is about specific discussions and topics concerning the *meaning of sport for society*. In the introduction of this part Steenbergen (chapter 2) presents the framework of the double character of sport. The next three chapters focus more specific on the conceptual and empirical relations between sport and health (Van Hilvoorde, chapter 3), sport and social integration (Elling, De Knop & Knoppers, chapter 4) and the pedagogical task of sport clubs (Biesta, Stams, Dirks, Rutten, Veugelers & Schuengel, chapter 5). Although the authors use different perspectives and methods, they all conclude that the often easily ascribed meanings of sport for society, can be contested and must be discussed contextual and in concrete terms instead of universal and abstract.

In the second part of the book – introduced by Buisman & Van Rossum (chapter 6) - several projects discussing *specific values in sport* are presented. In these chapters both dominant and more critical meanings assigned to fair play (Steenbergen, Buisman & Van Hilvoorde, chapter 7), Olympism (Timmers & De Knop, chapter 8) and the body (Knoppers & Elling, chapter 9) are discussed. By clarifying and discussing these specific values it becomes more and more clear that sport is a complex social practice in which several values are manifested.

The third part of the book handles with explicit and implicit *values in structures and organisations*. Anthonissen (chapter 10) introduces this part by characterizing 'the heart' of Dutch sport: amateur sport clubs. The other chapters in this part discuss values, standards and power relations with respect to groups such as administrators (Boessenkool, chapter 11) and coaches (Knoppers, chapter 13) and topics like communication (Anthonissen, Vermeulen & Verweel, chapter 12) and media (Knoppers & Elling, chapter 14).

A common finding of these different projects is that sport has changed a lot over the years, but that the traditional hegemonic norms and power structures have remained relatively stable.

In the last part of the book De Martelaer, De Knop & Buisman (chapter 15) argue for specific attention to (conflicting) *values in youth sport*. The meaning of sport for young children and possible conflicts between the way sports are offered and the interests of children are further discussed with respect to several different sports (Baar, chapter 16) and martial arts in particular (Theeboom, chapter 17). Sport is still popular among young people, but instead of resting on its laurels organized youth sport must continually invest in its future. One of such an investement can be based on the different experiences of children and youngsters with their sport, trying to create a child-friendly sport.

The book ends with a short conclusion (chapter 18) of the results and some reflections about the future of research in values and norms in sport.

References

Anthonissen, A. & Boessenkool, J. (1998). *Meanings of management*. Utrecht: ISOR. (in Dutch).

Buisman, A. J. (1987). *Youth sport and Fair Play*. Haarlem: De Vrieseborch. (in Dutch).

Buisman, A. J. (1993). Content and implementation of a youth sport policy. In: W. Duquet, P. De Knop, L. Bollaert (Eds.), *Youth sport: A social approach.* (pp. 206-222) Brussel: VUB Press.

Crum, B. (1991). *About the sportification of society*. Rijswijk: WVC. (in Dutch).

Elling, A. & Knop, P. De (1999). *According to one's own wishes and possibilities*. Arnhem: NOC*NSF. (in Dutch).

Gaell, B. & Boom, A. ten (2000). *Ways to prevent extreme dependency in top-level youth sport*. Arnhem: NOC*NSF. (in Dutch).

Kearney, A.T. (1992). *Sport as a source of inspiration for our society*. Arnhem: NOC*NSF. (in Dutch).

Knop, P. De (1989). *The role of parents in sports education*. Brussel: Koning Boudewijn Stichting. (in Dutch).

Knoppers, A. & Bouman, Y. (1996). *Trainers/coaches; A question of quality?* Arnhem: NOC*NSF. (in Dutch).

Knoppers, A. & Bouman, Y. (1998). *Always better than my athletes*. Arnhem: NOC*NSF. (in Dutch).

Knoppers, A. (Ed. 2000). *The construction of meaning in sports organizations: Management of diversity*. Maastricht: Shaker. (in Dutch).

NYSCA (1999). National Standards for Youth Sports. West Palm Beach (Fl): NYSCA.

NOC*NSF (1993). *Values and norms in sport. Research program and grant application*. Arnhem: NOC*NSF. (in Dutch).

Rokeach, M. (1973). *The nature of human values*. New York: Free Press, McMillan.

Steenbergen, J., Buisman, A.J., Knop, P. De & Lucassen, J.M.H. (Ed. 1998). *Values and norms in sport. Analyses and policy perspectives*. Houten: Bohn Stafleu Van Loghum. (in Dutch).

Steenbergen, J., Vos, N.R. de & Tamboer, J.W.I. (1992). The double character of sport. *Lichamelijke Opvoeding*, 14, pp. 638-641. (in Dutch).

Tamboer, J.W.I. (1994). About old values and modern sport. *Lichamelijke Opvoeding*, 1, pp. 4-6. (in Dutch).

Ven, J.A. van der (1985). *Education in values and norms*. Kampen: Kok. (in Dutch).

2 THE DOUBLE CHARACTER OF SPORT

Johan Steenbergen

Introduction

Sport is a complex social practice in which several values are manifested. Many, predominantly German, authors identify these days a dramatic change of values in sport, movement culture and society (Crum, 1991; Dietrich & Heinemann, 1989; Digel, 1986; Heinemann, 1980). The phrase 'changing values in sport', however, is not an equivocal term, but the expression refers to several developments which took place in both society and sport (ibid.).

Sport nowadays has become a 'variously shaped reality' in which new concepts of sport can be recognized. Therefore, it is more appropriate to speak of different concepts of sport, instead of one concept of sport. Concepts of sport, such as fitness sport, health sport, adventure sport, show sport, commercial sport or private sport, include sport-like activities in which the classical principle of citius-altius-fortius is abandoned. So, the panorama of contemporary sport looks more pluriform than just competitive sport. Also the offerings of sport are diversified and so more different groups of people enter sport nowadays – disabled, elderly and more women. The changing of values manifests itself also in the diverse and new motives of sport participants. Traditional values - and motives for participation – such as competition, discipline and achievement are accompinied by 'new' values such as health, adventure, pleasure and excitement. The changing values in sport are also revealed in the ranking of sport in the cultural value structure. Sport is valued higher than it used to be. Sport has become so important that it seems to be moved from the margin to the centre of society – the current society has become 'sportified'.

In this book several topics concerning values and norms in sport are discussed (critically). To systematize the discussion about the broad spectrum of values and norms in sport it is fruitful to use a framework. This framework – called 'the double character of sport' – will be described in the last part of this chapter. In the first part of this chapter the question 'what is sport?' will be considered critically by looking at two procedures regarding the possibility to clarify sport. At the end of this first part, and based on Wittgenstein's anti-essentilistic ideas concerning defining concepts, three members of the sport family are designated.

2.1 What is sport?

The first question to begin with in the clarification of sport is not "what is sport?", but "what sort of concept is sport?" and consequently "which procedure is most fruitful to clarify this concept?". Two extreme positions (procedures) can be identified in the clarification of sport: *essentialism* and *anti* or *non-essentialism*. Both these procedures concerning the possibility to define sport, reveal different views about the type of concept sport is.

2.1.1 An essentialistic position

How the nature of sport can be demarcated from other domains of human activity is a question which has been amply discussed in particularly philosophical literature of sport (Gerber & Morgan, 1979; Morgan & Meier, 1995). In many of these sport philosophical accounts the emphasis lies on the so called 'autonomy of sport' ('nature of sport' or 'ontology of sport') of which, based on certain characteristics or elements, sport can be sharply demarcated from non-sport. In this procedure of defining, characterizing or classifying sport one presupposes that sport has a describable essence – a position which can philosophically be considered as 'essentialistic' (Gerber & Morgan, 1979, p.1). Operating from this essentialistic position the conviction is that different phenomena are designate by the same concept or word because they posses a common property or properties – they share a common essence.

From an essentialistic philosophical position sport is considered as having certain necessary and sufficient conditions. For example, an activity is sport if and only if this activity is (i) physical, (ii) competitive, (iii) rule governed, (iv) a game, (v) institutionalized and (vi) globalized. These six properties – called the intension of the concept – are the criteria for belonging to the class of things designated by that word (e.g. sport). The class of all activities which possess these six properties is called the extension of the concept. The intension of 'triangle', as classic example, consists of the properties of a) having three sides, and b) having three interior angles equal to 180 degrees. The extension of 'triangle' consists of the class of all geometric figures which possess these properties.

Sport considered, like a triangle, as a concept whose boundaries are concisely drawn and whose membership is clearly limited means that sport is regarded as a so called closed concept. It is supposed that based on certain necessary and sufficient criteria sport can be demarcated clearly from other concepts. There are no borderline cases – every conceivable activity either is or is not sport. Both the intension and the extension of the concept 'sport' is concise. Is this essentialistic position a tenable one?

2.1.2 The essentialistic position criticized

The essentialistic position, and the applied procedure, concerning the definition of sport is not an unquestionable one – it is criticized by several authors. This group of analytic philosophers is inspired by the anti-essentialistic ideas stemming from Wittgenstein's famous 'Philosophical Investigations'. Within this group at least two positions can be recognised. In this section a brief outline is given of the first and most extreme position considering the possibility to define sport - in the next section the second and more moderate position is outlined. The most extreme position, which is outlined in this section, is denoted here as sceptical. These authors consider it possible to define precise concepts (like geometric figures) but impossible and unfruitful to define imprecise social concepts like 'freedom', 'democracy', 'art' and 'sport' (Kleinmann, 1968; McBride, 1979).

The linchpin of their severe criticism is the essentialists consideration of sport as a so called *closed concept* – sport, in their view, must be considered as an *open concept*. This openness manifests itself for example in the possibility of unforeseeable or novel conditions which are always forthcoming or envisageable. Consider just a few activities called (although not unanimous) 'sport' in ordinary language these days such as soccer, football, chess, bridge,

fitness sport, health sport and basketball and it becomes clear that
there is not one group of features based on which concise boundaries
can be drawn between these sports and other activities? Basketball,
soccer and football are competitive based sports, but this is not the
case with activities such as fitness sport and health sport. These sport-
like activities can be regarded as non-competitive-based concepts of
sport. In the German sport literature particularly these non-
competitive based concepts of sport are considered as alternative
concepts of sport (Dietrich & Heinemann, 1989; Digel, 1986;
Heinemann, 1980). This tendency to a wider view of sport than just
competitive sport, does not exist in the Anglo-Saxon literature. Fitness
and health sport are not considered sport, but conventionally thought
very closed 'related movement forms' of which the primary objective
is not the competition between contestants, but total fitness:
flexibility, muscular endurance, increase of the circulatory capacity
(Osterhoudt, 1996; Thomas, 1983).

    And the element 'physical skill'? Can this be regarded as the
common property in the aformentioned activities? Physical (or bodily)
skill is an element that is continuously (almost unanimously)
proposed as a criterion for distinguishing sport from other fields of
action (Morgan & Meier, 1995). Sport, with respect to this
characteristic, is at least partially distinguishable from other domains
because of it's physical character. If this element is considered as a
necessary element of sport practices, activities such as chess and
bridge are not included in the category of sport because they lack the
characteristic of physical skill. Although these activities are for
example on the sports pages, competitive in character and games,
most philosophers of sport (not all!; see Tamboer, 1992, 1994)
consider these activities non-sport because they lack the element
'physicality'. According to McBride and Kleinmann there is no single
common element or group of elements in virtue of which a sharp line
can be drawn between sport and other, not sportslike, activities. Sport
is an elusive concept which reveals a certain openness – and as a
consequence it seems impossible to set out essential criteria for sport
exhaustively. The central question, however, is if this conclusion must
lead to McBride's bald recommendation that 'Philosophers of sport
ought not waste their time attempting to define 'sport'' (1979, p.51)
and Kleinmann's view that 'it is logically impossible to formulate

necessary and/or sufficient properties for sport' (1968, p.151). An alternative in the demarcation of sport from non-sport can be found in a more moderate critical position concerning the possibiliy to define sport: sport is a Wittgensteinian family concept.

2.2 Sport and family resemblances

With respect to the contemporary plurality of sport it seems more fruitful not to speak of the concept of sport, but of different concepts of sport (Crum, 1991; Dietrich & Heinemann, 1989; Digel, 1986; Heinemann, 1980). No essential characteristic or set of characteristics can be identified based on which sport can be demarcated from non-sport (see also the foregoing). Sport seems best viewed from the Wittgensteinian perspective of a 'family-model', whose members are related to each other in all sorts of different ways and where no characteristic is common (essential) to all of these members (Crum 1991; Fogelin, 1979; Lenk, 1980; McNamee, 1995a; Wertz, 1991). Although their position is anti-essentialistic and these authors are more or less inspired by the later Wittgenstein, they do not consider it 'a waste of time' trying to answer the question 'what is sport?'. But contrary to the essentialists they are not exclusively preoccupied with commonality and similarities between sport activities, they also look for dissimilarities and the diversity of 'sport' in ordinary language.

If 'sport' is substituted for 'games' in Wittgenstein's famous and often quoted passage from the Philosophical Investigations, we can get a fairly clear picture of what these authors come up with (1967, § 66):

> Consider for example the proceedings that we call "games". I mean board-games, card-games, ball-games, Olympic games, and so on. What is common to them all? - Don't say: "There must be something common or they would not be called 'games'" - but look and see whether there is anything common to all. - For if you look at them you will not see something that is common to all, but similarities, relationships and a whole series of them at that. To repeat: don't think, but look! ... And the result of this examination is: we see a complicated network of

similarities overlapping and criss-crossing: sometimes
overall similarities sometimes similarities of detail.
I can think of no better expression to characterise these
similarities than "family resemblances"; for the various
resemblances between the members of a family: build,
features, colour of eyes, gait, temperament, etc. etc. overlap
and criss-cross in the same way. - And I shall say: "games"
form a family.

The family resemblance-model can be displayed in the following,
simple manner (Bambrough, 1966; Fogelin, 1979; McNamee, 1995a):

a	b	c	d	e	f
ABCDE	BCDEF	CDEFG	DEFGH	EFGHI	FGHIJ

The letters a, b, c, d and e are the names of certain games (or sports)
and the capitals beneath these letters are their characteristics. By
virtue of this schematic illustration of the family resemblance-model it
becomes apparent that (i) there exists a strong resemblance between
certain games (i.e. between a and b; b and c; e and f and so forth), (ii)
a less stronger (i.e. between a and e; b and f) or even no resemblance
(a and f) between other games, and (iii) above all that no single
common characteristic holds all games together. Hence the same term
– in our case the term 'sport' – can (or is!) be applied in ordinary
language to a number of activities between which there is no common
(essential) element. Although the family resemblance-model makes
clear that in conceptualizing sport we must not look for essences, the
question still remains how this model can be applied to sport.

2.2.1 The family resemblance-model considered critically

Although the 'family resemblance-model' is a strong thesis, it is
misleading to assume that this model is a universal panacea,
conveniently applicable to any concept which proves to be somewhat
elusive. Although some authors advocate the application of this
model, they hardly reflect critically on the nature of the resemblances
– these are left unclear, or more usually, pre-supposed.

Best puts this point less abstractly (1974, p.31):

> Consider a competitive musical festival. A group of musicians, perhaps a choir or a string ensemble, might be competing against other groups of musicians. On what basis do we decide that the model of family resemblances justifies our referring to such activities as "music" or "art" rather than "games". It could surely be plausibly argued that this situation bears an equally close resemblance to competitive team games.

Wittgenstein's theory of family resemblances states that concepts are shared under the same general term because they resemble in a number of overlapping ways. This becomes apparant in the way he considers language. In discussing what he refers to as language, Wittgenstein (1967, § 65) says:

> Instead of producing something common to all that we call language I am saying that these phenomena have no one thing in common which makes us use the same word for all – but they are *related* to one another in many different ways. And it is *because of this* relationship, or these relationships, that we call them all "language". [Second Italics mine]

So it is "because of" certain relationships which obtain amongst a set of activities that we apply the one general term to them all. But how could overlapping likeness between two or more activities suffice to justify their sharing the same general term? For example, although boxing and street-fighting resemble in a number of ways, only the former is in our ordinary language called sport. One could, however, always find some overlapping resemblance between any case of boxing and any case of street-fighting, so it would (following literally Wittgenstein's passage) always be correct to describe any case of boxing as also a case of street-fighting, and any case of street-fighting as also a case of boxing.

The two terms would thus become synonymous and, by parity of reasoning, since we can always find resemblances between instances of one concept and those of another, one could end up with the following (McNamee, 1995a, p.93):

g	h	i	j	k	l	et cetera
GHIJK	HIJKL	IJKLM	JKLMN	KLMNO	LMNOP	

Wittgensteins claim that we subsume a number of activities under the concept 'game' (or 'sport') because of resemblances is not tenable because the family resemblance-model lacks sufficient grounds to limit the extension of the concept. Since this objection claims that resemblances under-determine the extension of a concept, it is called the 'Problem of the Under-Determination of Extension' (Bellaimey, 1990). The main argument is the following: '... since we can always find resemblances between instances of one concept and those of another, if resemblances were the ground of the distinctions among concepts we would have no distinctions among concepts. Of course, we do have many concepts distinguished one from another, and so family resemblances cannot be the ground of these distinctions' (Bellaimey, 1990, p.31). So the logical consequence is that firstly the (sports)family has to be limited in order to know were to look for (family) resemblances.

Although in the application of the family resemblance-model an essentialistic position in demarcating sport from not-sport is avoid, an uncritically use of the model brings us to another, even unsatisfactory, position in defining sport: relativism. A position in which is stated that sport can not be demarcated from non-sport because there are no limiting criteria. Said in other words: there are no necessary and/or sufficient conditions based on which the sport family can be demarcated from other families. Both these positions – essentialism and relativism – are considered unfruitful. In the next section it is claimed that in defining sport it is more worthwhile to consider an alternative position – a position which goes beyond essentialism and relativism. This position considering the possibility to define sport is denoted as *moderate essentialism* (Beal, 1974, p.203).[1]

---

[1] This moderate essentialistic position is similar, at least comes close, to what Lenk (1980, p.421) denotes as 'relative essentialism' (in German: 'relativen Essentialismus') and Kretchmar (1998, p.20) typifies as 'soft metaphysics'.

2.2.2 Sport, Family resemblances and moderate essentialism

The essentialists regard sport, implicitly or explicitly, as a closed concept (see the foregoing). The assumption underlying this closeness is that sport can be demarcated from other activities in virtue of certain necessary and sufficient characteristics – e.g. play, game, competition, physicality, etc.. The 'scepticals' criticized this position by claiming that something which reveals and demands its openness is on arbitrary grounds closed. Hence, sport from this sceptical view is an open concept of which it is impossible to specify the necessary and/or sufficient conditions or properties that govern the use or application of sport. Thus we have two considerations of sport corresponding with two types of concepts: closed and open concepts. And two positions regarding the possibility to define sport: essentialism and anti-essentialism.

Following Beal (1974) it can argued that such a division of concepts and positions misdirects the inquiry into the possible ways of analyzing or elucidating concepts in terms of necessary and sufficicient conditions. Instead of only two types of concepts there exists a great variety of concepts explicable in terms of necessary and sufficient conditions – a diversity that reflects different degrees of being open and close (Beal, 1974, p.191). The two concepts are just the two extremes: wide open and tightly closed concepts. The sceptical authors consider sport as a concept which is, following the terminology of Beal (1974, p.197), *wide open*. This is a position in which it is assumed that there is no one property that is necessary and/or sufficient for an activity being sport. To avoid this extreme (relativistic) position, however, we are not forced to accept a doctrine of closing concepts tightly of a kind the essentialists are arguing for. Basically, the position in this chapter is that we can agree with Wittgenstein that it is preferable to move away from hard-core essentialism, but not to the extent that we must consider sport as a wide open concept as the only alternative. To deny that there is something common, as Wittgenstein does, does not entail the denial that we can specify a set of necessary and sufficient conditions governing application, as the sceptical authors suggest. It is possible to identify certain necessary and sufficient criteria without also closing the concept of sport by claiming that there must be something common (Beal, 1974).[2] As such we (try to) avoid both essentialism and relativism in conceptualizing sport and end up with a moderate rather than a strict essentialistic position. So the question is how this moderate essentialistic procedure can be applied to the demarcation of sport?

2.3 Three members of the sport family: paradigmatic cases and borderline cases

The question is which sport members can be recognized within the sport family? If, in following Wittgenstein's adage, the ordinary language is taken as the point of departure the first question is what in ordinary language is called 'sport'?[3] From this point of departure, the next question is to achieve a transparant description of the members of the sport-family and their inter-relationships and resemblances. Within the wide spectrum of activities which are called 'sport' in ordinary language nowadays, three concepts of sport can be recognized – one paradigmatic member and two borderline cases. The paradigmatic members are called as such, because of the common sense in calling these members 'sport'. Considering the two borderline cases this common sense concerning the question if these activities are or are not sport is less apparent.

The first paradigmatic member can be denoted as 'physical games'. In sport as a physical game two criteria are considered to be constitutive to demarcate sport from other activities: sports are (i) games which involve (ii) physical skill. In considering sport as a game one often refers to Suits' notion of a game (1978). He characterizes a game as a rule-bound goal-directed activity in which the rules agreed upon limit the permissible means of goal attainment. A game (and so sport) has a so called *gratuitous logic* – a term which indicates to the logically inefficiency that is characteristic for sport practices (and

---

[2] For a more detailed outline of the way in which Wittgenstein's family resemblance model can be recognized in this moderate essentialistic position, see: Beal (1974, pp.200-202).

[3] Maybe the first, and main question, should be what counts as 'ordinary language'. The sort of thing written about on sport pages, sport magazines or sport journals? The sort of thing talked about in sport programs, by sport organisations or by sport fans? In this chapter the ordinary language is considered in it's most broad sense - everything which is called 'sport' nowadays. This important question is considered critically by Lenk (1980) and Wertz (1991).

games) (Morgan, 1994). Morgan accentuates that the manifold sporting practices share in common that they are all contrived pursuits that seek to overcome unnecessary obstacles. Following the earlier Suits all sports are considered games – e.g. a rule-bound goal directed activity in which the rules agreed upon limit the permissible means of goal attainment.[4] As Suits and others have argued, the constitutive rules always prohibit the simplest, easiest, most direct ways to achieve the goal of the game in favor of more complex, more difficult, more indirect ways to achieve it.

The second criterion which marks out sport from other activities (and games) is that sport is concerned with physical skill and prowess. This characteristic is continuously proposed as a criterion for distinguishing sport from other fields of action. This characteristic entails that sport is always concerned with the testing of physical or bodily skill. It is crucial for an enhanced understanding of the three members of the sport family to discuss briefly the notion of 'physical skill'(see: Kretchmar, 1992; Osterhoudt, 1996, 1996, Tamboer, 1992, 1994). According to Tamboer (1992, 1994) it is important in the interpretation of physical skill to distinguish between bodily movements and motor actions. The conception of bodily movements considers human movement in terms of displacement of certain parts of the body. In everyday language one generally speaks of bodily (or physical) movements (Tamboer, 1992, pp.37/38). Kretchmar (1992, p.51) gives an example of the way in which movement can be described in terms of bodily movements:

> Every skillful movement in sport requires a remarkably complex coordination of body parts, some of which serve the function of anchor or base against which the movement of limbs occurs. In principle, the anchor is asked, as it were, to be the stable or non-moving part that makes movement possible and effective elsewhere. A baseball batter's feet, for instance, provide a relatively motionless foundation against which hip, torso and arm movements can be made.

---

[4] With the 'earlier Suits' I mean Suits before his publications in the Journal of the Philosophy of Sport in 1988 and 1989. Before this publications his position was: 'all sports are games'. A dozen years ago he changed his position. In two publications on this particular issue, Suits (1988, 1989) argued that not all sports are games. He contended that Olympic Games sports such as gymastics, diving, or ski jumping are definitely not games.

These words do not describe the actions, which together constitute the game of baseball, but the bodily movements that attend these actions (Tamboer, 1992, p.42). In view of an adequate description of human movement (and as a result sport), the concept of bodily movements should carefully and explicitly be distinguished from that of 'motor actions'. A motor action can be understood as a specific way of "knowing-the-world-in-action" (ibid. p.40). Human intentionality in motor actions is perceived and described as primarily displacing-directed (ibid. p.41). The concept of intentionality necessarily implies a directedness towards the world (or "environment"). Walking, for example, is always walking on or over something, and such a relational specification should not be confused with descriptions in terms of displacements of the legs with respect to the hip or trunk (Tamboer, 1994, p.86). Thus, unlike bodily movements, motor actions implies that the world is a defining element in its description.

If physical skill is interpreted in terms of motor actions an important differentiation can be made between two members of the sports-family – physical games and non-physical games. In physical games the goal of the activity is defined in terms of a movement problem, in which movement must be described in terms of certain movement actions. Most of the activities called 'sport' in our ordinary language are games in which the goal in the activity is characterized as the way in which the displacing is realised in a certain environment. To be the fastest in swimming, skating and running, to score more points in basketball, football or volleyball, to jump further or higher etc.. These physical games can be considered as the hard core of activities which are called sport in ordinary language.

These hard core, or paradigmatic, members of the sport family can be distinguished from the first borderline case – the non-physical games (Tamboer & Steenbergen, 2000). In the sport philosophical literature these activities are (almost unanimously) called non-sport because they do not require physical skill. The general argument is that chess, bridge and checkers appear to have all features requisite for something to qualify as sport, except that they are not games of *physical skill*. So the dividing line between sport and nonsport coincides with that between physical skill and non-physical skill. Although in ordinary language these activities are mostly (that is not unanimously) called sport, most philosophers of sport consider these activities as non-sport because they lack the element of physical skill. Even though in non-physical games as chess or bridge the lusory goal is indeed not characterized in terms of the way in which the displacing is realised in a certain environment, the question still remains why sport has to involve motor actions skills (Tamboer, 1992, p.43).

Following Wittgenstein's family resemblance-model with respect to his departure from ordinary language and considering the moderate essentialistic position, there is, however, no reason for considering chess, bridge and checkers as non-sports. If these activities were, in the light of the Wittgensteinian assumptions in the previous sections, excluded from the sport family an essentialistic position can not be avoided. Although motor actions are of logical necessity inherent to one member - 'physical games' - they are contingent to the sport family as a whole. So non-physical games can be regarded as a borderline member of the sport family which is a game for which motor actions are not constitutive.

Another member, and also a borderline case, of the sport family are the 'physical activities'. These are activities which are physical, but lack the four game elements as outlined by Suits. For example fitness and health sport can be considered as such borderline members, which most philosophers of sport do not consider as sport, because they lack competition and are inherently instrumental (e.g. Osterhoudt, 1996, p.98). Sport is in their view a game and as such the movements are intrinsically compelling. Fitness sport is a form of exercise in which the most expedient material means for achieving its material ends are preferred over less expedient means. In such activities one's principal concern is not with the movements themselves; it is not with the intrinsically compelling the edifying, the fulfilling possibilities of the movement themselves. It is instead with the instrumental, the extrinsic consequences of movement; the movements of such activities are therefore formed and valued as means to ends without themselves; which is to say, the movements of such activities are formed and valued in extrinsic terms (Osterhoudt, 1996, p.93). And because of the 'instrumental logic' and the 'search of the most direct ways to achieve the goal' (e.g. a physical fit body) exercise must be distinguished from sport members which have a gratuitous logic. Physical activities are – because of their lack of this gratuitous logic - of a fundamentally different order than the previous sport members. Although physical activities lack the four game elements, they possess the element 'physical activity' - so they are physical but not 'physical games'. Is physical in 'physical games' interpreted as to solve very specific movement problems; in physical activities physical means intensive bodily movements and the effect of these bodily movements on, for example, muscle power, endurance, heart rate and the muscular tonus.

The main conclusion is that 'the' sport does not exist (anymore). In this section Wittgenstein's family resemblance-model was applied to define sport – as a result three sport members were differentiated within the sport family. In the next and last part of this chapter sport will be viewed from a wider perspective.

2.4 The double character of sport

In the first part of this chapter the possibility to define sport is discussed thoroughly. Based on Wittgenstein's family resemblance-model three concepts of sport were distinguished, (i) physical games, (ii) non-physical games and (iii) physical activities. In this characterization of the sport family emphasis is laid on what can be called 'the autonomy of sport'. Sport, according to this view, is a domain which can be demarcated form other sorts of activity by certain predominant characteristics.

However, this characterization of sport merely by its autonomy is insufficient and rather limited. It was Franke (1978, 1983) who stresses the importance of the recognition of sports' 'relative' autonomy. Sport cannot only be defined by its autonomy, but is always embedded in a wider network of values that are current in a given society. Although such values are of influence on the autonomy of sport, they do not come from sport itself. As such, the relation of these values to the concept of sport is, by definition, considered to be of an external nature: the relation between sport and those values is not a logically necessary one, but merely contingent. Sport can be considered from an internal and external perspective, and both of these ways of viewing sport are necessary for understanding sport.

Hence sport is characterized by (i) a certain autonomy, (ii) being embedded or ensconed in a wider network of institutional interests, and (iii) influenced (and constructed) by values and norms that are current in society at large. Sport is characterized by what is called a 'double character' (Franke, 1983, Steenbergen & Tamboer, 1998; Tamboer & Steenbergen, 2000).

2.4.1 The autonomy of sport as a social practice

The autonomy of sport can best be regarded as a sport-specific conception of a social practice as defined by MacIntyre (1985, p.187).[5] He defines a practice as:

> Any coherent and complex socially established co-operative human activity through which goods internal to that form of activity are realized in the course of trying to achieve those standards of excellence and human conceptions of the ends and goods involved are systematically extended.

Like art, sciences or architecture, sport is a practice because it is a specifically co-operative human activity in the course of which goods internal to that activity are realized to achieve a specific state of affairs. In the given examples of what are and are not practices, MacIntyre distinguishes between technical skills and institutions. Tic-tac-toe is not a practice, nor is throwing a ball with skill, but the game of football is, and so is chess. Bricklaying is not a practice; architecture is. And similarly planting turnips is not a practice; farming is (MacIntyre, 1985, p.187). Other examples of practices are arts, games, sports and the enquiries of physics, chemistry and biology. These practices cannot be reduced to the various skills which are required to exemplify and sustain them without remainder. So practices are not synonymous with the various skills required to achieve 'standards of excellence', on the other hand practices must not be confused with institutions which give rise to them. Tennis, soccer and medicine, for example, are practices which must not be confused respectively with the ITF, FIFA or the American Medical

---

[5] MacIntyre's After Virtue is used in many sport philosophic publications. See for example: McNamee (1994, 1995) and Morgan (1994).

Associations. The notion of internal goods is a crucial element of MacIntryre's definition of a practice and its distinction from institutions. This notion can be exemplified by distinguishing them from those goods which are external. MacIntyre considers the example of teaching an intelligent young child how to play chess to clarify the distinction between internal and external goods. The child is motivated by giving a candy if she plays, and if the child wins she will receive an extra 50 cents worth of candy. As long as the candy is the primary motivation to play, the child has no reason not to cheat and every reason to cheat since the game itself is not relevant for the childs motivation. But there will come a time when the child will find in those goods specific to chess, such as a certain kind of analytical skill, strategic imagination, competitive intensity, the primary reason to play chess. These goods are internal to the practice of chess, because they '... cannot be had in any way but by playing chess or some other game of that specific kind' (MacIntyre, 1993, p.188).

This example shows that there are goods which are externally or contingently related to the practice of chess (the candy) and there are those which are internal to that practice (analytical skill, strategic imagination). Internal goods are called internal for two reasons. Firstly, they can only be defined, characterized or specified in the language of the practice(s) in question. Secondly, they can only be identified and recognized by the experience of participating in the specific practice; those who lack this experience are not competent to judge the internal goods of the practice in question. For analytical purpose it is important and necessary to make a sharp distinction between both goods, and consequently between the internal and external in sport. The external goods come into view when considering the second aspect of the double character of sport – 'sport as a means'.

2.4.2 The institutional embeddedness of sport

The distinction between internal and external goods becomes crucial in the account of the relationship between practices and institutions. It was noted in the previous section that a pratice must not be confused with institutions. Chess, physics and medicine are practices: chess clubs, laboratories, universities and hospitals are institutions. Institutions are characteristically concerned with the external goods. They are involved in acquiring money and other material goods; they are structured in terms of power and status, and they distribute money and power as rewards. Nor could they do otherwise if they are to sustain not only themselves, but also practices of which they are the bearers (MacIntyre, 1985, p.194).

Sport, in this view, is used as an instrument for so called extrinsic values. This instrumental view of sport considers sport as a means or instrument by which certain external (or extrinsic) values can be achieved. Traditionally the several instrumental values of sport are often used as a justification for the importance and value of sport (Seppänen, 1991). If sport is considered from this external perspective, more specific sport as a means for external purposes, the various social and cultural meanings come into view - the utility aspect of sport is emphasized (Bockrath & Franke, 1995, pp.290-292). These values, purposes or goods are called extrinsic because they are not inextricably bound up with engagement in a particular practice: there are always alternative ways for achieving such values. For example sport can be used by (local) governments as an instrument for social integration of different social-groups. Although these integrating potentials can be promoted by using sport, also work and school are practices in which social integration can be realized (see chapter 4 of this book). There are, in other words, alternative ways to realize social integration and so the relationship between sport and social integration can be regared as extrinsic - the extrinsic value for which sport is used lies outside the activity itself. Although sport can be detached from these extrinsic values on an analytical level, on an empirical level this distinction is in the actual practice of sport in society less transparent. This is what Breivik has in mind when he writes: 'Sport is not locked in its own world. Both intrinsic values (i.e. tennis joy!) and extrinsic values (i.e. a stronger heart!) flow from sport into other contexts and areas of persons' lives and society (my work, my family). And there is a flow back again' (1998, p.105).

Not only on an institutional level is sport used as an instrument for external purposes, also on an individual level can sport be used as a means for external purposes. These external purposes – such as 'feeling healthy', 'to be with other people' or 'to lose weight' – can be defined as extrinsic motives. These extrinsic motives serve as the answers to the question of why people take part in a particular activity. These extrinsic motives, however, should be distinguished from intrinsic motives. These motives serve, just as the extrinsic motives, as an answer on the 'why-question', but contrary to the extrinsic motives these motives are inextricably bound up with the

internal goods of the practice. The activity is valued intrinsically if
motives are given which flow from the internal goods associated with
the activity, i.e. these motives do not derive from anything beyond the
activity. An activity is valued extrinsically if the given motives are
related to the external goods of that activity. For instance, if a subject
values the game of soccer for reasons such as 'strategic skill', 'co-
operation' or 'competitive intensity' (to mention just a few possible
internal goods of this practice), then soccer is valued intrinsically by
the agent. Conversely, if someone values soccer because of reasons
such as earning money, status or prestige (possible external goods),
then it can be said that soccer is valued extrinsically by a person.
According to McNamee this kind of valuing is called 'relational
valuing' (1994, p.303). It can be presumed that the motives of
individuals are in principle unlimited and intrinsically and/or
extrinsically related to a particular practice. For analytical reasons,
however, it is important to make a clear distinction between extrinsic
and intrinsic motives. Hence, with respect to the frame of reference
'the double character of sport' it is important to make a distinction
between institutional external purposes (functions) and individual
external purposes (external motives/meanings). Sport too is not
always too a construction – sport is embedded in a certain socio-
cultural context.

2.4.3 The socio-cultural embeddedness of the autonomy of sport

In considering sport as a social practice it is acknowledged that sport
is socially and historically situated. The social-historical rootedness of
sport, however, does not mean that the sport practice cannot be
conceived independently of the organizing principles (institutional
embeddedness) or disjoined from its social setting, as Gruneau (1983,
p.60) argues. Following Morgan (1985, p.62) it is stated that '… the
constitutive rules really do partition sport off from the whole round of
social activities and practices'. But instead of a lapse back in an
(ahistorical and acultural) essentialistic account of sport it is
emphasised that ' … the formal rules of sport, and the formal
properties which they found … do not fall like manna from the
heavens, for they are neither historically arbitrary nor socially
inexplicable. These rules are fashioned, like everything else, out of the
social-historical experience of human agents' (Morgan, 1985, p.62).
So, sport has clear historical and social precedents, but this social-

historical rootedness '… does not warrant tying them too closely to the rest of life' (Morgan, 1985, p.63).

Many sports have their roots in the social world. Sports such as diving, skiing, skating and foot-racing originally met practical needs (Van Bottenburg, 1996). At one time however these activities are '… transformed by the superimposition of the gratuitous logic of the constitutive rules, a superimposition which adds on to and modifies the existing social layer of values and meanings with a formal layer of values and meanings' (Morgan, 1985, p.63). The ends within these practices are not social ends, but intrinsic ends of a specific sport, of which the constitutive rules prohibit the most efficient means in which the intrinsic goal is attained (Morgan 1994, pp.210-234).

So the autonomy of sport, as social practice, is not absolute but always relative. With respect to the double character of sport, and the discussion about values and norms in sport, this means (also) that the autonomy of sport and its formal rules can always be changed based on values and norms in society (sport is a social construct and so can be changed). These broader view on sport and its rootedness is more fundamental than may appear on first sight. Let's have a closer look at this broader view on sport. The formal rules of the sport practice can be seen as a standard for criticizing or justifying sporting behaviour. The rules of sport are therefore the basis upon which one can decide whether actions are justifiable: this is what is generally meant by the notion of formal fair play (see chapter 7 of this book). But in the words of Digel: 'Obeying the rules must be separated from the founding of these rules' (1982, p.82). As such, rules of sport are not self-founding: more needs to be said.[6] Expressed in MacIntyre's vocabulary, then, '… more must be said of the place of a practice in a larger moral context (1985, p.200).

For example, we may act fairly in a boxing match, but this does not necessarily mean that boxing, as such, is a morally good practice. It is conceivable that the rules of boxing are changed for reasons of health or humanity. In the light of the aforementioned frame of reference – the double character of sport – one may argue that there is a certain tension between the goal or purpose of boxing, the knock-out or intentional injuring of an opponent, and values, such as 'not doing harm', 'preventing harm or removing harm' (commonly referred to as beneficence), which are common in our society (Parry, 1998). So the

---

[6] The founding of the rules is never value-neutral, but always influenced by certain dominant values and value-structures (see chapters 9, 12, 13 and 14 of this book).

discussion about boxing is not merely in terms of whether the boxers play fairly or unfairly (or viciously), but may also concern the embeddedness of this practice in a wider network of commonly held values and norms.

From this broader point of view, we can also examine the sport-transcending discussion on children and (top level) sport (Grupe, 1985) and the pedagocial meaning of sport (see about the pedagocial questions concerning sport chapters 3, 5, 15, 16 and 17 of this book). Top level sport for children confronts us with questions about 'systematic training and planned competition programs into the period of childhood combined with the corresponding organization of the everyday life of the child and its social environment' (Grupe, 1985, p.9). A number of educational questions, which are first and foremost sport-external in nature, can be brought up. Grupe raises some of these questions: '... how are these children affected by the advancement of an adult conditioned, planned and organized sport into childhood? What is educational in that and what criteria can we use to determine whether this is useful or damaging, "suitable" or not "suitable" for the child's development and education? Which educational problems arise in this context? Thus, sport is faced with questions that are based on educational, in an analytical sense sport-transcending, values.

The normative judgements or justifications of sport given in the (two) examples above arise from a sport-transcending perspective. With this perspective in mind, the relative autonomy (its socio-cultural rootedness) of sports comes into sight – that is, the broader network of commonly held values and norms in which sport practices are embedded.

Conclusion

To discuss systematically the several values and norms which are related to sport it is important to make clear distinctions. By using the frame of reference 'the double character of sport' it is posssible to reveal the relationality of these values and norms. The different relationships of the values (or goods) norms with the sport practice in question – internal or external – come to the fore if the concept of sport itself is made sufficiently explicit.

The double character of sport can be used as a frame of reference based on which a systematic focus on the broad spectrum of values and norms concerning sport can be offered. In the remainder of this part, and other parts of this book, these different values and norms are brought to the fore thoroughly and discussed in more detail.

References

Bambrough, R. (1966). Universals and Family Resemblances. In: G. Pitcher (Ed.), *Wittgenstein: the Philosophical Investigations* (pp. 186-204). Anchor Books.

Beal, M.W. (1974). Essentialism and closed concepts. *Ratio*, 16, pp. 190-205.

Bellaimey, J. (1990). Family Resemblances and the Problem of the Under-Determination of Extension. *Philosophical Investigations*, 13, pp. 31-43.

Best, D. (1974). *Expression in Movement and the Arts*. London: Lepus Books.

Bockrath, F. & Franke, E. (1995). Is There Any Value in Sports? About the Ethical Significance of Sport Activities. *International Review for the Sociology of Sport*, 30, pp. 182-188.

Bottenburg, M. van (1996). Huizinga's thin Ice. In: A. Elling, J. Steenbergen & J.H.M. Lucassen (Eds.), *Values and Norms in Sport* (pp. 25-29). Arnhem: NOC*NSF. (in Dutch).

Breivik, G. (1998). Sport in High Modernity: Sport as a Carrier of Social Values. *Journal of the Philosophy of Sport*, XXV, pp. 102-118.

Crum, B. (1991). *About the Sportification of Society*. Rijswijk: WVC. (in Dutch).

Dietrich, K. & Heinemann, K. (1989). *The non-sportive Sport*. Schorndorf: Hofmann. (in German).

Digel, H. (1986). Concerning the Changing Values in Society, Leisure and Sport. In: K. Heinemann & H. Becker (Eds.), *Die Zukunft des sports* (pp. 14-43). Schorndorf: Hofmann. (in German).

Digel, H. (1982). *Understanding and Shaping Sport*. Hamburg: Rowohlt. (in German).

Fogelin, R.J. (1979). Sport: The Diversity of the Concept. In: E.W. Gerber & W.J. Morgan (Eds.), *Sport and the Body* (pp. 58-62). Philadelphia: Lea & Febiger.

Franke, E. (1978). *Theory and Meaning of Sportive Actions*. Schorndorf: Hofmann. (in German).

Franke, E. (1983). Non-goal-directedness versus Goal-directedess of Sport – or how the ordinary language Misleads. In: H. Lenk (Ed.), *Actual Problems in the Philosophy of Sport* (pp. 108-117). Schorndorf: Hofmann. (in German).

Gerber, E.W. & Morgan W.J. (Eds. 1979). *Sport and the Body: A Philosophical Symposium*. Philadelphia: Lea & Febiger.

Gruneau, R.S. (1983). *Class, Sports, and Social Development*. Amherst: University of Masachusetts Press.

Grupe, O. (1985). Top-Level Sports for Children from an Educational Viewpoint. *The International Journal of Physical Education*, 22, pp. 9-15.

Heinemann, K. (1980). *Introduction in the Sociology of Sport*. Schordorf: Hofmann. (in German).

Kleinmann, S. (1968). Toward a non-theory of Sport. *Quest*, pp. 29-34.

Kretchmar, R.S. (1992). Reactions to Tamboer's 'Sport and Motor Actions'. *Journal of the Philosophy of Sport*, X, pp. 21-32.

Kretchmar, R.S. (1998). Soft metahysics: a precursor to good sports ethics. In: M.J. McNamee & S.J. Parry (Eds.). *Ethics and Sport* (pp. 19-34). London: E & FN Spon.

Lenk, H. (1980). Toward an analytic Philosophy of Sport. *Sportwissenschaft*, 4, pp. 417-436. (in German).

MacIntyre, A.C. (1985). *After Virtue*. London: Duckworth.

McBride, F. (1979). Toward a non-definition of Sport. In: E.W. Gerber & W.J. Morgan (Eds.). *Sport and the Body, A Philosophical Symposium* (pp. 48-52). Philadelphia: Lea & Febiger.

McNamee, M.J. (1994). Valuing Leisure practices; towards a theoretical framework. *Leisure Studies*, 13, pp. 288-309.

McNamee, M.J. (1995). Sporting Practices, Institutions and Virtues: A Critique and a Restatement. *Journal of the Philosophy of Sport*, XXII, pp. 61-82.

McNamee, M.J. (1995a). Sport; Relativism, Commonality and Essential Contestability, In: S. Eassom (Ed.). *Sport and Values* (pp. 86-119). Bedford: Casper.

Morgan, W.J. (1985). 'Radical' Social Theory of Sport: A Critique and a Conceptual Emendation. *Sociology of Sport Journal*, 2, pp. 56-71.

Morgan, W.J. (1994). *Leftist Theories of Sport. A Critique and Reconstruction.* Chicago/Urbana: University of Illinois Press.

Morgan, W.J. & Meier, K.V. (Eds. 1995). *Philosophic Inquiry in Sport.* Champaign: Human Kinetics.

Osterhoudt, R.G. (1996). Physicality: One Among the Internal Goods of Sport. *Journal of the Philosophy of Sport*, XXIII, pp. 91-103.

Parry, S.J. (1998). Violence and aggression in contemporary sport. In: M.J. McNamee & S.J. Parry (Eds.), *Ethics and Sport* (pp. 205-224). London: E & FN Spon.

Seppänen, P. (1991). Values in sport for all. In: P. Oja & R. Telma (Eds.), *Sport for All* (pp. 21-32). Elseviers Science Publishers B.V.

Steenbergen, J. & Tamboer, J.W.I. (1998). Ethics and the Double Character of Sport: An Attempt to Systematize Discussion of the Ethics of Sport. In: M.J. McNamee & S.J. Parry (Eds.), *Ethics and Sport* (pp. 35-53). London: E & FN Spon.

Suits, B.H. (1978). *The Grasshopper: Games, Life and Utopia.* Toronto/Buffalo: University of Toronto.

Suits, B.H. (1988). Tricky Triad: Games, Play and Sport. *Journal of the Philosophy of Sport*, XV, pp. 1-9.

Suits, B.H. (1989). The Trick of the Disappearing Goal. *Journal of the Philosophy of Sport*, XVI, pp. 1-12.

Tamboer, J.W.I. (1992). Sport and Motor Actions. *Journal of the Philosophy of Sport*, XIX, pp. 31-45.

Tamboer, J.W.I. (1994). On the Contingent Relation Between Motor Actions and Sport: A Reaction to Kretchmar. *Journal of the Philosophy of Sport*, XXI, pp. 82-90.

Tamboer, J.W.I. & Steenbergen, J. (2000). *Philosophy of Sport*. Leende: Damon. (in Dutch).

Thomas, C.E. (1983). *Sport in a Philosophic Context*. Philadelphia: Lea & Febiger.

Wertz, S.K. (1991). *Talking a Good Game: Inquiries into the Principles of Sport*. Dallas: Southern Methodist University Press.

Wittgenstein, L. (1967). *Philosophical Investigations*. Oxford: Blackwell.

3 CAN HEALTH IN AND THROUGH SPORTS BE A PEDAGOGICAL AIM?

Ivo van Hilvoorde

Introduction

Our attention for health and exercise and for the relationship between movement and our bodies seems to have a paradoxical character. On the one hand, our bodies have become 'redundant'. 'Movement' has grown into a concept with a variety of different (among which: virtual) meanings and dimensions. But on the other hand we passionately try to compensate, and to resist 'body-hostile' working circumstances with an expanding variety of exercises and sports. According to the health experts however, a great part of the Dutch community does not compensate enough. Worse still, not many people meet their constructed standards of daily exercise. Children not in the least. In spite of the fact that almost 80% of the youth frequently participates in sport (which did not decrease over the last 25 years), recent figures indicate that the same percentage (that is: 80%) of the youth between 16 and 25 does not fulfil the constructed norm for daily exercise (Hildebrandt, Ooijendijk & Stiggebout, 1999; L'Abée, 2001). Many modern pedagogues, hesitant to formulate clear pedagogical aims, contrast with health experts who, without any hesitations, 'prove' scientifically the norms to which a healthy child must aspire. The need to exercise is being proclaimed simply because it is healthy. Health and (moral) goodness have almost become synonymous in the discourse of the health expert. An unhealthy lifestyle is as reprehensible as the indecent in the 19th century. Scientists play an important role by constructing these standards of health and fitness.

In the first part of this chapter we discuss the relation between the 'body- and motionless' society and its over-compensation in the form of extreme attention for corporality and health. We establish that on the one hand parts of the sports system start fusing together with the medical system (cf. Cachay & Thiel, 1999), and on the other hand extreme escapes from a healthy existence are being sought. This leads to the question what are the possibilities and limitations of a health policy that preferably likes to see the practising of a healthy and safe sport by as many people as possible? We also wonder to what extent scientific research can be independent and critical in this debate, or whether it acts as a continuation of political goals. Finally, we look at a number of pedagogical consequences, for example by asking how pedagogically oriented is health education. The question is whether there can be a more pedagogical perspective within health-educational programs. This question will be posed in terms of a short (and at this moment preliminary) historical account on developments of sport pedagogy as an academic discipline.

3.1 The paradox of 'body-hostility' and social hypochondria

In modern Western society many people collectively perform the same bodily movements by participating in activities such as running, stepping, skating and aerobics. At the same time, in the same society, more and more people climb mountains, explore caves, dive from high cliffs and bridges, with the help of an elastic band (bungee jumping). Is there a sociological relation between these extremes of conformism of movement on the one hand and on the other hand the cultivation of boundless contempt of speed, height and other activities that the public in large will associate with perilous adventure? At first sight this relation seems to be existent in terms of social pressure; just as the person who is doing his work-out and is jogging in water is performing these activities with the double purpose of to see and be seen, the solitary climber, diver or cyclist, is doing the same, by preparing photos and stories of his adventures for his or her homecoming. It is the same 'looking' person as Laermans (1993a) describes, someone who sees himself in an (imaginary) mirror while doing his workout or hanging on a climbing wall. "The awareness doubles. Beside the subjective awareness, 'the looking-man' forms a second awareness of object, besides the particular awareness an awareness-of-the-others evolves, besides the private self a public 'looking-glass self' grows" (1993a, p.67). The role that the practice of sports plays for this 'looking-glass self' turns out to be of paradoxical nature. On the one hand sports belongs pre-eminently within a healthy, good life style. On the other hand there is no field where health can be put at risk so explicitly, and voluntarily as is the case of sport.

If you ask people why they practice sport, most people refer in their answer to health as a primary value. Health is the fundamental condition to live, work, enjoy and to consume. Health is important for the quality of life. It also means that it is good to live a life that doesn't endanger health. For centuries the health effect of bodily movements has also been propagated in moral-ethical terms. In the eighteenth century it was the pedagogue Salzmann who institutionalized gymnastics, hoping that as a consequence he could banish sexual immoral behavior in youth. At the beginning of the 19th century Friedrich Ludwig Jahn laid the foundations for the German practice of gymnastics. Gymnastics made able-bodied men out of individuals, who were then able to fight for the health of a whole (German) nation.

The collapse of the religious worldview from the 19th century on, was partly filled up by doctors, the experts of a healthy life style. The competence of doctors, the science of illness and health, started to compete with the competence of the clergy, the doctrine of good and evil. 'Living means to be healthy' and 'Living means to be good' became two similar discourses (Rolies, 1987). Modern forms of sin are indicated in terms of not being fit or slender. A quasi-objective scale to measure this is the so-called Quetelet- or Body Mass Index. This index gives us the norms for obesity and overweight, but simultaneously expresses a body image, determined by western cultural values. The healthy (and therefore sporty) person is slender, fit and also socially productive. From a sports sociological perspective the current health cult is indicated in terms of compensation for a lack of movement in ordinary life, or as a modern form of giving meaning.

Nowadays, most people believe that health does not depend on coincidence and fate, but think that they are responsible for it themselves. It is a relatively new phenomenon that we take our health in our own hands and make it subject to our action. The individual has discovered that he has to act in order to stay healthy. The belief in progress has made a shift from society to people's own health. The current attention for health and sports can be seen as a reaction to the industrialized society and the growing absence of the body (Bette, 1989). To an increasing extent the body has been made superfluous, redundant, in a society in which moving from one place to another becomes less essential for communication or even surviving.

Talking about the present attraction of the practice of sport, one can point to the concrete experiences that sport can offer. The demand for naturalness and sensitivity is getting louder in a body-alien or, even stronger, body-hostile society (Rittner, 1985). A paradoxical consequence of this absence is the upgrading of the same body. The body proximity represents a place of refuge of permanent presence and authenticity. The body is an important symbol for a still controllable, impressionable reality. When running, we feel our heartbeat, hear our panting and experience pain, that can be associated with the improvement of fitness. The jogger knows that jogging causes a certain sensation, a sensation of being alone, fighting against pain, which can become a pleasure or even addictive (Vosman, 1993, p.41).

Objectified health parameters create the image of a body that is under total control. Numbers create the belief in health as something measurable, a status that can be described in terms of 'more or less'. This meets the wish of an objective inspection of one's own health. The practice of sport turns out to be a suitable means in order to achieve this. The longing for knowledge of 'objective' risk factors has also been nourished by what Beck (1991) calls the speculative era. An enormous attention to, and knowledge about, an abundance of toxic influences and carcinogens stimulates the fear for the invisible. The invisible and threatening risks can be 'suppressed' with the help of the objective arithmetic of the fitness-machine.

In addition to this concept of health, determined by usefulness and efficiency, sport also shows an unhealthy drawback. This can be denominated as a - however different - form of compensation. This concept of health has another rationality than the health of the objectified parameters. It is the concept of health, shown by the dangerous jump with an elastic rope, the fall and the dive from a high cliff. It is health as the victory over fear, the exceeding of boundaries, a victory over gravity or physicality. It is the concept of health referring to the flight from and victory over the motionless monotony of the open-plan office. It is the creation of the unique person, by the thought uniqueness of the sporty heroic deed, never performed before. But it is also the exceeding of social mores, the use of violence and aggression and, whether or not deliberately, the injuring of the other person.

The sociologist Norbert Elias described the process of civilization as an increasing aversion to an openly act of violence, and the growing monopoly on violence of the government. Nowadays there have been doubts about this increasing civilization. An increasing amount of control is needed in order to maintain an even inferior form of civilization. During the past years the world of sport has been confronted frequently with themes that are grist to the mill of those who share the opinion that in sport also it is just a matter of increasing aggression and decreasing a sense of values. Football vandalism, offending crowd chants, aggression on the football pitch, lethal accidents in boxing, and new violent sports (like *free fight* and *ultimate fight*), are examples of this. An almost hypochondriac focus on our health is alternated with the most absurd attempts to put this health at risk. The question is how government and the world of sport can go along with both the sunny side and drawback of this situation.

3.2 Possibilities and limitations of health-policy

Propagating and stimulating a healthy sport practice has been self-evident for decades. From the sixties and seventies on we are familiar with broad social campaigns like 'Jog yourself fit' (by which the running and jogging craze started), 'Sportreal' and 'Sport, even I do it'. Currently we see campaigns aimed at a more specific target group. An example of this is a project, which started in the nineties, called 'Youth in Motion'. Both the sport organizations and the government benefit from spreading this positive health value, and from pushing back the possible undesirable health effects of sport. The most important cornerstones of policy concerning sport and health are to anticipate the necessity of more physical exercise, to force back (the consequences of) sport injuries and to control and map the use of drugs in sport.

Although research on the consequences of physical activity was initially done because one expected an adverse influence between sport and life span, afterwards the conviction grew that sport and physical exercise have a broad spectrum of healthful influences. With the broadly used (that is: in The Netherlands) term 'movement-poverty' a cultural awareness is indicated that our ancestors must have been much richer in terms of moving, than is the case for the present mailing- and electronically surfing generation. The present time offers health scientist sufficient trends towards 'immobility' and examples to demonstrate that we never exercise enough (cf. Hildebrandt et al., 1999). With this appeal it seems that both politics and science agree on this issue. More than that, many health-scientists seem to be as obedient as Lalonde, pioneer in health-politics, wanted them to be.

In 1974 he wrote: "The spirit of enquiry and skepticism, and particularly the scientific method, so essential to research, are, however, a problem in health promotion. The reason for this is that science is full of 'ifs', 'buts' and 'may be's' while messages designed to influence the public must be loud, clear and unequivocal." (p.6).

From the fact that many of the present health-scientists are loud, clear and unequivocal we might conclude that they are not scientific, or else that they have found a fruitful, symbiotic relation with health-politics. But in spite of this apparent unanimity, one can cast a doubt on several objects of policy. It is not uncommon that romantic and cliché reflections about the healthy and primitive man are being used to strengthen the idea of a movement deficit of the present human being. Do we need to compare ourselves however with this hunting prehistoric (wo)man? From a critical reflection on the social role of health scientists and on the various campaigns a few questions can be formulated: Who, for example, doesn't exercise enough? And what are the norms to establish this? Who is responsible for the determination of these norms, and what knowledge is used as a basis. What, and whose interests are connected with this knowledge? How can target groups be identified? And how can people be stimulated to change their movement behavior structurally? In addition to the desirability also the feasibility of health education plays an important role.

The measuring of fitness is not neutral, but creates norms that distinguish people as 'fit' or 'not fit'. Nowadays, to comply with the norms of fitness means: a smaller chance to become ill, less absence through illness, higher productivity, decreasing risk of sport injuries, attractive, active, vigorous and (quantifiable) advantages for the economy. With this the concepts of health and fitness get more (moral) significance; they've become more than just a neutral, objective measurement. Fitness and slimness become associated not only with energy, drive and vitality but worthiness as a person; a fit and healthy body comes to be taken as a sign of prudence (cf. Featherstone, 1991).

Simultaneously with the measuring of fitness, it is therefore meaningful to ask oneself what will happen with these data. Fitness is increasingly associated with suitability for society, and is to a growing extent a necessary condition for this suitability. Legal developments, such as the 'privatization of responsibilities', for example, contribute to the increasing risk-selection in application procedures. This trend is strengthened by a growing knowledge of genetics and risk-orientated, predicting medical science. As soon as we know better what a person should do, or (on the contrary) should leave, one experiences a high temptation to introduce this person to the supposed free choices, or even to approve or disapprove the behavior of a person on these grounds. "Crucially, the ideology of healthism also tends to place responsibility for bodily vigilance solely on the individual, and deflects attention away from the social and cultural conditions which shape and constrain health." (White, Young & Gillet, 1995, p.160).

Increasing pressure on collective costs of health care reinforces the development of 'being-fit as a civic duty'. Laermans (1993) calls this new civic duty a modern sense of sin or a sense of guilt. The health value of sport is interpreted more often in terms of social, or (macro)economical interests. Especially when several interested parties (like for example insurance companies) benefit from specific research results, the question of the extent of autonomy of the scientists involved becomes relevant. Being-fit (which means being measured as fit) can, to put it briefly, have increasingly bigger consequences. The role of science here is not neutral, and neither is the choice for the criteria to measure fitness free of values.

Is fitness as a consequence of possible misuse for external purposes less worth aiming for? No, not at all. Fitness is also a fundamental condition for parts of the quality of life. But the meaning of 'being-fit' is not the same for everyone, in spite of an enormous amount of social pressure associated with this topic nowadays. Although fitness can be seen as an expression of a similar 'exciting less' society, it can also mean that we may risk our health to a great extent. The competition with others, the comparison of our achievements, the proof of our fear and the tendency to maintain our health will remain, in defiance of what health professionals say, very important motives for the modern sport practice.

3.3 Contextualized health-policy

The more practical question remains, if we agree on the necessity of a less immobile lifestyle, what means are available to make people sweat for fun? And what scientific expertise can be used to help doing this? Campaigns like *active living* and *The Netherlands Exercises*! are recent examples of a long tradition in health-education. But the question is how much flexibility is left, to be able to change the health-attitudes and behavior of adult people structurally. Research shows that campaigns based on rational knowledge on health risking behavior have little or no effect. The extent to which we can really influence our health, depends on many different lifestyle factors (cf. Lüschen, Cockerham & Kunz, 1996; Van Hilvoorde, 1998). Furthermore, much of our behavior - relevant for our health - has a rather stable character, and depends strongly on both genetic features as well as socio-economical living conditions and (sub)cultural values and norms. Given these large differences it is hard to expect all people to conform equally to a kind of self-responsible health ideology. The utility that some people gain from sport practice can be much higher than the potential utility of the still non-active persons (Wagner, 1987).

More important than the message that people should exercise more, is the question what it is that people are being restrained from doing exercise; what possible (financial, cognitive or other) thresholds are of importance in an 'immobile lifestyle'. To spread knowledge on behavior that possibly influences health is just a small link within a larger, more complex system of health-education. Modern campaigns could benefit more by integrating knowledge from different disciplines (like health-psychology and sociology) and research done on the question which factors determine changes in lifestyle (cf. Read, 1997; Balm, 2000).

Nilsen (1996) states that many of the present programs for health-education have little or no effect, because there has been too little concern with the local context and with the social and spatial reality of a specific community. Too little energy has been invested in developing a conceptual understanding of the community as a context of implementation. Little attention has been paid to daily life interpretations of risk- and other health-related behavior. An important question, often overlooked, is how cultural trends impinge on local cultures and personal identities. Especially the mediation of images and ideas by mass media is influential in creating a community-related identity. Communities, groups of people sharing values and institutions, share a certain identity, and behavior that helps constructing this identity. To be able to get insight into the mechanisms that influence the possible effects of a health program, it is important to understand the mechanisms by which people interpret cultural trends or mediated images. One of the important factors is the so-called *health belief*; how large is the belief that one can (and want to) really influence their own health? Another factor is the support of the environment.

Thus, with what kind of images does a certain community identify with? And, how are these images produced? Large firms of sports equipment for example, know how to attract youthful subcultures by cultivating the connection between high-risk sports and images of individuality, autonomy, freedom and non-conformity. In this case it would be useless to implement a knowledge-based health-program. Instead of following behaviorist principles of stimulus-response it is important to show how the health-related activities are part of a specific *life world*. Knowledge of these identifying mechanisms can be used for a more realistic implementation of health-programs.

With questions concerning learning-mechanisms and health-education we move towards the expertise of the educational sciences. Especially when asking to what extent the regular physical education in schools needs to be complemented with special health-education? There is currently a trend towards health-promoting schools. Reiss (1996) found that in Great-Britain health-education is much more a matter of health training. A training moreover that often produces no effect or is even contra-productive. The difference is that training is no more than learning the customs and habits, based on a clear distinction between healthy-unhealthy. Education tries to integrate this knowledge within a pattern of other values, like responsibility and respect for autonomy. Reiss observes one-sidedness within health education. "Much of school health education fails to acknowledge that life consists of rather more than trying to live for as long as possible" (ibid., p.95). Unhealthy behaviour may become one of the means students adopt to distance themselves from the values espoused by their schools. At its worst, health training may lower self-esteem and increase disaffection with schooling (ibid., p.102).

The health training based on images of 'what terrible things may happen, if we don't exercise enough' often has the same logic as driving lessons in American schools. In some American states it is allowed to drive at sixteen years of age, but one has to be twenty-one to drink alcohol. Because of problems with drinking and driving one tries to frighten the children during driving lessons at school. Films are being shown with horrible images of accidents; fifteen-year-old children watch their peers, dying in wrecks. This 'knowledge' of the dangers of drinking and driving however, does not stimulate a responsible use of alcohol, which still has to be 'learned' illegally. This kind of health training is based on the assumption that knowledge about future risks of present behaviour is sufficient.

Information and education however can also be based on a more reflexive way (cf. Kolb, 1996). Without imparting to insight into the individual and future significance of a responsible lifestyle, and without giving insight into the dominant role of an environment, health training will have little or no effect. It needs to be linked with the personal context and with that of a specific community. For a child, the message: 'each person should engage in a regular program of aerobic exercise of 3-5 sessions per week of 30-60 minutes each', is of little meaning. Nor does a child need to know the possible health value of new ramps and safe places to skate in the neighbourhood.

Because of changes in the spectrum of illnesses in the modern Western society the attention shifts from cure to prevention of the modern diseases of civilization. Knowledge grows on the relation between preventative behaviour and illness to prevent. This rationality of prevention and predictive medicine is the same rationality that leads to the school-game, 'who is the fittest pupil of the class?' (as has been 'played' in Germany). From a more pedagogically perspective however, health-education needs a more reflective and differentiated perspective, than this purely physiological one. That means a perspective that integrates knowledge on learning, teaching and moral education (cf. Read, 1997; Rütten, 1998). This begs the question, to conclude, of the present role and status of sport pedagogy. Following on recent discussions in Germany, we question the lack of pedagogic perspective in these matters of health-education and sport in The Netherlands. Again, this will only be a preliminary account, meant for further research.

3.5 Pedagogical reflection on sport and health

Traditionally, questioning values and standards scientifically is done within the field of ethics. With an accent on the world of the child, pedagogy claims expertise as well, with regard to (practical) questions on values and norms. One of the fields in which pedagogy can use its expertise is sport. As an important social and cultural phenomenon, the expanding world of sport does not escape from the increasing complexity regarding moral judgements, and themes asking for ethical and, also pedagogical reflection. Historically, pedagogues have been (also philosophically and psychologically) engaged in the concept of 'play', and also in the distinction between play and sport.

Within a culture-historical conception, play is being thought of as the basis of many manifestations of culture (Huizinga, 1938). In the fifties and sixties the world of sport went through many changes in terms of professionalization (the ideal of amateurism disappeared) and commercialisation. Critics of these developments saw this as an indication of the final disappearance of the element of play in sport. The attention of pedagogues for sport during this period however, remained little in The Netherlands. Given the strong pedagogical tradition in the reflection on 'play', as well as the strong scientific tradition closely related to various practical fields, it is remarkable that in the Netherlands, sport pedagogy - as a scientific sub-discipline - plays a marginal role in relation to other sport sciences. Just as remarkable is the relatively small attention of pedagogues themselves for the world of sport (of course with exceptions; see for example Buisman (1987) and Crum (1988)).

Sport pedagogy has often been characterized as an applied science in relation to its mother science, pedagogy. It deals with unplanned and intentional possibilities and limitations of education to and through movement, play and sport (cf. Haag, 1994). Contrary to the Netherlands, it seems that this academic sub-discipline is growing into a serious science in several countries. "Having gone through academic adolescence, sport pedagogy is now entering adulthood" (Kang, 1994, p.91). The longer existence of specialized journals in this area indicates that this is not only a recent development. A meaningful institutional moment for sport pedagogy was the introduction of a special interest group in 1986 within the American Educational Research Association (AERA) (Bain, 1997). These merely Anglo-Saxon developments however are hardly comparable with Continental traditions. From way back sport in the United States has been substantially integrated within the school-system. Without a sharp distinction between physical education and sport, pedagogical theorizing also developed closer to sports than was the case in Europe.

In the course of many years in Germany sport pedagogy had a central position in relation to other sport sciences. But from the nineties on the disappearance of this central role gave reason for ample discussion on the status and rationality of this loss. Especially the question if sport pedagogy should be an independent discipline, or a more integrated part within and among other sport sciences was initiated in *Sportwissenschaft* and also discussed in several other journals (cf. Cachay, 1991; Cachay & Bähr, Court, 1996 1992; Kurz, 1992; Prohl, 1994).

Three different positions can be roughly discerned in this discussion:

1. *Interdisciplinarity*: sport pedagogy should leave its isolation and strive for more integration with other disciplines.
2. *Metadisciplinarity*: sport pedagogy should strengthen its roots, or even return to its philosophical origin.
3. *Sub-disciplinarity*: sport pedagogy should strive for homogeneity and recognition, possibly by sub-disciplining its own expertise.

Cachay & Bähr (1992) plead from the perspective of constructive system theory for pragmatic interdisciplinarity in sport pedagogic research. According to the authors it would give pedagogic thinking a higher standing within sport science again. In the Netherlands however, there is a sharper – historically grown – distinction between physical education and sport, and with that also between pedagogical reflections in each of both fields of application. Therefore a combination of striving for more integration with other disciplines as well as for more homogeneity and recognition would be the obvious means to be able to bridge the gap between sport and pedagogy.

Another gap of interest here is the relation with the mother discipline, in this case pedagogy. From the moment onwards that educational science was strongly influenced by the 'empirical turn' during the sixties and seventies, the philosophical and pedagogical reflection in the field of physical education still depended on phenomenological and anthropological oriented reflections (cf. Grupe & Krüger, 1994). That this gap remained can be found within recent pedagogical publications, in which for example the philosophical anthropological paradigm is being called "as good as dead" (Koops, 2000, p.66).

Such a gap prevented a fruitful exchange of expertise, for example in the field of learning processes or between philosophically and empirically oriented research. Besides a period of left-oriented sport-critical research, pedagogical and philosophical theorizing on sports remained closely attached to theories of subject, and had fewer eyes for the social embeddings of sport. Themes like play and physicality remained important anthropological hobbyhorses. Cachay (1991) found the same focus on theories of subject in Germany, where social theory has also been predominantly avoided. "As a result, the pedagogy of physical education has hardly dealt with problems of society from the perspective of learning processes." (ibid., p.51).

Current themes like the conflict of sport and environment (and the limits of the sport for all-ideology), the pedagogical possibilities of risk- and adventure-sports or, returning to the theme of sport and health, the desirability of fitness as a pedagogical goal, can benefit from modern insights in learning and education. From a pedagogical point of view the legitimisation of research in sport must not refer to the value of alleged autonomous sport but to criteria which consider responsibility for a rising generation. 'Therefore "anthropological, ideological-critical and ethical reflection on the everyday purposes of sport" is required' (Beckers, In: Court, 1996, p.142).

To give an example, the enormous boom in the practice of adventure-sports did not get an equivalent yet in theorizing on the pedagogical meanings of these risk-full activities (Neumann, 1999). Stimulating individual responsibility, self-confidence, trust in others, communication, cooperation, tolerance, handling authority and criticism, experience of corporality, dealing with competition and pressure to perform, ecological conscience, stimulating imagination and intellect are possible (not necessary) benefits from 'outward bound' (ibid., p.161). And thus, possibly, pedagogical fields of interest. Such a broad spectrum of pedagogical values cannot be reduced to a discussion about 'fitness'.

Conclusion

Given the multiversity of contemporary sport, with all extreme manifestations, from large conformism in performing exercises to a growing craving for new "kicks", makes it impossible to discuss the health-value of sport in a one-dimensional, in one monopolized, discourse, or just in terms of epidemiological or physiological effects. It seems however, that the modern health-promoter has taken a firm position on the pulpit. But instead of preaching a religion, or pronounced ideals, he uses 'objective facts' to preach for the healthy human being. The gap is getting larger between timid attempts to clear up modern values and on the other hand the health-scientists who are loud, clear and unequivocal in prescribing and propagating their norms. That this clarity sometimes inevitably denies the complexity of learning mechanisms and educational goals, could be a stimulant for more reflexive, sport pedagogical research.

References

Bain, L. (1997). Sport Pedagogy. In: J. Maasengale & R. Swanson (Eds.), *The history of exercise and sport science* (pp. 15-37). Champaign: Human Kinetics.

Balm, M.F.K. (2000). *One can learn to move healthy. Behavioural changes by ergo-, physio- and remedial therapists.* Utrecht: Lemma. (in Dutch).

Beck, U. (1991). *Politics in risk society.* Frankfurt am Main: Suhrkamp Verlag. (in German).

Bette, K.H. (1989). *Corporal traces: Semantics and Paradoxes of modern Corporality.* Berlin: De Gruyter. (in German).

Buisman, A.J. (1987). *Youthsport and Fair Play.* Haarlem: Vrieseborch. (in Dutch).

Cachay, K. (1991). Sport Pedagogy and Societal Theory. *Spectrum der Sportwissenschaften*, 3, 1, pp. 51-66. (in German).

Cachay, K. & Bähr, H. (1992). Sport Pedagogy – Scientific Subdiscipline or Integrative Core of Sport Science? *Sportwissenschaft*, 22, pp. 283-303.

Cachay, K & Thiel, A. (1999). From Medicine- to Healthsystem – Professionalization chances for male and female Sport scientists? *Sportwissenschaft*, 29, pp. 143-157. (in German).

Court, J. (1996). German Philosophy of Sport. *International journal of physical education*, 33, 4, pp. 138-148.

Crum B. (1988). Concerning the development of research in sport pedagogy. *Sportwissenschaft*, 18, pp. 176-184.

Featherstone, M. (1991). *The Body in Consumer Culture. The Body: social process and cultural theory*, pp. 170-196.

Grupe, O. & Krüger, M. (1994). Sport Pedagogy : The anthropological Approach. *Sport Science Review*, 3, 1, pp. 18-27.

Haag, H. (1994). State-of-the-Art Review of Sport Pedagogy. *Sport Science Review*, 3, 1, pp. 1-10.

Hildebrandt, V., Ooijendijk, W. & Stiggebout, M. (1999). *Trend rapport Exercise and Health 1998/1999*. Lelystad: Koninklijke Vermande. (in Dutch).

Hilvoorde, I. van (1998). *Sport and health; An analysis of scientific constructions and social standardization*. Arnhem: NOC*NSF. (in Dutch).

Huizinga, J. (1938/1985). *Homo Ludens. On the origin of culture in play*. Groningen: Wolters-Noordhoff. (in Dutch).

Kang, S. (1994). Research and Practice in Sport Pedagogy. *Sport Science Review*, 1994, 3(1), pp. 91-102.

Kolb, M. (1996). Promotion of Health and Sport. *Sportwissenschaft*, 26, pp. 335-359.

Koops, W. (2000). *Failing adulthood. On destinations of development and goals of pedagogy*. Houten/Diegem: Bohn Stafleu Van Loghum. (in Dutch).

Kurz, D. (1992). Sport pedagogy as a discipline or as the nucleus of sport science? *Sportwissenschaft*, 22, pp. 145-154.

L'Abée, D. (2001). *Moving figures. An overview and analysis of quantitative data on youth, sport and moving*. Arnhem: Stichting Jeugd in Beweging. (in Dutch).

Laermans, R. (1993). *Individual flesh. On Body images*. Amsterdam: Uitgeverij De Balie. (in Dutch).

Laermans, R. (1993a). The mannequin-society. On 'look', lifestyle and corporality. In: F. de Wachter (ed.). *About use and disadvantage of postmodernism for life* (pp. 65-79). Kapellen: Uitgeverij Pelckmans. (in Dutch).

Lalonde, M. (1974). *A new perspective on the health of Canadians. A working document*. Ministry of Supply and Services, Canada.

Lüschen, G, Cockerham, W, & Kunz, G. (1996). The Sociocultural Context of Sport and Health: Problems of Causal Relations and Structural Interdependence. *Sociology of Sport Journal*, 13, pp. 197-213.

Neumann, P. (1999). Between adventure orientation and experience orientation – Sport Pedagogical considerations by example of a risk-education in Sport. *Sportwissenschaft*, pp. 158-174. (in German).

Nilsen, Ø. (1996). Community health promotion: concepts and lessons from contemporary sociology. *Health Policy*, 36, pp. 167-183.

Prohl, R. (1994). Sport Pedagogy as Advisory Science. *Sportwissenschaft*, 24, pp. 9-28. (in German).

Read, D.A. (1997). *Health Education. A Cognitive-Behavioral Approach.* Sudbury: Jones and Bartlett Publishers.

Reiss, M.J. (1996). Food, Smoking and Sex: Values in Health Education. In: J.M. Halstead & M.J. Taylor (Eds.), *Values and Values Education in Schools* (pp. 92-103). London: The Falmer Press.

Rittner, V. (1985). Sport and Health. To differentation of the Health-motive in Sport. *Sportwissenschaft*, 15, pp. 136-154. (in German).

Rolies, J. (1987). *The healthy citizen. Health as the norm.* Nijmegen: Sun. (in Dutch).

Rütten, A. (Ed. 1998). *Public health und Sport.* Stuttgart: Verlag Stephanie Nagelschmid. (in German).

Vosman, F. (1993). The Body: fate nor choice. In: *The divided body. Experience and imagination of corporality in a fragmented culture.* Baarn: Uitgeverij Gooi en Sticht. (in Dutch).

Wagner, G. (1987). Sport as a means for reducing the cost of illness – Some theoretical, statistical and empirical remarks. *International Review for Sociology of Sport*, 22, 3, pp. 217-226.

White, Ph., Young, K. & Gillett, J. (1995). Bodywork as a Moral Imperative: some Critical Notes on Health and Fitness. *Society and Leisure,* 18, 1, pp. 159-182.

4 THE INTEGRATING AND DIFFERENTIATING SIGNIFICANCE OF SPORT

Agnes Elling, Paul De Knop & Annelies Knoppers

Introduction

Sport participation and watching sports are among the most popular leisure activities of the Dutch population. Not only, as it used to be, for wealthy young men, but for many men and women of varying ages, social-economic and ethnic backgrounds (CBS, 1996). Not only the sport population has become more differentiated in the last few decades, the structure and organisation of sport have also changed. There used to be a relatively small number of sports which were mainly organised in (voluntarily) sport clubs. Nowadays a wide range of individual and team sports exist which are increasingly practised in differently organised settings like (commercial) sport centres or in public spaces (squares, parks, et cetera; Van Bottenburg & Schuyt, 1996; Crum, 1991).

Since the development of modern sport in the Netherlands in the nineteenth century, several integrating values and functions have been ascribed to the practice of sport (Van Bottenburg, 1996; Stevenson & Nixon, 1972; Vanreusel & Bulcaen, 1992). Sport is seen as bringing people together, as fostering identification with teams and athletes and can contribute to the social cohesiveness of a team, a social group, a town or a whole country. Since several developments like increased immigration, pluralist value orientations, secularisation and individualisation have lead to a perceived lack of social integration and social cohesion in society at large, the instrumental use of sport with its integrating potentials is increasingly promoted by (local) governments and (sport) organisations (Council of Europe, 1995; Kearney, 1992; VWS, 1996). The national men's soccer team in which men from different ethnicities play together is seen as a 'perfect' example of these functions. Because of its low threshold, its uniform character and its international standardised rules, many people regard sport as a perfect activity in which people of different social and ethnic backgrounds seem to mingle automatically, which leads to mixed friendships and more tolerance for cultural diversity. Projects to stimulate sport involvement are often legitimated by claims that sport is a good instrument for socialisation of youth and social integration of different minority groups like ethnic minorities, the physically challenged and the elderly (Elling, De Knop & Theeboom, 1998).

There is, however, little empirical evidence about positive effects of sport participation on broader social integration. And although some social traditional distinctions in society and sport seem to be weakening, others (like gender and nationality) are explicitly made and reinforced within competitive sport. In contrast to the view of sport as an ideal vehicle for social integration, sport can also mirror or magnify other processes in broader society. Sport not only brings people together, but also differentiates and discriminates among teams, social groups, towns and countries. Except illustrating ethnic diversity and integration, national men's soccer leagues can also illustrate ethnic differentiation and discrimination, e.g., the overtly racist crowd chants (Merkel & Tokarski, 1996). Furthermore there are still many differences in the participation rates of specific social groups, cultural connotations and power structures (e.g. related to gender and ethnicity) between specific types of sport. These examples raise questions about the uni-dimensionality and uniformity of integrating meanings and potentials of sport: do all sports in all organising contexts have the same integrating meanings and functions for all social groups?

The central question in this chapter is: in which ways is sport (participation) related to values and processes of social integration and differentiation with regard to different social groups? We will present a conceptual framework for (critically) analysing the processes of social integration in sport and broader integration through sport in society. We will also present some results of an empirical research project among young people in which we have looked at different integrating and differentiating values and norms with respect to gender and ethnicity.

4.1 What is social integration?

'I think sport is one of the most important factors for integration. In sport you meet everyone. It should be used as a means to increase acceptance. But unfortunately that is not always the case. On the [soccer]field you act different and are focussed on winning. Therefore it can go wrong sometimes.' (Surinam man, Elling & De Knop, 1999, p.140)

'Aren't we integrated enough? We work all day, shop and do all kinds of things together with straight people all day.' (member of gay sport club, idem, p.138).

Although many policy makers refer to the importance of sport in improving (the lack of) social integration in society, it is used in many meanings and with reference to different social groups and sporting contexts (Elling & De Knop, 1999). We argue that more dimensional analyses are necessary, due to broad and differently used conceptualisations of both sport and social integration and increased differentiation in the population and value orientations in and outside the realm of sport. We understand social integration as a multidimensional process which is continually related to processes of social differentiation, segregation and discrimination. We make a distinction among three, interrelated, dimensions (Elling & De Knop 1999; Engbersen & Gabriëls, 1995; Jenson, 2000): structural (participation), socio-cultural (values & norms) and socio-affective (social contacts & friendships). We will discuss each of these dimensions in further detail, both *within* the social practice of sport and in relation to 'external' social integrative meanings and effects *through* sport participation.

Structural integration *within* sport means participation in more or less integrated institutional forms. A person can participate with some one, against an other or in different groups and competitions. There are different lines of argument in favour or against certain ways of structural integration, they can be more functional, moral and/or expressive in nature. In mainstream organised club sport different ways of structural integration/segregation are mainly based on *functional* arguments, which are related to age, gender and sport specific skills. This line of argumentation is solely based on 'intrinsic' principles assigned to sport like fair competition and equal opportunities (Steenbergen, Van Hilvoorde & Tamboer, 1995).

Moral arguments plead for equal opportunities for all groups to participate in sport. Physically less abled people, for example, confront more structural and cultural barriers than abled people. Compared to the physically less abled, ethnic minorities and women confront fewer structural barriers to participating in mainstream organised sport, but still more than the white ethnic majority or men respectively (Elling & De Knop, 1999). The inclusion of young children in sport clubs can be encouraged both on the basis of functional arguments (to spot and select talents as early as possible) and based on moral arguments (young children should be given the opportunity to learn and develop sport skills within a save and (semi-professional environment).

Expressive arguments for specific forms of structural integration are used by people who choose to participate in a particular sport group. Examples are teams and clubs which are not (mainly) formed on the basis of sport specific skills, but which are (also) related to social connections and/or identities: a group of friends who form a team, ethnic minorities or gays and lesbians who choose to participate in their own sports clubs. Expressive arguments seem to gain more meaning with age, when not only sport performance but especially social contacts and feelings of 'belonging' and meeting 'equals' increase. Although the forming of new 'separate' clubs, based on social identities like ethnicity or (homo)sexual orientation is increasing, most people who belong to these minority groups seems to be structurally integrated in 'regular', ethnically/sexually mixed, tournaments or leagues (Janssens, 1999; Stöpler & Schuijff, 1997). Not all people have the same opportunities to be structurally integrated in different ways: although many people belonging to different social majority and minorities groups have a choice to participate in either 'mixed' and/or 'own' clubs and competitions, physically less abled people and the elderly often have little choice. They can only participate within 'own' groups, based on specific physical abilities and/or age.

Different stages of structural integration are mostly related to the extent to which minority groups are integrated within the activities and organisations of majority groups. One can, however, also stimulate 'reverse' integration: e.g. the participation of physically able people within 'adapted sports like sit-volleyball or wheelchair basketball, or the membership of white or straight people within an ethnic minority, or gay and lesbian sport clubs.

Structural integration *through* sport can be explained as upward social mobility or as broader participation in other sections of society as a result of involvement in sport. Social integration of (ethnic) minorities in the Netherlands is mostly measured in participation rates in levels of education, housing and labour and less in socio-cultural variables (Engbersen & Gabriëls, 1995). Involvement in sport has different opportunities for upward social mobility. Professional sport is most visible through the media, but too difficult to reach for most athletes. Only the 'lonely few' who reach the highest ranks can actually make a living from participation in sports and even for them it is usually only temporary. With the increased general participation in sport over the last twenty-five years, however, there are many more possibilities to work within the sport branch nowadays: as a teacher, coach, manager, journalist, researcher, etc.. These are structural integrating possibilities both in and through sport. Other structural integration processes through sport are connected to socialization, like learning certain skills and values which can be used outside the realm of sport. This process is often referred to by policy makers as a function of sport participation, but is not based on solid empirical evidence (Patriksson, 1995; Sabo, Melnick & Vanfossen, 1993). Participating in sport might, nonetheless, be an important (first) step for many people to feel confident and learn social skills, which can help them to move upwards in society. Immigrants, for example, might learn the (Dutch) language, norms and styles of communication quicker and therefore have increased possibilities in other social sectors. Sometimes sport participation can also be an important element in the (re)integration of (male) delinquent youth or in preventing others from 'deviant' behaviour (De Knop & Theeboom, 1991).

In the process of **socio-cultural** integration *within* sport, aspects as norms and values and construction of ideologies and representation are central to the discussion. In our pluralist society we regard a multicultural climate as more integrative than a dominant and normative climate, directed at assimilation of minority values and groups. In a multicultural climate, tolerance, the development- and the experience of identity, acceptance and respect for a plurality of values are of great importance (Struijs, 1998; Taylor, 1994).

Since sport in general has become more plural (e.g., with respect to value orientations and motives), it is difficult to define thé culture of sport. Nonetheless, especially in traditional sport clubs, one can distinguish dominant values and norms which are presented as 'neutral' and 'intrinsically linked to sport', but are in fact constructed by white (older) men (Anthonissen & Boessenkool, 1998; Knoppers & Bouman, 1998). Integration by minority groups is often only possible and accepted, as most *functional*, when they 'assimilate' to the existing white, male culture. Different value orientations and motivations have, nonetheless, developed within the world of sport as a whole, over the last few decades. And especially social groups like women, the elderly and ethnic minorities have contributed to this evolution of a more pluralist sport landscape. *Moral* arguments, based on the principles of justice and equality (e.g. Coakley, 1998; Lumpkin, Stoll & Beller, 1994), would therefore plead for greater understanding of different value orientations instead of the existing hierarchy in which white, male values and norms are hegemonic. Although sport brings people together and can stimulate the exchange of different values and norms; we stress that (competitive) sport itself is not value free and often is perceived to be more 'open' and tolerant by the dominant group than by minority groups. Racist outings like 'dirty Turk' or 'go back to your own country' in the heat of the game might be used and interpreted as strategic psychological intimidation, similar to the use of 'carrots' (Meloen & Eersteling, 1994). It is often also seen as natural that women receive less attention and payment in sports because they perform 'less well than' men. Whose norms and values are used here?

Socio-cultural integration *through* sport, the transmission of norms and values from the world of sport to society (and vice versa), is not a transparent process (Coakley, 1998, Mielke & Bahlke, 1995). This is partly due to the different social identities that are ascribed to and are experienced by people in certain sectors in society. Professional sports, but also competitive and recreational sport, can have exemplary and de-constructive functions. White female (and heterosexually 'feminine') soccer players, or black (male or female) golf players, for example, might deconstruct dominant images related to gender and ethnicity, respectively.

A professional black athlete or soccer player can contribute to processes of self-identification and emancipation for young black people, but can at the same time confirm dominant stereotypical ideas about ethnicity (as 'naturally fast and strong') and lead to exclusion or discrimination (Coakley, 1998; Jarvie, 1991).

Socio-affectionate integration is above all connected to expressive aspects and stands out clearly in the establishment of different social contacts, friendships, love affairs and marriages. Most sports are social leisure activities in which people with very different social backgrounds, voluntarily engage. The specific leisure context and the pursuing of similar (competitive) goals together are seen as important aspects to stimulate (intimate) social contacts between people with similar and different social backgrounds in sport (e.g. Vanreusel & Bulcaen, 1992).

Apart from 'performance' and health', 'sociability' is an important motivation for many people, to participate in sport. One can participate together with friends and/or meet new friendships through sport. Especially, when moving into another town sport can be a good instrument for meeting other people and stimulating the process of (affective) social integration (Van der Poel & Roques, 1999).

It is often thought that good team work requires friendly informal contacts among team members. Therefore, specific social activities are planned to stimulate the team cohesion. In that context friendship among sport group members is seen as *functional* to sport performance. But social contacts among sport group members do not automatically develop into sport related or sport transcendent friendships (Elling & De Knop, 1999). Especially when the sport group members are from various social groups, since social relations and friendships are also structured by e.g., social class, gender and ethnicity (Adams & Blieszener, 1994; Saharso, 1992). Some studies showed that having more inter-ethnic or other 'mixed' contacts *in* sport doesn't necessarily translate into having more 'mixed' friendships *through* sport (Chu & Griffey, 1982; Poisson, 1999).

Although sport is a place where other people and 'the other' can be met; individuals with explicit social motives like 'making friends' mostly do not want to meet 'the other', but people with similar backgrounds (Elling & De Knop, 1999; Janssens, 1999). For minority groups this means that they mostly join 'separate' clubs, based on a specific social identity (e.g., sport clubs for Turkish, Surinam, gay and lesbian, or deaf people). This illustrates that sport participation can function as a means of social expression and *integration* within a particular group and as a means of *differentiation* between specific groups and subcultures (Brinkhoff, 1998; Donnelly, 1993).

We conclude that on the one hand, sport provides many opportunities for informal contacts between people with varying social characteristics and is therefore often regarded as a good 'instrument' for meeting 'the other'. On the other hand, sport can be seen as a social practice in which most of all contacts between people with similar interests and social backgrounds are stimulated. Therefore it is difficult to speak of sport as a very effective (let alone, ideal) instrument for 'mixed' social (affective) integration.

Nuances and contradictions
The three dimensions of social integration are not independent, but interrelated. There are continuing, but complex interactions between different integrating and differentiating processes in and through sport like participation, representation, discrimination, emancipation, group cohesion, identification and conflicts.

We have given some examples and will further try to show that integrating potentials and effects depend on which type of sport and which social group is involved, and are mediated by several other factors, like structural and cultural barriers, motivations, constructions of social identities and social networks. In the next paragraph we will further illustrate the complex relations between sport and social integration by focussing on the results of a research study we conducted among young people.

4.2 The empirical research project

4.2.1 Methodology

Questionnaires, which consisted of several open and closed questions about sport participation, social networks and value orientations (related to gender and ethnicity), were collected among 1025 young people in the age between 14-20 years in the towns of Amsterdam and Tilburg, from January to April 1999. The respondents were students in six schools, which varied in ethnic population ('white', 'black' and 'mixed' school)[1] and included all four types of secondary education (vbo, mavo, havo, vwo). The questionnaires were filled out within regular school hours, which lead to a 99% response; completion took approximately thirty minutes. In addition to the questionnaire, we held a total of 25 semi-structured interviews with 31 boys and girls of varying ethnicities, who were involved in sport in different ways. Most interviews were held with individual respondents and some with small groups (two or three persons) and lasted approximately 45 minutes.

Respondents
A total of 1016 questionnaires were available for analysis; the respondents group consists of 53% girls and 47% boys. Most respondents follow the two median education levels and the mean age is 16 years. Nearly two third of the research population belongs to the ethnic majority and about one third belongs to ethnic minority groups. Only respondents who or of whom one or both parents were born abroad (the first and second generation) of ethnic minorities from non-western countries, and/or those who are defined as target groups in Dutch integration policies, are classified as ethnic minority. This excluded (white) respondents who, or whose parents were, born in countries like Germany or the USA. On the basis of these definitions the largest ethnic minority groups among the respondents – as within the Dutch population at large - are Moroccan (10%), Surinam (8%),Turkish (6%) and Indonesian (4%) youth.

---

[1] A school was classified as 'black' or 'white', when more than 75% of the population belonged to ethnic minorities or to the ethnic majority, respectively. About half of the respondents attended an ethnic 'mixed' school; 'black' and 'white' school were both attended by a quarter of the research population.

4.2.2 Sport participation: degrees of structural integration

Nearly two third of the respondents participates actively in sport in their leisure time, about six hours a week and mostly in the organised setting of a sport club (see table 1). Most gender and ethnic difference affirmed other research (e.g. CBS, 1996; DSP, 2000; Duyvendak, Krouwel, Boonstra & Kraaijkamp, 1998).

In general, more boys than girls and more ethnic majority than minority youth participate in sport. When we look at interactions between gender and ethnicity, there is only an ethnic difference among girls. The sport participation level of the ethnic minority boys is similar to the ethnic majority boys; the first group is even involved more hours per week. Both among ethnic majority and ethnic minority youth, girls participate less and less frequent than boys (p<0.001).

Table 1: Sport participation, frequency and organisational form by gender and ethnicity

	total	gender		ethnicity		boys		girls	
	total	boys	girls	e.min	e.maj	e.min	e.maj	e.min	e.maj
n	(1002)	(465)	(537)	(349)	(653)	(157)	(308)	(192)	(345)
participation (%)	64	75***	54	53***	70	71	77	39***	63
n	(640)	(348)	(292)	(185)	(456)	(111)	(237)	(74)	(218)
frequency									
hours a week	5.8	6.6***	5.0	6.5*	5.6	7.6**	6.2	5.1	4.9
organisational form									
club (%)	59	64**	52	42***	66	50**	71	29***	60
comm. sport org (%)	19	14***	26	28***	15	18	12	45***	19
public space (%)	19	26***	11	29***	15	37**	20	18*	9
different (%)	16	11***	21	17	15	13	10	21	22

(* p < 0.05; ** p < 0.01; *** p < 0.001)

We also looked more specifically at different ethnic minority groups. Although other research found similar low levels of sport participation between Turkish and Moroccan girls (e.g. DSP, 2000), we found a higher level of sport participation among Moroccan girls (40%; similar to Surinam girls), than among Turkish girls (18%). Indonesian girls participate to a similar level than ethnic majority girls (63%). There are hardly differences in levels of sport participation between boys of different ethnic minorities.

There are also several similarities and differences in the organisational forms of sport participation. The largest percentage of most groups are involved within organised club form. An exception are ethnic minority girls, who practise their (fitness) sports mainly in commercial sport centres. Although the overall sport participation of ethnic minority boys is higher than ethnic majority girls, the latter group is more often involved in organised club sport.

How should these findings with respect to the general participation and different types of structural integration be interpreted? Do ethnic minority girls, and specifically Turkish girls, have to be stimulated to participate more in sport? Do ethnic majority boys have to be stimulated more to be involved in organised club sport? We argue that one should be careful with such conclusions, because then the sport participation of 'white' boys is taken as a norm (Elling, 2001). In a multicultural society, one should respect different norms about the 'good life', especially with regard to leisure time. Nonetheless one should also take possible constraints in consideration: do specific groups not want to participate, are they not able to or are they not allowed to? (Schuijt, 1997). Boys and girls not only differentiate in general sport participation, but distinctions are even stronger with respect to specific sports.

Type of sport
A total number of 60 different types of sports are mentioned by the respondents that participate in sport. More than half of the sport participants are involved in soccer (34%) and/or fitness/aerobics (22%). These are the only two sports that occur in the top five of four different groups differentiated towards gender and ethnicity, although the relative popularity still differs between groups. In table 2 the ten most popular sports are shown, differentiated by gender and ethnicity.

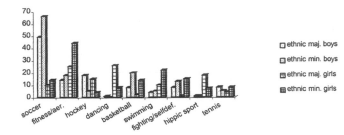

Table 2: Ten most popular sports, differentiated by gender and ethnicity

(Field)hockey is mainly played by the ethnic majority boys and girls (in Tilburg) and basketball and fighting/self defence sports are more popular among ethnic minority boys and girls (in Amsterdam). Dancing and hippic sports are mainly participated in by ethnic majority girls.

A question that arises from these results is whether differences in the popularity of sports are only influenced by individual and group possibilities and preferences, or also by values and norms among and about social groups. Although several Dutch studies about sport participation showed similar differences in sport participation between social groups (CBS, 1996; DSP, 2000), hardly any attention has been paid to interactions with social networks and value orientations. Exceptions are some more ethnographical studies, e.g., among young soccer players (e.g. Elling, 1999). International research has showed that (non)participation in sport is also used by youth subcultures as a means of self expression and differentiation (e.g. Brinkhoff, 1998).

4.2.3 Value orientations towards sport, gender and ethnicity: socio cultural integration?

In the questionnaire, respondents were asked in different ways about their value orientations towards specific sports. They were asked whether they would like to participate in a number of, fifteen, different sports, and also more explicitly whether all sports were 'suitable' for boys and girls and for 'blacks' and 'whites'. There seems to be general understanding among all groups about the overall popularity of some sports (e.g. swimming, tennis, basketball and soccer) and the unpopularity of others (e.g. skateboarding, golf and korfball).[2] Further, most respondents, although more girls than boys (p<0.001), agreed that both boys and girls (79%) and both 'blacks' and 'whites' (91%) could practise all sports.

Gendered value orientations

'I was teased a lot, especially by the boys. That I was a girl and a sissy. Just teasing all day... My brother and some other boys left the sport, because they were teased a lot at school.' (Dutch male gymnast)

Although young people in general agree about the popularity of specific sports, only some sports are relatively gender neutral (e.g., tennis, hockey). More boys (70%, rank 2) than girls (46%, rank 6), for example are willing to play soccer. From the girls who do not want to participate one out of ten explicitly mentioned social arguments like 'it is not a sport for girls' or 'it is a boys sport'. Soccer and fighting sports were also most often mentioned as sports that are less or not suitable for girls. On the contrary dance/ballet and gymnastics were most often mentioned as less or not suitable for boys. Figure skating and gymnastics are much more popular among girls (54%, rank 3 and 38%, rank 8, respectively) than among boys (8%, rank 15 and 15%, rank 13, respectively). Many of the boys who do not want to participate in these sports used gender related arguments like 'it is a girls sport', or a 'sissy sport'. Although korfball, a sport in which boys and girls participate together, is not popular among both male and female respondents, only boys used gender specific arguments for not willing to participate. Boys not only referred to gender, but also to sexuality ('sport for gays/queers/faggots'), as reasons not to participate in the specific sports. This is similar to findings of Laberge & Albert (1999) who studied relations between hegemonic masculine values and sport (see also chapter 9 of this book). Although several studies from a cultural studies and/or feminist approach showed

---

[2] The general ranking order is: swimming (61%), tennis (58%), basketball (57%), soccer (57%), formula 1 racing (54%), baseball (49%), volleyball (45%), boxing (35%), figure skating (33%), field hockey (29%), track and field (29%), gymnastics (28%), skateboarding (27%), golf (24%) and korfball (18%).

that perceived gender differences in the suitability of specific sports are social constructions (e.g. Hargreaves, 1994), most (young) people referred to 'natural' biological differences like 'not built for it' or 'unnatural' or to socio-cultural –aesthetic- aspects: 'ugly', 'doesn't look good'.

From the results we conclude that gendered norms and values structure sport participation; they can both positively and negatively influence personal choices. Above all traditional 'masculine' sports are valued more positive than traditional 'feminine' activities and in addition gender-'inappropriate' behaviour among boys is more negatively valued than among girls.

Ethnic value orientations

"Because of their length, they are relatively long and I recently heard it has to do with the equilibrium point of those people. Therefore you hardly see black swimmers. They are good at sprinting and their physicality is just better for those sports." ('white' Dutch boy)

"I always thought that brown people were better at dancing than whites. But then I saw a white person dancing very well and when you look at golf, you see a brown person who is good at it as well. It's more interests, I think, culture and background." (Surinam girl)

Most of the fifteen sports are more popular among ethnic minorities than among the ethnic majority, although they hardly differ in ranking. Exceptions are basketball and boxing which rank higher among ethnic minorities than among ethnic majority youth. It was interesting that we found no significant ethnic difference in the level of agreement that all sports are suitable for 'white' and 'black' people. Track and field and basketball were mentioned most often as sports that are 'less suitable' for 'white' people. Mostly biological arguments like 'blacks are faster/bigger/stronger', were used to explain differences, which confirms stereotypical images about black people as 'natural' athletes (Coakley, 1998). Fewer youngsters mentioned one or more sports that they thought of as less suitable for blacks; (speed)skating was most often mentioned. In addition fewer biological and more socio-cultural arguments were made, which actually strengthened the idea of the 'natural' athletic superiority of black people. Compared to the questionnaire, explanations for ethnic/racial differences in athletic abilities during the interviews were more complex and more often included socio-economical and socio-cultural arguments. In general socio-critical arguments were more often made by ethnic majority girls and ethnic majority boys and girls than by ethnic majority boys. Nevertheless most respondents gave only explanations for the (better) performances of black athletes as 'the other', which made 'whiteness' more or less invisible.

The results show that sport not only might stimulate more respect for different social groups, as is often considered in governmental policies (e.g. Raad voor het Jeugdbeleid, 1995), but is also used to distinguish and discriminate between groups. Many (young) people believe that sport is relatively neutral with respect to gender and ethnicity and that participation in (a particular) sport is a personal choice. Some of the findings can indeed be interpreted as illustrating a relatively high level of socio-cultural integration through the emergence of a global (youth) culture[3] (Wilson & Sparks, 1996). However, the results also show the expression of stereotypical 'naturalised' images related to gender and ethnicity, especially by male youth. These cultural images and ideologies influence 'free' choices and may constrain personal development and social equality in sport and society (Hargreaves, 1994; Messner & Sabo, 1990).

Degrees of socio-cultural integration do not only interact with specific forms of (non)participation in particular sports, but is also related to socio-affective integration. In what ways do young people participate in gender and ethnic mixed sport groups and to what extent do (mixed) friendships occur through sport?

---

[3] The number one position of Michael Jordan as their sport hero illustrates this globalisation process. Nonetheless Michael Jordan was more often chosen by ethnic minority youth than by the ethnic majority (Elling, 2001).

4.2.4 'Mixed' social contacts and friendships in sport: aspects of socio-affective integration

"I have different friends, from work, from school, from sport and from going out... The friends from sport are not very close, I don't go out with them as well, but they are good friends nevertheless." (Dutch boy)

"Most of the friends I have, I met through sport, by playing soccer on the streets. I don't do other things with them, except saying hello when I see them. With my [best] girl friend I do everything." (Moroccan girl)

More than half of the respondents and interestingly more girls than boys, participate in a 'mixed' gender context; most often in (commercial) sport centres (57%), compared to clubs (30%) or public spaces (25%). It is possible that girls more often than boys regard some contexts (like sport centres) as 'mixed'. From the ones that don't participate in mixed gender contexts, girls more often than boys would like to, mostly because it's *'nicer'* or *'more enjoyable'*. Boys more often say they don't like to, because *'girls are not as good'* or *'boys are better'*.

Compared to the ethnic majority, about twice as many Surinam, Turkish and Moroccan respondents participate in an ethnic 'mixed' group (see table 3). Most of these 'mixed' groups include (other) Euro-Dutch youngsters (92%), although more often with regard to Euro-Dutch respondents than with regard to respondents of ethnic minorities. About one out of ten ethnic minority respondents participate with people from their 'own' ethnic group. The Indonesian respondents confirmed their 'official status' of being more similar to the Euro-Dutch group, compared with other ethnic minorities.

Table 3: Mixed sport participation (in %)

	Ethnicity							Total
	Moroccan	Surinam	Turkish	Indonesian	Other min	Ethnic min	Ethnic maj	
N	*(45)*	*(37)*	*(19)*	*(21)*	*(31)*	*(152)*	*(420)*	*(572)*
						***		
Mixed	82,2	81,1	84,2	47,6	61,2	73,7	40,7	**49,5**
Dutch	4,4	5,4	5,3	52,4	32,3	16,4	58,3	**47,2**
own ethnic group	13,3	13,5	10,5	-	6,5	9,9	1,0	**3,3**
Total	100	100	100	100	100	100	100	**100**

(*** p < 0.001)

When the respondents were asked with whom they prefer to participate, most respondents indicated that they would like to play in an ethnic 'mixed' setting or that they 'don't mind'. A similar group of ethnic minorities and the ethnic majority (12%), but more boys than girls, indicate they prefer their 'own' ethnic group.

The ethnic majority often views separate ethnic groups as processes of separation which provocates increased inter-ethnic tensions and inhibits the integration process (Duyvendak, et al, 1998; Janssens, 1999). But as our results show, many people belonging to the ethnic majority themselves are not active in 'mingling' or even prefer to stay separate. They often seem to regard integration, or 'assimilation', as the sole responsibility of ethnic minorities.

'Mixed' friendships through (club)sport?

About two third of the young respondents, with hardly any differences between groups, regards most or some of the other people with whom they participate in sports as friends. Interestingly, only among the ethnic majority youth are most social activities undertaken more often with their 'other' friends than with their sport friends, especially more 'intimate' activities like visiting each other and talking. Among the ethnic minorities the activity pattern between sport friends and general friends is more similar. This could indicate more overlap between these social networks among ethnic minorities than among the ethnic majority, who more often participate within an organised club context.

Of the three best friends of the respondents, only 9% are met through sport. School (59%) and neighbourhood (14%) are most often mentioned as 'meeting place'. When controlled for sport participation, as many boys as girls meet their friends through sport (clubs), but ethnic majority youth more often than ethnic minorities. The last group more often meet friends 'on the street', which can also include public sport activities. The representation of ethnic populations at the school seem to be of most influence in the forming of 'mixed' ethnic friendships. For the ethnic majority respondents a relatively equal amount of friendships formed through either school, neighbourhood or sport have a 'mixed' ethnic character. The number of friendships formed through sport by ethnic minorities in our study was too small (n=13) to draw conclusions. Girls who play sport more often have a best opposite-sex friend, than girls who don't play sport. With respect to boys, no difference was found. These results question or at least nuance common sense ideas like the 'fraternisation through sport'; seemingly ideal contexts, like sport, do not necessarily lead to more ('mixed') friendships (Chu & Griffey, 1982; Poisson, 1999).

Conclusion

We have argued that both sport and social integration are complex processes, which are not similar for all social groups. To claim that 'sport integrates' is an 'empty' statement which is equally valid as stating that 'sport discriminates'. Especially when specific types of sport, the organisational structures, the social characteristics of the sport groups and the interactive social relations and images are taken into account, the complex character of integrating and differentiating dimensions in and through sport become more visible. The primary results of our empirical study among young people show that gender and ethnicity (still) influence sport participation, social networks and sport related images and are differently related to processes of social integration and differentiation. Dominant perceptions about different 'natural' athletic abilities between men and women and between 'blacks' and 'whites' seem to structure social networks and sport participation. On the one hand, specific sports (e.g. like soccer) play an important role in the social networks of (male) ethnic minority and majority youth. On the other hand, however, sport only seems to play a marginal role for them in the making of good friends. Above all, some sports (e.g. soccer) tend to be integrative in some respect, but can be judged differently when another frame of reference is used. For individuals, participation in sport might reflect or enhance social integration in society, but our research indicates that instrumental approaches with regard to the social integrative functions of sport are to be viewed and analysed critically.

References

Adams R.G. & Blieszner, R. (1994). An integrative conceptual framework for friendship research. *Journal of Social and Personal Relationships*. 11, pp. 163-184.

Anthonissen, A. & Boessenkool, J. (1998). *Meanings in management: Diversity in managerial performance in amateur sport organizations*. Utrecht: Isor (in Dutch).

Bottenburg, M. van (1996). Huizinga's thin ice. In: A. Elling, J. Steenbergen & J.H.M. Lucassen (Eds.), *Waarden en Normen in de sport* (pp. 25-29). Arnhem: NOC*NSF. (in Dutch).

Bottenburg, M. van & Schuyt, K. (1996). *The social meaning of sport*. Arnhem: NOC*NSF (in Dutch).

Brinkhoff, K-P. (1998). *Youth sport and socialization* Weinheim: Juventa.

CBS (1996). Sport involvement 1995. *Sociaal Culturele Berichten* 96/16. (in Dutch).

Chu, D. & Griffey, D.C. (1982). Sport and racial integration: The relationship of personal contact, attitudes and behaviour. In: A.O. Dunleavy, A.W. Miracle & R. Rees. (Eds.), *Studies in the sociology of sport* (pp. 271-282). Fort Worth: Texas Christian University Press

Coakley. J.J. (1998). *Sport in society. Issues and controversies*. (6th ed.), St. Louis: Mosby.

Council of Europe (1995). *The significance of sport for society, health, socialisation, economy*. Committee for the Development of Sport, Council of Europe Press.

Crum, B. (1991). *The sportification of society*. Rijswijk: Ministerie van WVC. (in Dutch).

Donelly, P. (1993). Subcultures in sport. In: A.G. Ingham & J.W. Loy (Eds.), *Sport in social development* (pp. 119-145). Champaign ILL: Human Kinetics.

DSP (2000). *Sport participation statistics for Amsterdam, 1999.* Amsterdam: Gemeente Amsterdam (O+S). (in Dutch).

Duyvendak, J.W., Krouwel, A. Boonstra, N. & Kraaijkamp, R. (1998). *Integration through sport.* Rotterdam: Bestuursdienst. (in Dutch).

Elling, A. (1999). 'A bit rough, I like that'. Images of and experiences in women's soccer. *Tijdschrift voor Genderstudies* 2/4, 25-35. (in Dutch).

Elling, A. (2001) *Fraternisation through sport: truth or myth?* Arnhem: NOC*NSF. (in Dutch).

Elling, A. & Knop, P. De (1999). *According to one's own wishes and possibilities.* Arnhem: NOC*NSF. (in Dutch).

Elling, A., Knop, P. De & Theeboom, M. (1996). Social integration in sports policy in the Netherlands and Flanders. In: J. Steenbergen, A.J. Buisman, P. De Knop & J.M.H. Lucassen (Eds.) *Waarden en normen in de sport.* (pp.261-279). Houten: Bohn Stafleu Van Loghum. (in Dutch).

Engbersen, G. & Gabriëls, R. (Eds.) (1995). *Areas for integration. Towards a differentiated immigrant policy.* Amsterdam: Boom (in Dutch).

Hargreaves, J (1994). *Sporting females. Critical issues in the history and sociology of women's sport.* London: Routledge.

Janssens, J. (1999). *Ethnic division in sport.* Den Bosch: Diopter. (in Dutch).

Jarvie, G. (Ed.), (1991) *Sport, Racism and Ethnicity.* London (NY): Falmer Press.

Jenson, J (2000). *Labour, care and social cohesion.* Paper presentation Symposium Social Cohesion, June 14, Amsterdam.

Kearney, A.T. (1992). *Sport as a source of inspiration for society.* Amsterdam: A.T. Kearney. (in Dutch).

Knop, P. De & Theeboom, M. (1991) Sport as instrument for integration for social vulnerable youth. In: P. De Knop & L. Walgrave (Eds.), *Sport als integratie: Kansen voor sociaal kwetsbare jeugd* (pp. 37-58). Brussel: Koning Boudewijn Stichting. (in Dutch).

Knoppers, A. & Bouman, Y. (1998). The trainer/coach as a carrier of culture. In: J. Steenbergen, A.J. Buisman, P. De Knop, J.M.H. Lucassen (Eds.), *Waarden en Normen in de sport*. (pp. 223-237). Houten. Bohn Stafleu Van Loghum. (in Dutch).

Laberge, S. & Albert, M. (1999). Conceptions of masculinity and of gender transgressions in sport among adolescent boys. Hegemony, contestation, and social class dynamic. *Men and Masculinities*, 1/3, pp. 243-267.

Lumpkin, A., Stoll, S.K. & Beller, J.M. (1994). *Sport ethics: Applications for fair play*. St. Louis: Mosby.

Meloen, J.D. & Eersteling, P. (1994*). 'People call names sometimes': Discrimination of immigrants in amateur sport*. Utrecht: Jan van Arkel. (in Dutch).

Merkel, U. & Tokarski, W. (1996). *Racism and xenophobia in European football*. Aachen: Meyer und Meyer.

Messner, M.A. & Sabo, D.F (1990). Introduction: Toward a critical feminist reappraisal of sport, men and the gender order. In M. A. Messner & D.F. Sabo (Eds.), *Sport, men and the gender order: Critical feminist perspectives* (pp. 1-15). Champaign, ILL: Human Kinetics.

Mielke, R. & Bahlke, S. (1995). Structure and preferences of fundamental values of young athletes. Do they differ from non-athletes and from young people with alternative leisure activities? *International Review for the Sociology of Sport*, 30, pp. 419-435.

Patrikson, G. (1995) Scientific review (II) of Socialisation. In: I. Vuori, P. Fentem, B. Svoboda, G. Patriksson, W. Andreff & W. Weber. *The significance of sport for society. Health, socialisation, economy*. Committee for the Development of Sport (CDDS), Council of Europe Press.

Poel, H. van der & Roques, C. (1999). *Connected through sport? The meaning of sport for the building of community in a new housing estate*. Tilburg; Vrijetijdwetenschappen, KUB. (in Dutch).

Poisson, (1999). *The contact hypothesis and a middle school boys' basketball team*. Paper presentation NASSS, November 3-6, Cleveland, Ohio.

Raad voor het Jeugdbeleid (1995). *Youth in movement. Sport is fun which makes you healthy*. Utrecht: SWP. (in Dutch).

Sabo, D., Melnick, M.J. & Vanfossen, B.E. (1993). High school athletic participation and post secundary educational and occupational mobility: a focus on race and gender. *Sociology of Sport Journal*, 10, pp. 44-56.

Saharso, S. (1992). *'Jan and everybody'. Ethnic minority youth about ethnic identity, discrimination and friendship*. Utrecht: van Arkel. (in Dutch).

Schuyt, K. (1997). *Social cohesion and social policy*. Amsterdam: De Balie. (in Dutch).

Stevenson, C.L. & Nixon, J.E. (1972). A conceptual scheme of the social functions of sport. *Sportwissenschaft* 2, pp. 119-132.

Steenbergen, J., Hilvoorde, I. van & Tamboer, J. (1995). *Fair Play*. Arnhem: NOC*NSF. (in Dutch).

Stöpler, L. & Schuijf, J. (1997). *Sexual identity unknown: An exploration of the integration of gay and lesbian sport clubs and national sport federations*. Utrecht: Homostudies. (in Dutch).

Struijs, A. (1998). *Minorities policy and moral*. Assen: Van Gorcum. (in Dutch).

Taylor, Ch. (1994). *Multiculturalism*. Princeton (NY): University Press.

Vanreusel, B. & Bulcaen, F. (1992). *The social meaning of sport participation*. Leuven: Institute for Physical Education, Catholic University. (in Dutch).

VWS (1996). *What moves sport: The shapes and main objectives of national governmental policies*. Den Haag: Sdu. (in Dutch).

Wilson, B. & Sparks, R. (1996). 'It's gotta be the shoes': youth, race and sneaker commercials. *Sociology of Sport Journal*, 13: pp. 398-427.

5 DOES SPORT MAKE A DIFFERENCE? AN EXPLORATION OF THE IMPACT OF SPORT ON THE SOCIAL INTEGRATION OF YOUNG PEOPLE

Gert Biesta, Geert-Jan Stams, Evelien Dirks, Esther Rutten, Wiel Veugelers & Carlo Schuengel

Introduction[1]

Young people do not engage in sport activities or become a member of a sport club in order to get an education, let alone a moral education. Education is primarily a responsibility of parents and, to a lesser extent, of schools. Yet there can be no doubt that each social practice in which young people take part - sport included - will exert an influence on them. By taking part in sport young people learn. Not only do they learn the skills and knowledge needed to 'do' their sport. They also learn sport-related rules and norms. And they learn - often more 'implicitly' than 'explicitly' - the values which underpin these rules and norms, and the values which are at stake in the wider context of their sport (such as the values that inform the 'climate' or 'culture' of their sport club). While it cannot be claimed, therefore, that sport is an educational practice, there can be no doubt that sport, like any other practice in which young people take part, is an educationally significant practice (for this idea see Biesta, 1997a; 1997b).

The fact that sport is educationally significant raises the question in what way(s) and to what extent (taking part in) sport exerts an influence on young people's orientations, attitudes and behavior, especially their normative and moral orientations, attitudes and

[1] The research reported in this chapter was partly conducted as a project of the research program 'Waarden en Normen in de Sport-II' ('Values and Norms in Sport II) (project leader Dr Gert Biesta, University of Exeter, UK). The research was further sponsored by the Dutch Youth Information Institute (Stichting Jeugdinformatie Nederland) (in a project led by Dr Gert Biesta and Prof Dr Paul Verweel, Utrecht University). A follow up study, also sponsored by the Dutch Youth Information Institute (SJN), is currently being conducted (project leaders Dr Gert Biesta and Prof Dr Carlo Schuengel, Free University Amsterdam).

behavior. An adequate understanding of this is not merely interesting for reasons of intellectual curiosity. Once it is acknowledged that taking part in sport has a formative influence on young people (e.g. Arnold, 1994; Coackley, 1996, 1998; Shields & Bredemeier, 1995; for a negative influence, see Begg, Langley, Moffitt, & Marshall, 1996), it becomes possible and necessary to take responsibility for such influence - at least, that is, to the extent to which educationally relevant factors and dimensions can be 'controlled'. It becomes possible, in other words, to deal with these factors and dimensions in a more deliberate and more informed way instead of simply 'letting it happen'. Having an understanding of the ways in which sport is or can be 'educationally significant' is, therefore, especially important for those who are actually concerned with young people active in organized sport, either directly (such as trainers) or more indirectly (for example youth coordinators in a sport club).

The idea that sport is an educationally significant practice formed the point of departure for a research project which we conducted in several sport clubs in the Netherlands (see Biesta, Stams, Rutten, Scheltus, Veugelers, Verweel, Schuengel & Dirks, 2000). One of the aims of the project was to get a better understanding of the normative and educational orientations and expectations of young people (aged 12-18) active in organized sport, their parents, their trainers, and club officials with a special responsibility for young sportsmen and sportswomen. A further aim was to find out which factors and dimensions of organized sport for adolescents might especially be 'educationally significant' or 'formative'. A final aim of the project was to broach a discussion between all parties about their orientations and expectations and about educationally relevant factors and dimensions. The reason for this was not only to get a more detailed understanding of (possible) differences and discrepancies between the ideas and expectations of the parties involved; it was also to create an awareness among the participants of the normative and educational factors, dimensions, opportunities and responsibilities that exist in the context of sport for young people.

In this chapter we want to present and discuss some of the findings of this project. We will focus on the question as to whether there are reasons for assuming that young people's participation in sports makes a difference for them and, if so, which factors and dimensions are especially important. We will discuss the results of an explorative survey which we conducted involving 260 young soccer players and swimmers, age 12 to 18, in which we wanted to find out whether we could identify factors within sport that are related to the dimensions of prosocial and antisocial behavior of young people active in sport. We took prosocial and antisocial behavior as a measure for the social integration of young people, considering that lower levels of antisocial behavior and higher levels of prosocial behavior may be indicative of greater social integration in a (non-clinical) population of adolescents who are active in organized youth sport. On the basis of the survey we were able to identify three factors which correlated with the social integration of young sportsmen and sportswomen: (1) the quality of the relationship between adolescents active in sport and their trainers, (2) the sociomoral climate of the sport club, and (3) the adolescents' level of sociomoral reasoning in the context of organized youth sport. In the following pages we will first discuss some of the details of our survey and present a structural causal model in which social integration is hypothesized to be influenced by the three aforementioned factors. After that we will give an impression of some findings of follow up discussions which we had with young people, trainers, other club officials and parents about the findings of our survey.

5.1 Methods of the survey study

Participants
A total number of N = 10 sport clubs participated in our study: n = 6 soccer clubs (n = 187 adolescents) and n = 4 swimming clubs (n = 73 adolescents). The sport clubs were randomly drawn from the population of soccer and swimming clubs in the urbanized area of two Dutch cities, namely Amsterdam and Utrecht. All selected clubs agreed to participate. The mean size of the young persons' sections of the clubs was M = 224 youth members (SD = 204). The questionnaires were filled in by N = 260 participants (n = 153 boys; n = 107 girls), who were between 12 and 18 years of age. The mean age was M = 14.8 (SD = 1.5). The response percentage was excellent, that is, 90%.
The adolescents who participated in our study had low to lower-middle class backgrounds. Their level of formal education could be considered as middle to high. The mean family size was 2.8 children.

The percentage of single parent families was 18.4%, and the percentage of divorced parents was 15.1%. The sample consisted of adolescents with a Dutch (n = 208), Turkish (n = 15), Moroccan (n = 20) and Surinam (n = 17) background.

Measures
N = 260 adolescents completed questionnaires on antisocial and prosocial behavior, their relationship with the trainer, the sociomoral climate of their sport club, and sociomoral reasoning in the context of youth sport. For the purpose of interpretation, all scores were keyed to the names of the scales. For instance, a relatively high score on the scale for antisocial behavior is indicative of a high level of reported antisocial behavior.

[1] Antisocial behavior: The antisocial behavior questionnaire is a shortened version of the Anti Social Behavior Inventory, the ASBI (Wouters & Spiering, 1990). In a study of moral judgment development and delinquency in homeless and residential youth, carried out by Tavecchio, Stams, Brugman & Thomeer-Bouwens (1999), 4 factors emerged from a principal components analysis. These factors were petty crime (21 items, α= .93), vandalism (16 items, α = .92), violence (10 items, α = .86) and rebellious behavior and opposition to police authorities (7 items, α = .83). The overall scale could be considered as a measure of antisocial behavior (54 items, α = .96).

The shortened version of the ASBI was developed for the purpose of the present study, and contained 15 items: 5 items with the highest factor loadings on the overall scale for antisocial behavior, and 10 items representing salient antisocial behaviors as well as having sufficient prevalence in a non-clinical population of adolescents. The reliability of the shortened version was α = .91. As the total score was not normally distributed, this score was transformed to approach a normal distribution by carrying out the following procedure: $y = -1 * (1/x) + 1$ (Tabachnick & Fidell, 1996).

[2] Prosocial behavior: In order to assess prosocial behavior, we translated the Prosocial Behaviour Questionnaire, the PBQ (Weir & Duveen, 1981) and adapted the PBQ to be used as a self report measure of prosocial behavior in adolescents. Weir & Duveen (1981) and Janssens & Dekovic (1997) reported high reliabilities above α = .90. The prosocial behavior questionnaire contains 20 4-point Likert

scale items, ranging from "rarely applies" to "certainly applies". The items represent positive social behaviors such as helping, sharing and supporting others. Some examples are: "I spontaneously help to pick up objects, which another person has dropped", and "I take the opportunity to praise the work of those who are less able". In the present study, we found a reliability of $\alpha = .89$.

[3] Quality of the relationship between the adolescent active in sport and his or her trainer: The Quality of the Relationship scale is an adaptation of the Barrett-Lennard Relationship Inventory (Barrett-Lennard, 1962; Van IJzendoorn, Tavecchhio, Stams, Verhoeven & Reiling, 1998), and was construed to assess the quality of the relationship between the adolescent active in sport and his or her trainer in terms of empathic understanding, positive regard, congruence, i.e. "the degree to which one person is functionally integrated in the context of his relationship, such that there is absence of conflict or inconsistency between his total experience, his awareness, and his overt communication" (Barrett-Lennard, 1962, p. 4), and willingness to be known, i.e. "the degree to which one person is willing to be known as a person, by another, according to the other's desire for this; to be known as a person involves especially the sharing of experiences and perceptions of the self, perceptions of and feelings toward the other, and perceptions of the self-other interaction or relationship" (ibid., p.5).

The Quality of the relationship scale consists of 12 statements about how the adolescent active in sport and his or her trainer feel and behave towards each other. By means of 6-point Likert scales, ranging from totally disagree to totally agree, adolescents responded to statements concerning their present relationship with the trainer. Two examples of Quality of Relationship items are: "I appreciate this trainer" and "I nearly always know exactly what this trainer means". The reliability of the Quality of Relationship scale was $\alpha = .87$.

[4] Perception of the Sociomoral Climate of the Sport Club: Perception of the Sociomoral Climate is an adaptation of the School Culture Scale (Higgins, 1995, 1997; Veugelers & De Kat, 1998). It is a 17-item self report measure that purports to assess the sociomoral climate of the sport club in terms of normative expectations, social conduct, quality of communication, and opportunities for youth participation. Adolescents active in sport indicated on 5-point Likert

scales the degree to which statements regarding the sociomoral climate of their sport club were true or untrue. We will give some examples of items: "at this sport club, young people active in sport trust each other", "at this sport club, the trainers take interest in their sportsmen and sportswomen", "at this sport club, some of the young people active in sport suffer from bullying" and "at this sport club, young people active in sport can freely express their opinions". The reliability of the Sociomoral Climate scale was $\alpha = .86$.

[5] The Practical Sociomoral Reflection Objective Measure -- Sport (PSROM-Sport): This instrument was developed to assess practical sociomoral reasoning in the context of organized youth sport, and was derived from the Sociomoral Objective Measure Short Form, the SROM-SF (Basinger & Gibbs, 1987; Stams, 1994; Stams, Van Roosmalen, Høst, Brugman & Tavecchio, 1994) which is a multiple choice questionnaire with 2 moral dilemmas and 12 question arrays focusing on sociomoral norms. Each question includes a response option representative of Kohlberg's moral stages 1 through 4. The first two stages, indicative of unilateral and instrumental reasoning respectively, constitute the immature or preconventional level. The third and fourth stage, mutual-prosocial and systemic reasoning respectively, constitute the mature or conventional level (Gibbs, Basinger & Fuller, 1992; Stams, 1994; Tavecchio et al. 1999). The PSROM-Sport assesses the level of practical sociomoral reasoning in a similar way, using 12 questions about salient sociomoral dilemmas in the context of organized youth sport. As such, the PSROM-Sport rather assesses moral performance than moral competence. The reliability of the PSROM-Sport was sufficient, that is, $\alpha = .60$. Below, we give a full example of a PSROM-Sport question array - directly drawn from the questionnaire - including the sociomoral problem under consideration and all 4 response options. The first response option is indicative of stage 2 instrumental reasoning. The second response option is indicative of stage 4 systemic reasoning, also referring to fundamental sociomoral norms and values, such as being responsible or just. The third response option is indicative of stage 1 unilateral reasoning, which is characterized by a focus on immediate and concrete consequences, such as salient gains, losses, or punishment. The fourth response option is indicative of stage 3 prosocial reasoning, i.e. the more psychological and emphatic stage where relationships become increasingly important.

Example of a PSROM-Sport question array

Suppose that your friend is one of the best players in your team. Due to illness, he has not been able to play soccer for several months. You decide to help your friend to catch up, so that he might be ready in time for the most important match of the year, because:

		Close to a reason that you would give ?		
a)	Your friend has done things for you too	yes	no	don't know
b)	It shows that you feel responsible for your club	yes	no	don't know
c)	If you help your friend, you might win this match	yes	no	don't know
d)	If you don't , you don't act as a real friend	yes	no	don't know

Closest to the reason that you would give?	A	B	C	D

5.2 Results of the survey study

In this section we test a causal model by means of structural equation analysis, a way of statistical testing in which a specific causal model is fitted to the empirical data. If there is an adequate fit, which means that the causal model cannot be rejected ($p > .05$), one is allowed to conclude that the causal model holds. In the case of the present study, we hypothesized a model that accounts for the influences of sociomoral reasoning in the context of youth sport, sociomoral climate of the sport club, and quality of the relationship with the trainer on social integration in terms of antisocial and prosocial behavior. To complete the model, we included causal paths between quality of the relationship with the trainer and sociomoral reasoning, and between sociomoral climate and sociomoral reasoning. Finally, we added an association between quality of the relationship and sociomoral climate.

Table 1 presents the correlations between the variables that were entered in the model as well as the means and standard deviations. Except for the correlations between sociomoral climate and sociomoral reasoning, and between sociomoral reasoning and antisocial behavior, all variables that were included in the model were associated significantly. The mean level of sociomoral reasoning was 2.8, rounded 3, which indicated that adolescents active in sport reasoned at the prosocial and empathic level of sociomoral reasoning when they were confronted with sociomoral dilemmas in the context of organized youth sport.

Table 1: Means, Standard Deviations, and Correlations between Sociomoral Reasoning, Sociomoral Climate, Quality of Relationship, and Antisocial and Prosocial Behavior

	M	SD	1	2	3	4	5
1. sociomoral reasoning	2.8	.4	1.00				
2. sociomoral climate	3.8	.6	.08	1.00			
3. quality of relationship	4.7	.8	.22*	.47*	1.00		
4. antisocial behavior	0.2	.1	-.13	-.40*	-.39*	1.00	
5. prosocial behavior	2.7	.4	.24*	.35*	.29*	-.27*	1.00

Note 1: N = 237

Note 2: * correlations are significant at the level $p < .01$ (two-tailed)

In Figure 1 we show the observed variables - relationship with the trainer, sociomoral reasoning, and sociomoral climate - which are hypothesized to have an impact on social integration in terms of lower levels of antisocial and higher levels of prosocial behavior. Using structuring equation modeling (Bollen, 1989; Brown & Gudeck, 1993), we found an adequate fit - $X2 (2, N = 237) = 4.30$, $p = .12$, for a model that included significant paths linking quality of the relationship with the trainer (.36), moral reasoning in the context of youth sport (.22), and sociomoral climate (.54) with social integration, which indicated that social integration was facilitated by a higher quality of the relationship with the trainer, a higher level of sociomoral reasoning, and a more positive sociomoral climate of the sport club. Also, the model accounted for a positive and direct effect of quality of the relationship with the trainer on sociomoral reasoning (.23), and an association between quality of the relationship with the trainer and sociomoral climate (.47). All diagrammed paths were significant at $p < .01$.

Figure 1: Multiple Indicator Multiple Cause Model of Social Integration: The Observed Variables are Relationship with the Trainer, Sociomoral Reasoning, Sociomoral Climate (Causal Factors), Antisocial Behavior, and Prosocial Behavior. The latent Variable is Social Integration.

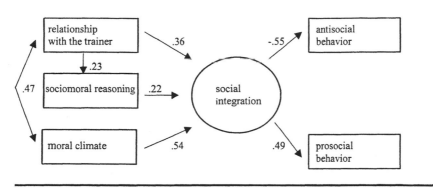

$N = 237$; $X2$ $(2, N = 237) = 4.30, p = .12$

All path coefficients are significant at $p < .01$

To summarize, we found statistical support for a causal model in which social integration was positively affected by a higher quality of the relationship between adolescents active in sport and their trainer, a higher level of adolescents' sociomoral reasoning in the context of sport, and a more positive (perceived) sociomoral climate of the sport club. A more positive sociomoral climate of the sport club was associated with relatively good relationships between the adolescents active in sport and their trainer, while trainers had a direct and positive influence on the level of sociomoral reasoning of their young sportsmen and sportswomen. On average, they reasoned at the prosocial and empathic level of sociomoral reasoning in the context of organized youth sport.

5.3 Follow up discussions

The findings of the survey suggest that if participation in sport indeed 'makes a difference' with respect to the normative orientations and attitudes and the behavior of young people, then three factors of their participation in organized sport might especially be important, namely, the quality of the relationship with their trainer, their level of sociomoral reasoning, and the sociomoral climate of the sport club. This conclusion is not only important for understanding how participation in sport might make a difference for young people. It is also important if sport clubs would want to review the quality of the 'educational' impact of their activities and/or develop a more pro-active attitude towards this. The findings of our survey study give, in other words, an indication of 'where to look' and 'what to look for'.

Yet one of the important questions is, whether and in what way the factors that we found in our survey are actually considered to be of importance by the young people themselves and by their trainers, their parents and by a club's youth officials. To find out more about this, we arranged group discussions in several of the clubs that were engaged in our survey study. In these sessions we systematically discussed the findings of our survey with young sportsmen and sportswomen from "competitive" teams, trainers, parents and club officials. In this section we want to give an impression of the ways in which the factors and dimensions that we found in our survey study were being addressed in these sessions. A full-blown analysis of the data is beyond the scope of this chapter: such an analysis will be published elsewhere (Biesta, Stams, Dirks, Rutten, Schuengel & Veugelers, 2001). What we want to present here, are some salient quotes and examples concerning the factors - quality of the relationship between adolescents active in sport and their trainer, sociomoral reasoning in the context of youth sport, and the sociomoral climate of the sport club - and dimensions - antisocial and prosocial behavior in the context of organized youth sport - we identified in the survey.

5.4 Quality of the relationship between adolescents active in sport and their trainer

Young sportsmen and sportswomen, trainers, coaches, parents, and club officials all agreed about the crucial importance of the relationship between the young people and their trainer. Firstly, the discussants saw the quality of the relationship as an important vehicle for good achievements. A swimmer said:

> If I have a good relationship with my trainer, he is able to motivate me to swim faster, to reach beyond the limits of my capabilities.

And a soccer player:

> When a trainer says you've played well, then you feel much better. And when he says that you've made a complete mess of it, then you don't show up again. It really hurts when a trainer says you haven't played well. But when you have lost and he says 'damn it', then you really won't turn up next time. If he says 'more luck next time', then you carry on. You've done the best you can, but you can't help it. Then you go on, you know.

A trainer added:

> It is a relationship based upon trust. We expect sportsmen and sportswomen to deliver enormous efforts, which requires a good rapport. We want our young people to go a bit further than they can. And if they do so, it is a sign of mutual trust.

And another trainer:

> A trainer should be able to communicate well with his sportsmen and sportswomen in order to make clear what he wants.

Secondly, a good relationship with the trainer was considered to be a major factor in the promotion of the adolescent's wellbeing. It was also considered to be important for reducing sport attrition. This is what a sportswoman said:

> I had a trainer whom I didn't like that much. So, I didn't want to swim anymore. I didn't agree anymore with what she said. I thought, I just let her bullshit, you see. I make up my own mind. You simply don't feel like doing it, you know, until you get a new trainer. Then you start doing your best again. I didn't put much effort in improving that relationship, because I didn't like her. In fact I never even spoke to her.

Thirdly, an adverse relationship with the trainer appeared to promote antisocial or aggressive behavior. A soccer player remarked:

> If there is a bad relationship between a player and a trainer, then things won't go well, of course. Then a player starts to mess around and be a loudmouth.

In contrast, a good relationship not only appeared to engender prosocial behavior. It was also seen as a basis upon which trainers could pay attention to their role as an educator. As one trainer put it:

> You must get on quite well with these lads. You're also sort of an educator. You must know what you're talking about. If you don't know anything about soccer, then you will never deserve their respect. But the most important thing is that you get along well. The whole point is creating a good atmosphere. And you need to pick the right moment to talk to them about their conduct; when they go beyond their bounds. You really ask a lot of self-discipline and self-control of those boys, you know.

Most trainers, parents, coordinators, and club officials were quite explicit about the educational task of the trainer, as is evidenced by the following remark, made by a trainer:

> You must educate each other; you must dare to talk to somebody about his conduct. Even if there are all kind of emotions involved.

A soccer player made it clear that the trainer may also have a negative influence:

> A coach really has an influence. When he says 'tackle him' or so. That really makes you aggressive.

The youth coordinator of this club responded:

> It's for sure that you have a large influence over those kids. There is always an element of education. They learn in all

kind of different ways. For example on the pitch where they learn rules, another kind of discipline than at school or at home. Interaction. You must learn to function properly in a team, to be tolerant, to know that you're not the most important one. A trainer always and inevitably has a role in that.

Finally, all participants agreed that the trainer should set an example for his young sportsmen and sportswomen.

5.5 Sociomoral reasoning in the context of youth sport

The discussants used sociomoral argumentation in most of their judgments about dilemmas concerning antisocial and social behavior in the context of sport. A striking example of such argumentation was found in the following remarks of a coach. In the dilemma between participation and selection he clearly made a choice for participation:

We used to have a really poor goalie, but at a certain moment we told them that calling him names really doesn't help. We told them that it is their task to prevent the other team from scoring. So make sure that you have a good defense. Be a team. In those cases you're constantly talking to these boys, both as a parent and a trainer. Norms and values. I prefer that they are a team and that they lose the game, than that they aren't a team and win it. Those norms are really much more important.

Sociomoral climate
There was general agreement among the discussants that a positive sociomoral climate consists in social support, in helping each other, sharing experiences, providing opportunities for participation, but above all that it has to do with mutual respect and clarity of communication. It transpired from the discussions that a positive sociomoral climate can have a strong impact on social integration in terms of less antisocial and more prosocial behavior.

One of the trainers gave the following explanation of how he thought the climate in his club 'worked':

> We hardly have any antisocial behavior. You do not need to put a lot of effort in that, because everybody sort of already has those norms and values. The older members of the club simply pass them on to the younger ones.

Another trainer said:

> It's a simple fact that if, for example, when some of them stay around to chat a bit and someone joins them who is aggressive and wants to start a fight, that it's much more likely that he will adjust to the group than that they will adjust to him.

5.6 Antisocial and prosocial behavior in the context of organized youth sport

Antisocial and prosocial behavior were an explicit theme in discussions about fair play (see chapter 7 of this book) The issue of fair play evoked many very lively debates. It became overwhelmingly clear that rough competition as can be found in contact sports like water polo and soccer, triggers forms of antisocial behavior. The evidence was abundant. A soccer player said:

> If somebody passes you again and again, then you just tackle him, you know. That's really wicked; you simply feel much better then. You lay one on him, and then he goes 'oh, oh, oh', and he just doesn't dare to do anything anymore. That's so much better.

And another soccer player:

> As soon as the match starts everyone changes. That's the whole point, you see. When the referee whistles, then you turn your bum. From that moment on you are enemies. Some really normal guys - a mate of mine from school, for example, who is in our team - they really get crazy. Totally

aggressive, shouting, really out of their mind. Completely different. You start to think "Who is this guy?" But after the match, he was just normal again. Talked normal, again, you know.

On the other hand, there was also abundant evidence of trainers who were quite able to deal with antisocial behavior. Fierce competition in physical contact sports provided them with an opportunity for teaching young people to deal with rules, values, and norms in stressful and ambiguous situations, and to exert self-discipline or control impulses in the face of adversity and severe provocation. This is how one trainer summarized it:

You should always try to keep your hands to yourself. Stay cool, don't react. Then you will always win. If you don't do anything, even if you let them hit you, it sounds odd, but then, in the end, you always win.

To summarize, we systematically discussed the findings of our survey with adolescents active in selection teams, trainers, coaches, parents and club officials. Firstly, we found evidence for the crucial influence of the trainer-adolescent relationship quality on the young sportswomen's and sportswomen's achievements in sport, their experienced wellbeing in sporting activities, and their social integration in terms of antisocial and prosocial behavior. Moreover, a good quality of the relationship between the adolescent and the trainer was identified as a vehicle for any supposed educational task of the trainer. In addition, most discussants argued that the trainer should be a good example for his young sportsmen and sportswomen.

The discussants used sociomoral argumentation in most of their judgments about dilemmas concerning antisocial and prosocial behavior in the context of organized youth sport, which indicated that sociomoral reasoning may be an important factor in matters that concern antisocial and prosocial behavior, that is, in issues of social integration. There was general agreement among the discussants that a positive sociomoral climate consists in social support, in helping each other, sharing experiences, providing opportunities for participation, but above all mutual respect and clarity of communication between club members. The discussions about antisocial and prosocial behavior in the context of organized youth sport all centered around the issue of fair play. It became clear that rough competition, as can be found in physical contact sports like water polo and soccer, triggers forms of antisocial behavior. At the same time, it became evident that many trainers were quite able to deal with this kind of antisocial behavior. The problematic situations as they were encountered in the context of organized youth sport provided trainers and coaches with an opportunity for carrying out their educational task in a more explicit way, that is, by teaching young people to deal with rules, values, and norms, and to cope with competition and high achievement stress.

Conclusion

Does sport make a difference? Does it have an impact on the orientations, attitudes and behavior of young people who take part in organized sport? The findings that we have presented in this chapter suggest that this may well be the case and, if so, that three factors - the quality of the relationship with the trainer, the level of sociomoral reasoning in the context of sport, and the sociomoral climate of the sport club - deserve our special attention, not only to understand the possible impact of sport, but also if we want to know where to begin when we would like to consolidate or improve the 'educational' quality of organized sport for young people. There are, of course, many research questions still unanswered. Our survey only established relations between the different factors and dimensions that appear to be educationally relevant in the context of organized youth sport, but further research is needed to establish the precise nature of these relations. Our research also raises the question whether participation in organized youth sports has a potential which other contexts in which young people take part (or spend their time), such as the family and the school, do not have. To put it differently: Is organized sport for young people a 'special' context and, if so, what is special about this context? A critical question, both for research and practice, is whether it is the sport activity itself which makes the difference, or whether it is the context of organized sport which is the decisive factor. There are reasons to believe that the sporting activity itself provokes rather more than less aggression and antisocial behavior in young people (see Begg et al., 1996).

Our research so far at least indicates that the most important 'positive' factors are to be found in the context of the sport (and not – or at least not necessarily – in the sport activity itself).

If sport is unique in its educational potential and in its possible positive influence on young people's social integration, it might well be that this is most of all because sport is one of the few settings in which adults and young people engage in relationships with each other on a voluntary basis (unlike the context of school and the context of the family) and, further to this, because the context of the sport provides opportunities for (educational) action which may be to a far lesser extent available in other contexts. Therefore: if sport makes a difference – or if we want sport to make a difference – there is every reason to focus our attention first of all on the organized context in which sport activities take place.

References

Arnold, P. J. (1994). Sport and moral education. *Journal of Moral Education*, 23, pp. 75-89.

Barrett-Lennard, G. T. (1962). Dimensions of therapist response as causal factors in therapeutic change. *Psychological Monographs*, 76, 43, p. 562.

Basinger, K. S. & Gibbs, J. C. (1987). Validation of the Sociomoral Reflection Objective Measure-Short Form. *Psychological Reports*, 61, pp. 139-146.

Begg, D. J., Langley, J. D., Moffitt, T. & Marshall, S. W. (1996). Sport and delinquency: an examination of the deterrence hypothesis in a longitudinal study. *British Journal of Sports and Medicine*, 30, pp. 335-341.

Biesta, G. J. J. (1997a). Education, not initiation. In: F. Margonis (Ed.), *Philosophy of education 1996* (pp. 90-98). Urbana, Ill.: Philosophy of Education Society.

Biesta, G. J. J. (1997b). Impossible education. Comments on the idea of education as transmission. *Comenius*, 17(4), pp. 312-324. (in Dutch).

Biesta, G. J. J., Stams, G. J. J. M., Rutten, E. A., Scheltus, H., Veugelers, W., Verweel, P., Schuengel, C., & Dirks, E. (2000). *Norms and values in youth sport*. Utrecht, The Netherlands/ Exeter, UK: Utrecht University/ University of Exeter. (in Dutch).

Biesta, G. J. J., Stams, G. J. J. M., Dirks, E., Rutten, E. A., Schuengel, C. & Veugelers, W. (2001). *The pedagogical task of the sport club*. Arnhem: NOC*NSF. (in Dutch).

Bollen, K. A. (1989). *Structural equations with latent variables*. New York: John Wiley.

Brown, M. W. & Gudeck, R. (1993). Alternative ways of assessing model-fit. In: K. A. Bollen & J. S. Long (Eds.), *Testing structural equation models*. (pp. 136-162). Newbury Park, CA: Sage.

Coakley, J. (1996). Socialization through sports. In O. Bar-Or (Ed.), *The child and adolescent athlete. Encyclopaedia of sports medicine, Vol. 6.* (pp. 353-363). Cambridge, MA, US: Blackwell Scientific Publications.

Coakley, J. J. (1998). *Sport in society*. Singapore: McGraw-Hill.

Gibbs, J. C., Basinger, K. S. & Fuller, D. (1992). *Measuring the development of sociomoral reflection*. Hillsdale, New Yersy: Lawrence Erlbaum.

Higgins, A. (1995). *Dimensions of the School Culture Scale: Measuring attitudes, norms and values in educational settings*. Fordham, Fordham University:

Higgins, A. (1997). Research using the school culture scale. *International Journal of Educational Research*, 27, pp. 558-564.

IJzendoorn, M.H., van, Tavecchio, L. W. C., Stams, G. J. J. M., Verhoeven, M. J. E. & Reiling, E. J. (1998). Attunement between parents and professional caregivers: A comparison of childrearing attitudes in different child-care settings. *Journal of Marriage and the Family*, 60, pp. 771-781.

Janssens, J. M. A. M. & Dekovic, M. (1997). Child rearing, prosocial moral reasoning, and prosocial behaviour. *International Journal of Behavioral Development*, 20, pp. 509-527.

Shields, D. L. L. & Bredemeier, B. J. L. (1995). *Character development and physical activity*. Champaing, IL: Human Kinetics.

Stams, G. J. J. M. (1994). *The sociomoral competence of secondary school students: A validation study of the Sociomoral Reflection Objective Measure Short form*. Leiden: University of Leiden. (in Dutch).

Stams, G. J. J. M., Van Roosmalen, M., Høst, K., Brugman, D. & Tavecchio, L. W. C. (1994). *Social Relationships Inventory: A Dutch translation of the SROM-SF*. Leiden: University of Leiden. (in Dutch).

Tabachnick, B. G. & Fidell, L. S. (1996). *Using Multivariate Statistics*. (3rd ed.). California State University, Northridge: Harper Collins College Publishers.

Tavecchio, L. W. C., Stams, G. J. J. M., Brugman, D. & Thomeer-Bouwens, M. A. E. (1999). Moral judgement development and delinquency in homeless youth. *Journal of Moral Education*, 28, pp. 63-79.

Veugelers, W. & De Kat, E. (1998). *Education in secondary schools: Students, parents and teachers report on the educational task of the school, and the attunement between the family and the school*. Assen: Van Gorcum. (in Dutch).

Weir, K. & Duveen, G. (1981). Further development and validation of the prosocial behaviour questionnaire for use by teachers. *Journal of Child Psychology and Psychiatry*, 22, pp. 357-374.

Wouters, L. & Spiering, W. (1990). *Questionnaire of Anti-Social Behaviour*. Amsterdam: GG & GD Amsterdam. (in Dutch).

PART TWO

SPECIFIC VALUES IN SPORT

6 VALUES AND VALUE CLARIFICATION IN SPORTS

Albert Buisman & Jacques van Rossum

Introduction

The term value has many different meanings. In the Dutch language we talk about the value of the dollar and the Euro, about a worthless (without value) soccer game with a missed penalty, valuable experiences in the sport matches, and about the demise of values and norms in our society today. Sometimes the values are specifically named, such as "respect for your opponent" in fair play issues. Sometimes values appear to be more hidden and have to be brought to light through interpretation, such as in the example below.

> In the last few years, a discussion has developed around the question of weather or not wheelchair bound athletes should be allowed to participate in the four-day endurance walk held each year in Nymegen in The Netherlands. The manager, along with several board members, was not for that idea. Strong intervention on the part of then-Secretary of Sports, Mrs. Erica Terpstra, lead to the fact that a limited group of wheelchair athletes was aloud to participate as an experiment. That ended up being a mixed blessing. Jan Troost, one of the initiative takers, reports that he was told: "Nice of you to join us, but I don't want to see you again next year." One other able bodied participant threatened to spread thumbtacks.

How can we interpret this example? Which values and norms become visible here? First we can ask the conceptual question of whether we are talking about competition type sport in reference to the four-day endurance walk. If it were a competition sport, it would be difficult to allow wheel chair participants to participate, as conditions would not be equal. But with the four-day endurance walk there is no competition between participants, so wheelchair bound athletes could participate. One could view the four-day endurance walk as an achievement walk in which a predetermined distance has to be covered in a predetermined amount of time. This could be done either on foot, or by wheelchair. The next conceptual question is whether walking and using a wheelchair are associated activities. This question is not easily answered. At first glance they really are different activities. Cyclists and in-line skaters are not allowed in this achievement walk since that would be against the rules of the walking sport. On the other hand one could argue that wheelchairs to this group of people are a necessary means for getting around, equivalent to walking to the non-handicapped person. From that point of view, walking and riding a wheelchair are equivalent activities and one could expect the board members to act more relaxed. The rules of the sport are a system of agreements that can be altered or adapted at will, if there is sufficient need to do so.

We can also look at this situation from an experience perspective. Then we view this as a group of athletes who are eager to show their athletic ability. The four-day endurance walk, with its big enthusiastic audience, is a prime opportunity for that. As it is, physically handicapped athletes encounter many restrictions in sport and this is a prime opportunity to align with a sport, to integrate. Such values could be made very explicit in phenomenological research of interpretive perspective.

The other side shows many walking participants who feel that athletes in a wheelchair do not belong at the four-day endurance walk. Several practical arguments are used to validate the exclusion of the wheelchair athletes: paths are sometimes to narrow, fear of being run into. Maybe the underlying thought here is one of segregation, kinds stick with kinds. Those handicapped people should organize their own endurance events with their own kind. Here, the discovered values are more at a social-psychological level: people belong, or they don't belong. Processes of inclusion or exclusion are at issue here.

We can also look at this situation from the angle of policy. How should organized sport boards and governments act, when faced with this type of issue? Does it make sense to conduct research on questions such as:

- How many participants are for and how many are against and why?
- How many athletes in a wheelchair wish to participate?
- Can the townships and municipalities handle any practical issues?

This type of research will answer the questions of logistics, but does not answer the question of how to proceed. Several options exist here.

The group of wheelchair participants could simply be excluded from the four-day endurance walk, with the argument that the majority of walking participants is against their participation. Additionally, values such as social integration of one group of people can not be forced upon the walking sport if it does not want that. However, social integration could be viewed as a goal of those who make policy. The board of the sport could be pressured, by stating that their policy can be viewed as an apartheid policy. By use of this terminology, the discussion can get very political.

Policy research can focus on the content of the policy, the values and norms identified by various parties. But research could also focus on the effects of the policy and that kind of research follows a completely different path then the first kind of research.

Here is an example of how values can be viewed in different ways. This was a typical example from The Netherlands. In the USA there is a similar example in golf where a player, who has a chronically diseased leg, is not allowed to participate in PGA golf tournaments. This case is currently reviewed by the US Supreme Court (USA Today, 18-1-2001).

While researching values and norms in sport, three alternating views will surface: conceptual, from an experience perspective and from the view of policy. The goal is to clarify values, as in the summarized analysis of the four-day endurance walk. With this analysis we hope to contribute to a more systematic and balanced discussion on this type of topic. It is not the case that these issues will be more easily resolved, however better conditions are created so that participants to this discussion will better understand themselves as well as others. And that is a valuable start. The second example shows a different kind of strained relationship, between organized competition sport with its sport specific values, and youth sport with values geared to the position of children. The example comes from the Canadian commission for fair play (Binder, 1990):

> Several years ago, Jarrod Barakett, was humiliated by a hockey coach obsessed with winning. The team and coach had agreed to a rotation that allowed each player a chance to play in every game. During a league game, when Jarrod stood up for his turn, the coach said to him: "Sit down, we want to **win** this game! Jarrod had had enough and hung up his skates for good. He was only eight years old.

From this example, the Canadian Commission lists its values for a good child's life in sports: sport participation, enjoyment in the game, social interaction and the learning of skills. Those values are at odds with winning the game in this example. Those are values that belong to a type of sport with older youth and adults. Sport specific values that can be identified here are the desire to win, to go to the edge to give all you got, permanent selection processes, in which the best always go first. The competition sport is "performance elitist" says Rijsdorp (1973, p.164). "Those who perform go first" (ibid.). This example is clearly a conflict in values. On the one hand the sport specific values (see chapter 2 of this book) and on the other hand the values belonging to a young child.

In this example it leads to a conflict. The eight-year old boy turned away from the sport in disappointment. A discussion about these values is clearly not simple in nature. It does not have to lead to conflict. Even those who think that youth sport should not merely be a derivative of the rules of adults (smaller ball, smaller goals) but that it has its own culture to see the trend that children are focussing more and more to the sport specific values. But at the same time they point out that the youngest group ages 4 to 8 have no concept of the need to win and that therefore the immediate emphasized goal in sport education should not be placed there. In the learning process a conscious effort needs to be made with older youth in team sports to not chose the biggest strongest player in a match in an effort to win, as the result then is that the other players do not get enough experience. Foppe de Haan, trainer of Heerenveen (a Dutch soccer club), says this in an interview with Dutch journalist John Volkers (De Volkskrant, 12-3-'97):

> People always talk about winning, but first you have to create the conditions otherwise winning is no more then an accident. You have to train hard, think of a concept. In the end, you will win more then you lose.

At first glance conflicting values can be tuned into each other, but a necessary condition would be a well thought through discussion about these values. With the discussion about these examples we have arrived at the heart of this chapter: How can values be described and how do they function in sports and sports research?
After discussing the various definitions of values you will find in this chapter discussions on several approaches in value research in sports.

This research is then placed in the strained relationship between passing on values and clarifying values.

6.1 About the term value

Beckers & Nauta (1983) stated that a generally accepted definition of value does not exist in the social sciences. They point to Lautmann who lists 120 definitions and descriptions of the term "value" (ibid., p.16). According to the authors, there are two trends to be identified. Values can be viewed from the individual perspective, tied to concepts such as need or motive. But one can also approach values as dictated by society and then we focus more on the guidelines and goals of human behavior. A discussion about definitions of values follows here. Sometimes those definitions are very close and sometimes they overlap one another.

6.1.1 Values as socially desirable

Beckers & Nauta (1983, p.28) gave this definition:

> Values are socially desirable things, living in a society, groups or individuals. They are detectable in verbal or written forms or can be deduced from the actions of instructions, organizations or people.

Central in this definition is the concept of social desirability in which the concept gets a positive meaning. Another author who views the term value as positive is Rokeach (1973). According to him (ibid., p.5) a value is an:

> Enduring belief that a specific mode of conduct or end-state of existence is personally or socially preferable to an opposite or converse mode of conduct or end-state of existence.

In this description he emphasizes the comparison of values, preferring one value more then another. When he then lists some values it becomes clear what this author means with 'value'. A central theme in his theory is the separation between "terminal values" and "instrumental values". After lengthy research Rokeach found 18 terminal values and 18 instrumental values.

- Terminal values, for example, are goals people hope to achieve in life, a comfortable life, equality, social recognition, a world of beauty, national and family security, freedom, happiness, true friendship and an exciting life.
- Instrumental values are more viewed as ways to reach the terminal values. Upon closer review they appear to be predominantly personal traits such as ambition, self respect, helpful, honesty, independent, obedient, polite, courageous, responsible, cheerful, self-controlled.

Kretchmar (1994) attaches values to what he calls "Good life". The life of a person is made up of a combination of individual values that are connected. In his definition of value he also identifies the (socially) desirableness. He (ibid., p.250) identifies two types of values:

> Moral values are certain personality traits and human motives. They describe what we often call a morally good person. These are traits like honesty, conscientiousness, affection, prudence, industriousness and courage. Non-moral values are things we desire from live. Rather than describing a person or a person's motives, they identify items that people want- things like pleasure, knowledge, wealth, security, excellence and friendship.

People constantly compare these values according to Kretchmar in order to determine their priorities. Professionals in the field of sport should have an overview of these values in order to prevent one-sidedness in policy. This approach to values, tied to the 'good life', can be called idealistic. Ideals are pursued and that gives life perspective. This interpretation of values tries to awaken the good in people and make it grow. However, this group of values is viewed critically by various writers. De Swaan separated, in an article in Trouw (1997, 14-10-1997) fresh virtues such as courage, honesty, and hard work from mushy virtues such as humbleness, obedience, nationalism and compassion.

De Swaan talks about virtues, but they mean about the same as values:

> The fresh virtues focus on character forming, the mushy
> values have to hold people together. They glue people
> together. In today's terms, they promote social
> cohesiveness.

The same criticism we find with the German literature scientist
Herzinger (1997), who argues against so-called communal values.
They do not necessarily have to have a positive effect on the moral
quality of the society. According to Herzinger, it makes a difference
whether the communal values relate to the voluntary firefighters or the
Ku Klux Klan.

It depends on which content these communal values have with
which the person feels associated. Despite the criticism, which can
also be applied to the individualistic values, we often run into this
interpretation of values as socially desirable. Values are presented as
ideals which people try to follow.

6.1.2 Values with a plus and values with a minus

The labelling of this interpretation of values comes from Hofstede
(1991). Hofstede describes values as "collective tendencies to chose a
certain path over a different path" (ibid., p.20). According to
Hofstede, values are feelings with a direction: a plus- and a minus
point. As examples he lists 'bad versus good', 'ugly versus pretty' and
'irrational versus rational'.

Here we find the acknowledgement that in values there are also
negative issues, which in the idealistic approach to values is not
usually made explicit. This definition clearly emphasizes a dominant
socialization pattern of a certain group or culture. It is necessary to
pause at the socialization processes, because the values and norms are
often cause of conscious reflection. In the description "collective
tendencies" it is pointed out that the members of a group can be
labelled by the value system of that group in which they have been
accepted. Many values and norms are attributed to them, without the
members of that group consciously aware of it. The issue here is that
positive values are placed against negative values and that can also
give direction for behavior.

This same thought is found with Maslow, (1971) who puts positive values such as honesty against mistrust and suspicion, good against bad. Kretchmer (1994, p.250) too emphasizes a contrast in values – called by Kretchmar "contrasting ethical traits".

Traits that promote good ethics	Traits that promote bad ethics
■ Honesty and integrity, an interest in achieving something of value. ■ A sense of fair play ■ Patience, a willingness to wait for the right opportunity	■ Drive and desire and interest in succeeding by whatever means ■ A win-at-all costs attitude ■ Opportunism, a tendency to jump at the first attractive offer one receives

In this interpretation of value it is acknowledged that people are often guided by values that can not be called socially desirable. "It is not the prettiest traits that get your far in this world" says Jan Loorbach, the captain of the Dutch Olympic delegation, in an interview with Trouw (8-11-1997). In that context he mentions ambition and vanity, values often viewed as negative, but values that can accomplish something. Loorbach even calls these values "fuel of progress".

This interpretation of the term value is called realistic because it more closely aligns to the tasks of very day life that people encounter. You can find many examples in sport. Holding a soccer player who broke through the defense line by his shirt while knowing that you could get the red card and get kicked out of the game. But the importance of winning is so great that the offence is made very consciously. This reality is usually not denied, but there is discussion about whether this should be viewed as a sacrifice for the good of the team or an unjustified offence of the rules. With this we point out that from one situation we can extract different values, mostly determined by the eye of the beholder.

6.1.3 Contextual values

Idealistic values are usually general in nature, they hold true for a large variety of situations that people encounter. On the other hand values can be connected to a certain context with which the scope of those values is limited. In the theory of the double character in sport, (Steenbergen, de Vos, Tamboer, 1992) the question is asked about those traits typical to that sport and the values associated with them such as competition, the desire to win, setting rules. Next this question can be asked of all branches of sport. What is so specific to golf where they use a handicap, and what is typical for gymnastics and handball. How are these sports different and how are they alike. We can conduct a conceptual analysis but an interpretive analysis can also help shed light on these questions. With boxing, for example, a conceptual analysis can give conclusion that may not be recognized by the participants of that sport. Contextual values can also be formulated with an eye on a specific focus group. Sport specific values from competition sport and adventure sport can not just be translated to sports for younger children. In sports for young children belong values such as the need for safety, care, a broad development and growth towards independence, and these should not be ignored.

6.1.4 The relationship between values and actions

In the preceding description of values the ideas were emphasized. There are also definitions where actions are specifically pointed out. A direct example of actions we find in Halstead (1996, p.5):

> The term values is used to refer to principles, fundamental convictions, ideals, standards or life stances which act as general guides to behaviour or as points of reference in decision-making or the evaluation of beliefs or action and which are closely connected to personal integrity and personal identity.

In the last part of the description the relationship to the identity of the person is pointed out. Values are lasting convictions, as Rokeach pointed out as well. People just don't switch values, their entire being is then compromised. But we are not saying that values never change. In modern western society adulthood is seen as much less constant and stable as a phase of life. People more often change the place they live, their job, or their spouse. This brings to light changes in values An author who places emphasis on actions is Van der Ven (1985), who introduces the term norm.

A norm is considered by this author (p.21) as a solidifying of values:

> One can perceive this as a guideline. In a conflict between
> two or more values in a category of concrete issues, it will
> indicate which value is preferred.

A separate discussion concerns the issue if whether or not the values
within a person should be somewhat consistent. This last thought we
find clearly in the description from Howe & Howe (1975). After they
concluded that values give direction to life, they immediately state
that those values have to be clear and consistent (p.17):

> Our values are the things that we are for and the things we
> are against. They give purpose and direction to our lives. If
> our values are clear, consistent, and soundly chosen, we
> tend to live our lives in meaningful and satisfying ways. If
> we lack values, or our values are confused and conflicted,
> we tend to live our lives in troubled and frustrating ways.
> Today, more and more people- especially the young- seem
> to be living their lives without clear purpose and direction,
> unable to decide what they are for or against.

All confusion, doubt and despair have been banished from life? Is this
not too much a portrayal of a harmonious person as that which is
desirable?

6.1.5 Values from a anthropological perspective

In the description of value used in the program "Values and norms in
sport" we are inspired by the description of Van der Ven (1985), who
describes a value as an appreciation (or interpretation) of the human
existence, that is viewed as a guideline for action. Value is limited
here to "appreciation of the human existence". Knowledge of issues or
events come into play when a view of the human picture can be found.
This anthropological approach attempts to shed light on the human
being, as giving purpose to its own existence. We also find these
anthropological accents with Valstar (1997). They view values as
"interpretations concerning human relations and exceed every day
objects and situations. Moral values are viewed as interpretations that
function imperative for behavior" (p.17). Values are rooted in the

affective domain and people tend to stay true all their lives to chosen values. This is the difference between values and terms such as views, wishes, and interests that are more easily changed.

There is a situational aspect attached to values. They are above a situation, but at the same time are tied to time and place. Values have to constantly be interpreted in the associated context and culture. "Values just are not available separately. In that sense a discussion about 'absolute values' is completely useless." (ibid). Within this anthropological narrowing the discussion can be about many different valuations of people, ranging from views of girls in sport, from the person testing his limits in adventure sport. There is a clear avoidance of a solid list of values, etched somehow in a specific view of life.

Values can not be unilaterally viewed as 'positive'. The issue is just as much about values viewed as not socially desirable, such as selfishness, sense of superiority of ones own kind, breaching rules. These are most certainly used as guidelines. No essential characteristics of humans are formulated within this train of thought, but the 'designs of the human being' is used, viewed in its time and culture.

6.2 Different approaches of values in research

From the description of the term value it becomes clear that research of values can be approached in a variety of different ways. Next a few approaches in summary. The approaches are not mutually exclusive and can not be placed in a good/bad schedule. The approach chosen will largely depend on the situation.

6.2.1 Idealistic value versus realistic value treatment

In an idealistic approach of values, ethical terms such as honesty, freedom, obedience, and equality function as starting points for research. You can give the respondents a list with these socially desirable items and ask them to rank them in order of importance. Athletes and non-athletes can be compared this way, seeing what the impact of the sport can be on its participants.

Lee (1997, pp.250-251) reports on this type of research:

> .... insofar as there are differences in the values of athletes
> and non-athletes, it is only that athletes tend to place more
> value on being good at what they do.

From this research was concluded that there were less differences then once was assumed. Realistic value treatment in research assumes positive as well as negative values. Values are placed in a negative setting as well. To be tested positive as well as negative interpretations are usually presented to the respondents in a certain balance, as they are experienced in daily practice of sport. We presented in the fair play quiz as educational tool to youngsters, positive as well as negative items about fair play. (Buisman, Steenbergen, Van de Langemheen, 1997). They had to give an opinion on it. As example:

> - Your coach orders you to injure a dangerous opponent during a
> championship. I do what I am ordered.
> - You must always, and under all circumstances follow the
> direction of the referee and the officials.

In the last research the objective was not so much the answers themselves as the arguments used in which the values came to light.

6.2.2 General social versus situational or context-bound value treatment

This separation falls in part under the above category, but has to be kept separate. With general social values we think more of values with a general reach, values that fit anywhere, positive as well as negative. We could be talking about honesty, nationalism or love of the motherland and tolerance. We could also think about research in which according to the theory of Kohlberg, several moral dilemmas are solved.

Kohlberg (1971) introduced a developmental theory of moral reasoning on three levels. At the pre-conventional level the child interprets good and bad, right or wrong in terms of physical or hedonistic consequences of action (punishment, reward, exchange of favors). At the conventional level, maintaining the expectations of the individual's family, group, or nation is perceived as valuable in its own right, regardless of immediate and obvious consequences, for example a law and order orientation. At the post-conventional level there is a clear effort to define moral values and principles which have validity and application apart from the authority of the groups of certain persons, (Galbraith & Jones, 1976, pp. 11/12), for example the universal ethical principle orientation. One can now begin research into at what level athletes and non-athletes solve moral dilemmas. The general universal theory of moral reasoning remains the research goal. This research was for example conducted by Shields & Bredemeyer (1998).

Next to that are the more situational- or contextual value treatments in research. An example of this can be found in the conceptual research of Steenbergen, De Vos & Tamboer(1992) about the double character of sport. Here several competition sport specific values are analyzed, such as the will to win, competition, contest, and to push to the edge of one's capabilities. But one can also analyze the context of the research group and situate value research there. An example of that can be found in the research of Van der Loo & Van Rossum (1997), in which the "sport education" of top-level-sport parents were compared to a control group, parents of children who played regular sports. Items listed were, for example, accepting direction from the referee, listening to the trainer, doing your very best, staying in shape, and improving technique.

Situational value treatment can also be pointed out in the research of Baar (1996) into the game interpretation of children in sport. Here the search is for values that belong to the life of a child within the context of the sport.

6.2.3 Values as individual needs or as a social product

This difference agrees with what was brought forward in the last paragraph by Beckers & Nauta (1983). Questionnaires can be given to athletes when researching whether they are motivated more intrinsically or extrinsically in their sport. It appears to be of great value to know how athletes value their sport and their surroundings, so that policy can be geared to that. Van Rossum (1996, 1998) has done various researches on this topic, mostly in hockey. Here we can also categorize experience oriented value research. Schröder & Meiling (1987) interviewed young athletes in water polo about their experience with fair play in their sport.

Some comments are:

> - and they were really pinching and I though, I don't have to take
> that, I am pinching back(girl, age 13)
> - when someone breaks through, you don't think about good
> sportsmanship, you go get him (boy, age 15).

The first comment can be heard in a variety of ways. The value behind this comment is " if you get me, I will get you back". Un-sportsman like behavior could be condoned this way: "They started, so…". An individual value statement becomes clear, and it is interesting to know how such a reaction compares to the club culture.

In research one can also focus on values as fallout of social convictions, such as the guidelines for sportsmanlike behavior. In the values and norms-program, for example, an analysis was done on fair play behavior codes in order to research the underlying values (Van de Langemheen & Buisman,1997). And Duyvenstijn (1997) researched values and norms in sport journalism. He concluded that Dutch newspapers such as the Volkskrant, Telegraaf, Trouw and a few regional newspapers pay little attention to female sport, handicapped sport or youth sport. The public has little interest in those, so say the journalists that were interviewed. However, journalism effectively ignored certain groups of athletes.

6.2.4 Goal values and values concerning human nature

Values are often seen as goals that they try to obtain mostly in pedagogical situations with children. In this context values are interpreted as input, discipline, respect for others, honesty, ability to plan and work with others. Children are often measured in sport by these values and then it becomes clear how much they can't do yet: children do not yet play well together, they are still egocentrical, they can not concentrate, they show little input and are quite playful. But in our example from the introduction we saw that there are values that belong well in a child's life.

The term 'good child life' is taken from Van der Zeyde (1963), who developed this concept based on her observations of children who were slow in their development. Values in the life of a still young child in sport are the playfulness, the still open assignment of meanings, the need for safety and security, the potential to explore and to grow into independence (Langeveld, 1979). These values belong to the nature of a young child. For puberty aged youngsters we could list: more physically aware, blossoming sexuality, one's own place among peers, experiment with authority, discovery of one's own ability in the sport. Lee (1993) researched values in sport among 93 young athletes in soccer (60 boys) and tennis (18 girls and 9 boys). The ages ranged from 12 to 16. The children were asked in a semi-structured interview about moral dilemmas in the sport. Content analysis of discussion protocols, produced 18 values given these young people, of which some are listed below (ibid., p.40):

Value	descriptor
Achievement	Being personally or collectively successful in play
Caring	Showing concern for other people
Companionship	Being with friends with a similar interest in the game
Equity / Fairness	Not allowing an unfair advantage in the contest/ judgement
Health & Fitness	Becoming healthy as a result of the activity, and in becoming fit to enhance performance.
Showing skill	Being able to perform the skills of the game well.
Winning	Demonstrating superiority in the contest.

When looking at these values one can conclude that most were formulated from the context of sport. But the values are hardly typical for youth between 12-16, they apply just as well to a group of adults. They are more geared toward goal oriented values. The sense-making of boys and girls at this age can hardly be found in this list. The results of such research give leaders and board members in sport little information about perception of this group of young people. That really should be a bigger focus of those making policy.

6.3 Value research between transfer of values and clarification of values

The example in the first paragraph about the question of whether or not wheelchair athletes should be allowed to participate in the four-day endurance walk can be viewed as a form of value clarification. However, that designation is not automatic because when reading between the lines of the analysis one can detect a moralizing undertone. Can it be conveyance of values too? In value conveyance, values are conveyed in the hope that the target group will take on these values. In value clarification, various values are openly offered for the target group to chose. The issue is to make the group aware of the values and norms that are already available (Praamsma, 1994, p.92).

Tamboer (1994) made, as mentioned in the first chapter of this book, an important distinction between the 'transfer' and 'clarification' of values. He argued that justice should be done to different views concerning value orientations in a multicultural society and try to clarify the different values. And this value clarifications means (ibid., p.4) "… an appeal to people to be accountable about their deepest convictions … Not to try, one way or another, to convince someone about their own correctness, as that would be the same as forcing the will of one onto others".

In the discussion of research about values, how does this discussion appear? It points out to researchers the tense relationship that is also present in their own line of work. On the one side is the danger that with help of a massive theory on values, delivered from a magician's hat, that was put there in advance. That could be with a functionalistic research approach (Coakley, 1994, p.35), in which the dominant values of current society are being confirmed. But it could just as easily be with a conflict theory where the research is about "how sport is related to alienation, coercion and social control, commercialism, nationalism, militarism, sexism and racism"(ibid.).

In sport one can encounter all kinds of closed value systems. Those are systems with a set pattern of values, hardly usable for discussion or testing. One could call competition a central feature for recreation sport and assign that to this group of athletes as well. Here too we find prejudices against specific groups of athletes. For example female athletes and athletes from ethnic minorities. One can view these prejudices as fixed values. In our description of values we do not always see values as "socially desirableness". Research into the under-representation of female coaches in the sport and the values on which that was based was done by Knoppers & Bouman (1996). In this research an attempt was made to maintain a certain nuance and a distant view when handling values. A careful attempt was made to ensure ethnic minorities were not only tested on values of Western society, but to understand the values from within these culture groups.

In the entire program an attempt was made to connect the various forms of research. A separate conceptual study was conducted into fair play in sport (Steenbergen, Van Hilvoorde & Tamboer, 1995) to which a policy research into the content of a fair play campaign could be connected (Van de Langemheen, Buisman, 1997). In research by Roose (1998) the need to clarify conceptual terms was identified so that they could be used to name those values for boys and girls active in gymnastics and volleyball.

On the other hand there are pitfalls to a too pluriform approach to value clarification. You run into values that can make children, youth and adults unhappy, or that can seriously compromise the health of the athletes, values that call up racism and fearful nationalism. Are we, as researchers done when the results have been communicated to society, or can society expect more from researchers in light of their science? In the WNS research these critical values were often found, such as when researching doping, cage fights, and top level sport for children. An attempt was made to gain attention of the press via articles sent. There are cultivation programs in which the results of the research are written and an attempt was made to show the practical side of value clarification (Buisman, Steenbergen & Van de Langemheen, 1997). There appear to be plenty of opportunities to be accountable to society for the contents that were found during research into values.

Description and evaluation in research of values: a tense relationship that will always be there and can never be resolved. On the one hand, the identified values need to be described with nuance and from a distant view, and at the same time remain very critical in reference to the (hidden) values in the methods and tools of the research. On the other hand, a certain sense of being connected is necessary and one should let one's own voice be heard in the research and take stands. Value research asks of the researcher how he or she compares to the identified values.

References

Baar, P. (1996). Drop-outs in boys-gymnastics. In: A.J. Buisman (Ed.), *Jeugdsport en beleid* (pp. 128-148). Houten/Diegem: Bohn Stafleu van Loghum. (in Dutch).

Beckers, J.W. & Nauta, A.P.W. (1983). Some facts about values in the Netherlands after 1945. In: J.W. Beckers & A.P.W. Nauta (Eds.), *Normen en waarden, verandering of verschuiving?* (pp.113-117). Den Haag: Vuga. (in Dutch).

Binder, D. (1990). *Fair Play for kids- a resource manual.* Canada: The commission for Fair Play and sport.

Buisman, A. J., Steenbergen, J. & Langemheen, J. van de (1997). *Fair Play in sport- How do you view that?*. Baarn: Bekadidakt. (in Dutch).

Coakley, J.J. (1994). *Sport in society. Issues and controversies.* St. Louis: Mosby.

Duijvestijn, P. (1997). *Sport in the media. Research into sports reporting in five Dutch newspapers.* Utrecht: Master Thesis Department Educational Studies, University Utrecht. (in Dutch).

Galbraith, R.E. & Jones, T.M. (1976). *Moral reasoning- A teaching handbook for adapting Kohlberg in the classroom.* Anoka (Minnesota): Greenhaven Press.

Halstead, J.M. & Taylor, M.J. (1996). *Values in education and education in values.* London, Washington, DC: Palmer Press.

Herzinger, R. (1997). The dictatorship of the community. *Filosofiemagazine*, 6, pp. 12-17. (in Dutch).

Hofstede, G. (1992). *Cultures and organizations. Software of the mind* London: Mc Grawhill.

Howe, L.W. & Howe, M.M. (1975). *Personalizing Education. Value clarification and beyond.* New York: Hart Publ. Company.

Kohlberg, L. (1971). Stages of moral development as the basis for moral education. In: C. Beck, E. Sullivan & D. Crittendon (Eds), *Moral Education* (pp. 16-32) Toronto: University of Toronto Press.

Knoppers, A. & Bouman, Y. (1996). *Trainers/coaches: a question of quality.* Arnhem: NOC / NSF. (in Dutch).

Kretchmar, R.S. (1994). *Practical philosophy of sport.* Champaign, Ill.: Human Kinetics.

Langhemeen, J & Buisman, A.J. (1997). *Does Fair Play score? Evaluation of the campaign "Fair Play always scores".* Utrecht: Vakgroep pedagogiek. (in Dutch).

Langeveld, M.J. (1979). *Psychology of development.* Groningen: Wolters-Noordhoff. (in Dutch).

Lee, M.J. (1993). Moral development and children's sporting values. In: Whitehead, J. (Ed.). *Developmental issues in children's sport and physical education* (pp. 30-43) Bedford: Institute for the study of children in sport.

Lee, M.J. (1997). *Values and responsibilities in children's sport.* Paper presented on the ICHPER-congress, June 1997, Vancouver.

Loo, H., van der & Rossum, J.H.A. van (1997). The family as an educational foundation for the development of youthsport talent. *Richting Sportgericht*, 51, pp. 225-231. (in Dutch).

Maslow, A.H. (1971). *The farther reaches of human nature.* New York: The Viking Press.

Praamsma, J.M. (1994). The environment question as an educational problem. *Vraagstelling - Tijdschrift voor de gamma wetenschappen*, 1, pp. 89-99. (in Dutch).

Rijsdorp, K. (1973). *Sport and society; a confrontation of the sport with societal questions.* Alphen aan de Rijn: Samson. (in Dutch).

Rokeach, M. (1973). *The nature of human values.* New York: Free Press, Mc Millan.

Roose, J. (1998). Play experience of children in competitive sport. In: J. Steenbergen, A.J. Buisman, P. De Knop & J.M.H. Lucassen (Eds.), *Waarden en normen in de sport.* (pp.163-183). Houten/Diegem: Bohn Stafleu van Loghum. (in Dutch).

Rossum, J.H.A. van (1996). Why children play: Do Dutch boys and girls value similar goals in playing games that US children do? *International Play Journal* , 4, pp. 51-58.

Rossum. J.H.A. van (1998). Why children play: American versus Dutch boys and girls. In: G. Hofstede (Ed.), *Masculinity and femininity: The taboo dimension of national cultures* (pp. 130-138) Thousand Oaks: Sage Publications.

Schröder, T. & Meiling, J. (1987). Youngsters about waterpolo. In: A.J. Buisman (Ed.), *Jeugdsport en Fair Play.* (pp. 81-87). Haarlem: de Vrieseborch. (in Dutch).

Shields, D.L.L., Bredemeyer, B.J.L. (1995). *Character development and physical activity.* Champaign, Ill.: Human Kinetics.

Steenbergen, J., Hilvoorde, I., & Tamboer, J.W.I. (1995). *Fair play.* Arnhem: NOC*NSF. (in Dutch).

Steenbergen, J., Vos, N.R. de & Tamboer, J.W.I. (1992). The double character of sport. *Lichamelijke opvoeding*, 14. (pp. 638-641). (in Dutch).

Tamboer, J. (1994). About old values and modern sport. *Lichamelijke Opvoeding*, 1, pp. 4-7. (in Dutch).

Valstar, J.G. (1977). *Fundamental document values and norms.* Zwolle: Lerarenopleidingen Basisonderwijs Overijssel. (in Dutch).

Ven, J.A. van der (1985). *Education in values and norms.* Kampen: Kok. (in Dutch).

Zeyde, N.F. van der (1963). *Serious educational problems of the child in education play-therapy.* Utrecht: Bijleveld. (in Dutch).

7 MEANINGS OF FAIR PLAY IN COMPETITIVE SPORT

Johan Steenbergen, Albert Buisman & Ivo van Hilvoorde

Introduction

In a discussion and policy about values and norms in sport one inevitably encounters the concept of 'fair play'. This concept expresses a moral criterion according to which a 'fair' sports practice can be measured. A century ago the same principle actually applied as presently. At the time the traditional sports ethics was ethics entirely based on 'fairness' (Meinberg, 1991, p.9), and nowadays 'fair play' is also often viewed as an umbrella that comprises the many aspects of moral values and norms in sport. However, in order to let the term 'fair' be meaningful and practical, for example for sports organisations in the event of a fair play-policy, it is first of all advisable to introduce a number of conceptual distinctions. These distinctions can be introduced by relating them to the previously mentioned context of 'the double character of sport' (see chapter 2 of this book). Referring to the aspect of the autonomy of sport, it is possible to refer to fair play in a more narrow sense. In addition, we distinguish fair play in a broad sense, whereby a connection is established with the aspect of embedding sport in various contexts.

However, the mere introduction of a conceptual clarity does not suffice. In sports practice it is often the case that the concept of 'fair play' has more meanings than assumed in the drawn up conceptual distinctions. If fair play is considered in relation with children and young persons in sport, entirely different values and norms are envisaged which are directly related to the specific characteristics of this group. In the latter part of this chapter the broadening of the concept of fair play will be discussed, resulting in a discussion on conceptual and pedagogical principles There it will also be advocated to avoid a too one-sided viewpoint regarding fair play, whereby particular individual sportsmen are called to account with regard to their responsibility for fair play. Institutions – sports associations, sports federations, sports clubs – are also responsible for promoting and creating fair sport. Moreover, we should not forget that trainers/coaches also have their own responsibilities with respect to values and norms and fair play .

7.1 Fair play in a narrow sense

The title of this section, and especially the phrase 'narrow sense', makes clear that fair play is restricted here to a well-defined description. That is, a description of fair play that is related to the autonomy of competitive based sport. More specifically, it is assumed that fair play is only relevant with regard to two members of the sports family – 'physical games' and 'non-physical games' (see chapter 2 of this book). The third member of the autonomy of the sports family, the so-called 'physical activities', is not relevant in a discussion about and clarification of fair play, because this member lacks competition and uniform rules to which every member should obey.

Traditionally the morality of sport has been described in terms of the notion of 'fair play'. This notion applies, in its most general sense, to 'playing according to and in the spirit of the rules'. With respect to this phrase, one often refers to the well known distinction between 'formal fair play' and 'informal fair play' (Lenk, 1964; Pilz & Wewer, 1987). A good start to understand the concept of fair play is to examine this distinction more closely.

7.2 Formal fair play

In defining and understanding formal fair play it is best to examine the concept of sport which underlies this notion. In the former section it is stated that fair play in the narrow sense, and thus by definition 'formal fair play', is only relevant with respect to two concepts of sport: physical games and non-physical games. As such, only those sports are relevant of which the autonomy is (partly) characterized by Suits' four game-elements (1978). Sport, as a game, is a rule-governed practice.

The predominant idea of rules in games is that they define the game practice. This set of rules has a necessary connection with the specific practice. They are constitutive for the action in question and so they are called constitutive rules (Searle, 1969, pp.33-34). These rules '... constitute (and also regulate) an activity the existence of which is logically dependent on the rules' (Searle, 1969, p.34). 'The rules of football or chess, for example, do not merely regulate playing football or chess, but as it were they create the very possibility of playing such games. The activities of playing football or chess are constituted by acting in accordance with (at least a large subset of) the appropriate rules' (Searle, 1969, pp.33/34).

So, one cannot engage in games (sports) such as chess, football, handball and the like unless the constitutive rules are accepted by the players. To enter into a (game) practice is, by definition, accepting the constitutive rules. More strongly, it is only against the background of these rules that the several actions within games can be described and understood. One can only perform the actions intrinsic to games if the constitutive rules of the game are accepted. As such, in the words of Rawls, (1955, p.25), these rules of practices are logically prior to particular cases. This means that rules which specify a form of action would not be described as that sort of action unless the rule-governed practice exists. This point can be illustrated by the game of baseball (Rawls, 1955, p.25). Many of the actions which are performed in a game of baseball can be done whether there is a game or not. For example, one can throw a ball, run, or swing a peculiarly shaped piece of wood. But one cannot steal a base, or strike out, or draw a walk, or make an error, or balk; although one can do certain things which appear to resemble these actions such as sliding into a bag, missing a grounder and so on. Striking out, stealing a base, balking etc., are all actions which can only happen in a game. No matter what a person did, what he did would not be described as stealing a base or striking out or drawing a walk unless he could only be described as to be playing baseball, and for him to be doing this presupposes the rule-like practice which constitutes the game. The practice is logically prior to particular cases: unless the practice exists, the terms referring to actions specified by the practice will lack a sense.

So, based on this brief outline it can be concluded that constitutive rules (i) define the autonomy of practices, and (ii) give meaning to the several actions within these practices. This interpretation of games in which various game derivative notions are defined solely in terms of the formal rules of a game is known as 'formalism' (d'Agostino, 1981, p.7). The linchpin of the formalistic account of games is the so-called logical incompatibility thesis (Morgan, 1987). This thesis holds that one cannot win in a game unless the formal rules are obeyed. Hence winning and cheating – constituted by intentional rule violation - are logically incompatible (Morgan, 1987, p.1). Cheating disrupts the agreed-upon mutual test and, from a logical point of view, the game. As Delattre (1975, p.136) says:

> ... from the point of view of logic, the need for the player's utter respect for the game is equally crucial. Competing, winning and losing in athletics are intelligible only within the framework of rules which define a specific competitive sport. A person may cheat at a game or compete at it, but it is logically impossible for him to do both. To cheat is to cease to compete.

Hence in order to justify the 'keeping of the formal rules of the game' it is not necessary to provide arguments extrinsic to sport. Formal fair play, defined as 'playing according to the formal rules', can be logically deduced from the autonomy of sport. Without acceptance of the constitutive rules one cannot, in a logical sense, play the game and so this notion of fair play comes close to or is even synonymous with Suits' expression 'lusory attitude'. That is '... the knowing acceptance of constitutive rules so the activity made possible by such acceptance can occur' (1978, p.40). Considered in this way, formal fair play is a necessary condition for or even a constitutive element of a game.

The question is, however, whether fair play is sufficiently defined solely in terms of 'keeping the rules'. No, only in a (rather) limited way. Formal fair play does not refer to all the rules, but only to the constitutive rules. These rules, upon which the existence of the game is logically dependent, must be distinguished from the regulative rules - rules which '... regulate a pre-existing activity, an activity whose existence is logically independent of the rules' (Searle, 1969: p.34). Although these rules presuppose the existence of constitutive rules and count as extensions of these rules, this does not mean that the breaking of these rules counts as 'not engaging in the game in question' (Morgan, 1987). Suits (1978, p.52) states with respect to the regulative rules: 'violating the [regulative] rule is neither to fail to play the game nor (necessarily) to fail to play the game well, since it is sometimes tactically correct to incur such a penalty for the sake of the advantage gained'. These rules, although different from constitutive rules, are still written game-rules, and as such they are by Loland (1998) like the constitutive rules denoted as 'formal playing rules'. These rules '… provide a conceptual framework necessary to realize a game in practice' (1998, p.85).

A strict formalistic conceptualization of fair play, in which fair play is regarded solely in terms of 'playing in accordance with the formal rules', is a rather limited account of fair play. Sport regarded as a social practices is always embedded in a broader context in which several unwritten rules (values and norms) reveal itself (see chapter two: the double character of sport). Although these unwritten rules are not established in the formal rules, they influence the way in which sport is valued from a moral perspective. The weakness of conceiving fair play as a formal conception of fair play is situated in ignorance of both the unwritten rules and the wider network of values and norms in which sport is embedded. And so fair play must be conceptualized in a broader sense than solely in terms of formal fair play.

7.3 Ethos of the game and informal fair play

With respect to formal fair play only the 'formalistic autonomy' – the 'specific nature' as defined merely by the written rules – of sport is described. Sport, however, is always embedded in a wider network of common held values and norms, which are (often) not formalized in the written rules. On the basis of these common held values and norms the written rules are interpreted. These shared values and norms which determine how the rules of a certain game are to be applied in concrete circumstances are defined by d'Agostino (1981) as the ethos of the game; that is the '… unofficial, implicit, empirically determinable conventions which govern official interpretation of the formal rules of a game (1981, p.13). This ethos of the games makes it possible to consider games and fair play more dynamically than the aforementioned formalistic account of these concepts.

Valuing a sport action as fair or unfair is not based solely on obeying the written rules. Fair play is also 'playing in the spirit of the rules' – and so fair play transcends the obedience of the prescribed rules. A few examples can illustrate this notion of 'playing in the spirit of rules'. The attitude, in which certain unwritten rules are dominant, was evident in two professional soccer matches in England. Two years ago (1999) during a FA-Cup match between Arsenal and Sheffield United, an Arsenal player became injured. In accordance with the unwritten rules, a Sheffield player kicked the ball out of play to make possible medical treatment of the injured player. At this level it is common that, after the injured player has been taken form the field, the ball is thrown back to the side, which was in possession of the ball (in this case: Sheffield United). The ball was thrown back to the Sheffield defense. The Nigerian international Kanu, however, intercepted the ball and scored a goal for Arsenal. In accordance with formal rules of soccer this was a legal goal – and this was also the decision of the referee. But although no rule was broken both sides were confused. The Sheffield players and coaches were outraged, the Arsenal players and managers embarrassed. Arsenal won the FA-match, but the coach of Arsenal (the Frenchman Wenger) made an appeal to the English Football Association for a replay of the match. So, although no formal rule was broken, for almost everyone it was clear that the ball should have been thrown back to Sheffield and that the action of the Arsenal player was in conflict with the fair play-principle.

We can give another example in which is illustrated that the concept of fair play transcends the codified rules of the game. In a Premier League match between West Ham United and Everton (2000) the West Ham player Di Canio demonstrated a form of playing in the spirit of the rules. In a duel between a West Ham player and the goalkeeper of Everton the latter got injured and as a result the goal was unguarded. After giving a cross by a West Ham player his team-mate, Di Canio, had a completely open goal and could score an easy goal. Instead of putting the ball in the unguarded goal he took the ball into his hands, so the goalkeeper could receive medical treatment. The Italian player received a standing ovation by players and fans for demonstrating this fair play-behavior.

A third example makes clear that on this level players not always play in the spirit of the rules. During the 1986 World Championship soccer game in which Argentina played against England, the well-known and excellent player Maradona scored by intentionally using his hand – leaving goalkeeper Peter Shilton staggered. Both the referee and linesman did not see that this 'goal' was scored in an unlawful way. Should Maradona have told the referee that he touched the ball with his hand instead of his head? The answer depends partly on what idea/concept Maradona has of the sport of soccer. With respect to formal fair play Maradona could have answered: 'why should I tell the referee? Is there a rule in soccer which says that a player should correct the referee'? On the other hand, with regard to the unwritten rules, he could have given the following answer: 'Yes, I should have told the referee that it was not a lawful goal. Although it is not imposed by a formal rule, the spirit or purpose of the soccer game is to find out which is the best side, not to measure the eyesight of the referee and linesman'. These different answers each partly depend on the way in which the particular sport is characterized or valued.

In the three examples it is indeed not a question of sticking or not sticking to the rules; the actions can nevertheless be characterized as fair (Di Canio) and unfair (Kanu, Maradona). Therefore, the judgment of these acts is not limited by the written rules. Informal fair play, as this aspect of fair play is often denoted, concerns an attitude towards the game, which is not prescribed by the formal rules. Important characteristics of this attitude, mentioned in the literature, are the following (Gabler, 1990; Lenk & Pilz, 1989; Loland, 1990):

- The idea of guaranteeing your opponent the same chances of winning or losing.
- Treating the other with 'respect'. The playing partner is not just an enemy with a formal role, but instead needs to be respected as a fellow human being.
- Playing only against players with a similar playing strength.
- The conviction that both parties play the game with total dedication, shown by the primary focus on the intrinsic aims of the specific game.

The three above-mentioned examples of informal fair play were connected with the features 'equal chances in playing and winning' and 'respect for the opponent'. The principle of similar playing strength forms the basis of initiatives to play several test matches at the beginning of the youth competition in order to determine the playing strength of the different teams.

As an example of 'playing the game with total dedication' we can think of former cycling champion Eddy Merkcx. In reply to the question why Merkcx, the guaranteed winner of the Giro in 1973, also wanted to win the green jersey in the same year, and thereby beating fellow-countryman De Vlaeminck in this sprinting contest, Merkcx answered: "I think it would be immoral to not have taken advantage of the opportunity."

Because of this attitude some people will label Merkcx as anti-social or even immoral. But that would deny the fact that 'playing the game with total dedication' and therefore 'wanting to win' is a central characteristic of informal fair play, and with that of the ethos of the game. The defeated opponent who remarked after the game that he didn't really play with his whole heart may also be accused of an unsportsmanlike attitude for the same reasons. From an informal perspective the dedication to win can also be interpreted in a different way. Yvonne Reinders, who was almost unbeatable in her time as world champion, explained that she regularly gave away races in order, as she explained "to stimulate bicycle racing for women" (Buisman, Cleymans & Van Essen, 1989, p.50):

> I never sold any races, I always gave them away just like that. I know how difficult it is to make a living in sport. I also experienced that I had spent my last penny, so that I could not do anything anymore. And then I sometimes said: 'Ah, well , that's clear, we'll arrange something.' However, at the time I gave away races to stimulate bicycle racing for women. Because people who, normally speaking, would never go to the race, may go more often if their favorite wins. Then you can promote the races.

But when the persons in question explained that Yvonne Reinders had let them win, the champion was quite irritated. It was sheer unsportsmanlike behavior. This means that in a special context of sport the meaning of concepts may drastically change. In the situation of the bicycle racing for women it was difficult at the time to get women with a similar strength together. And there was one woman who was head and shoulders above the others. According to this sportswoman, 'fair' meant considering the position of other women in the pack and serving the interest of cycling. In contrast with Eddy

Merckx, who at the time was also head and shoulders above other cyclists in the cycling pack, she did not (only) want to 'always try to win', but she showed that she had a broader attitude towards the cycling sport for women in its totality. In short, informal fair play is a concept that often leads to different and sometimes apparently contradictory interpretations, without being able to clearly state that one person or the other is acting fairly or unfairly. In order to understand and assess the attitudes of both cyclists, it is, for example, essential to gain an understanding of the (different) positions of men's cycling and women's cycling at the time, and maybe even now. These examples also show that you should be cautious to consider concepts such as 'fair' and 'unfair' as entirely ethical concepts. What Merckx did was fair in a formal (and partly informal) sense, but one can ask critically if this 'winning' attitude was the best one with respect to De Vlaeminck. What Yvonne Reinders did was unfair in a formal sense, but at the same time it was very social and very relevant for sport from a policy viewpoint and the propaganda for women cycling.

It will not cost a lot of effort to find more examples like these, but the examples make clear that informal fair play leaves enough possibilities for different interpretations. For example, how far should and can one go with the principle of equal chances to win and play. Was tennis fairer during the nineteen-twenties, when better tennis players got a handicap when they played against less able players? And why do we classify judokas and boxers on the basis of their weight, while players in volleyball and basketball are not classified on the basis of their height? Furthermore, how can the principle of equal chances of winning and losing be optimized, without ignoring the other feature of the game, namely to make possible that the inequalities in skills can be shown?

Similar questions can be posed in relation to the other characteristics of fair play. On the one hand every kind of sport has its own, historically grown, customs and conventions (d'Agostino, 1981). On the other hand, changes in values within society as a whole also influence customs and conventions of every specific sport in a particular way. In tennis, for example, it is unsportsmanlike to make a noise when one of the players is serving. This convention is unknown in volleyball, and also soccer fans won't hesitate to break the concentration of a player when taking a penalty. Especially Dutch soccer players know this convention quite well. Hockey and cricket players know other conventions than soccer, cycling or boxing; therefore one can talk of a sport-specific moral or subculture. Informal fair play in other words relates to a moral of a sport, which may indeed vary for any kind of sport, but still relies on the same kind of features (such as equal chances to win or lose or losing and respect for the opponent).

When referring to 'informal fair play', it always relates to the specificity of competitive sport. It concerns a whole set of values and norms that influence the course of a game. But there still is an important difference with the earlier discussed concept 'formal fair play'. The fact is, 'informal fair play' cannot logically be deduced from the specificity of 'the' sport. Sport-extrinsic values, concerning for example respect for the opponent, are of importance in the concretization of 'informal fair play'. Besides, this concept is influenced by values in society as a whole. But nevertheless, 'informal fair play' can only be understood when reasoning about the intrinsic perspective of competitive sport; therefore we classify both formal and informal fair play within 'fair play in the narrow sense'.

As explained in a previous part of this book, sport can be characterized by its double character. This means that the sport practice is always embedded within a broader network of values and norms. And although not necessarily connected with sport, they do influence this practice. With this we come to a broader definition of fair play, which will be discussed in the next paragraph.

7.4 Fair play in a broader sense

It is possible to give fair play a broader meaning than we did in the previous paragraphs. We will concentrate on the other aspect of the double character of sport: 'the social embedment of sport'. In this case fair play concerns both the ethos of the game as well as several sport-extrinsic aims and values. Aims therefore, which do not emanate from the autonomy of sport, but instead, arise from extrinsic valuing. On the one hand this broader meaning of fair play is expressed when using sport as an instrument, for example as a means for extrinsic values such as developing one's personality, social integration or health. On the other hand sport can be confronted with values stemming from the social-cultural embedding in which sport is being practiced. This can also include developmental values and giving meaning, as well as social issues such as equality or inequality in possibilities of participation, justice, sport injuries, discrimination, hooliganism and ecological awareness (Steenbergen & Tamboer, 1998). All these issues can be placed within the concept of fair play, which is often the case in policy.

It is clear that a broad spectrum of values and norms can be placed within the 'umbrella concept' of fair play. Values such as equivalence, justice and equality of chances are of importance for optimizing the ethos of the game. They are values that can be found within the autonomy of the game. This is not the case with respect to values as 'developing one's personality', 'health' and 'social integration'. Although these values (meanings) are probably indispensable for 'the good life', conceptually speaking they display an instrumental approach towards sport. To put it differently, sport is used as an instrument to achieve certain external goals such as health, social integration and character development.

Ecological questions and questions concerning discrimination can also be understood from a broader social-cultural embedment of sport in society. But they are not necessarily connected with the practice of sport. But sport, as a central social phenomenon, cannot distance itself from social values such as 'you must not discriminate' or 'you must be responsible for nature and the environment'. Although the aforementioned values often are placed under the concept 'fair play', the question remains if it is fruitful to place both the sport-intrinsic values and sport-extrinsic values under the umbrella of 'fair play'.

7.5 Fair play and educational meanings

Another example of a broad(er) conceptualizing of fair play can be found within (sport)pedagogical literature (Buisman, 1987). Besides formal ('following the rules') and informal ('respect your opponent') aspects, fair play can also be understood as an important pedagogical and didactical principle. Examples of these pedagogical principles within sport are: 'giving others the opportunity to score a goal', 'don't always play the ball to your friend' and 'give everyone an equal chance to play'. The judgement whether or not the game can be designated as 'fair' or 'unfair' is made on the basis of a sport-extrinsic perspective: in this case on pedagogical grounds. And so, in determining the meaning of fair play, not only sport-intrinsic values are of importance, but also criteria derived from pedagogical principles. The practice of sport can be judged by the following, pedagogical criteria: 'children should enjoy the sport they are practicing', 'the aim should be to make the experiences for the child as diverse as possible', 'sport should be geared to the child's perception of their environment', and an 'early and one-sided specialization should be avoided within youth sport'. Sport is fair, from this broader perspective, when it is suitable for children and when it is child-oriented.

From this conception of 'fair play in a broader sense' sport is regarded as being embedded in a wider network of common held values and norms. It is however questionable whether it is meaningful to place all values and norms, which are good aims for a 'good (youth) sport', under the concept 'fair play'. With reference to the last example, is it useful to discuss pedagogical values when talking about fair play? Or should we handle educational values separately? We think the answer can be both "yes" and "no".

In the first part of this chapter the focus is in particular on a conceptual interpretation of fair play – an interpretation with regard to which the meaning is slightly extended all the time. From a pedagogical perspective it is important to broaden this merely conceptual approach by not only assessing fair play from the perspective of the sports practice by adults. A conceptual analysis of fair play should not only focus on concepts such as 'making profits', 'observing the rules' and 'equal chances', but also consider them against an anthropological background. That is to say, in the meaning that is given to the practice of sport and fair play in a specific stage in the lives of young people.

In a discussion between conceptual thinkers in sport and sports educators, the latter always emphasize the special position of "a child in development" according to two meanings. In the first place it concerns the developmental-psychological perspective whereby fair play in sport is directly linked to the developmental phase of the child.

From this perspective fair sport may, for example, have the following meaning:

- Accepting that younger children like to crowd together in the field, because they want to be where the ball is.
- Letting all the children play the same amount of time, so that not only the best players are on the field, which means that it is not always the primary aim to win a game in youth sport.
- Giving children the opportunity to discover their talents and not letting them specialize in a certain sport too early.

These considerations can be illuminated with an example. A football trainer, Sjef Vergoossen (De Volkskrant, 6-3.1993) explained in an interview the following:

> A trainer who thinks that his youth team should primarily win is not doing the right thing. Winning itself is not important, but trying to win is. A game is a means, but never should be a target. Although children should always try to achieve a maximum result.

He gave an example of an Ajax youth team that was about to lose a match, so the coach directed a tall center back to a forward position. All balls went to him and Ajax won. 'I would never choose such a solution', according to Vergoossen. 'Ajax succumbed to the urge to win at all cost'. So he states that when children are in the learning period of sport, the will to win is not always the highest aim, certainly not in the long term. Winning or trying to win is an important distinction in the learning period of the young.

In this example the second orientation also becomes clear, that is the target perspective. The focus is not only on the development and degree in which children mature in this process. There are also clear targets in sport and people try to realize these targets through influencing. In this example the important thing is to learn the sport well. This target is more important than winning a match. And the important thing is also to promote independence. Fair play does not only mean that you adapt to the rules of sport, but at the same time also learn to have a critical judgment about this.

Children and young people learn different things in sport. They increasingly participate in the sports culture: trainers teach them attitudes and skills. Sometimes these aspects are presented to them as targets that are explicitly stated, but sometimes this also happens more implicitly in a socialization process. Examples are:

- They learn to view things from the perspective of the other, as a result of which a concept such as 'respect for the opponent and co-player' can be explained.
- They learn to know their place in sport, they learn about their specific skills, as a result of which they are able to accept selection processes better.
- Older youth also learn about the other side of competitive sport, in which an extreme commitment is required to achieve a good result. This other side of sport is not always so nice and so the fair play idea should be presented realistically here.

From a developmental-psychological perspective it is therefore clear that fair play will be interpreted in a broader context than 'playing according to and in the spirit of the rules'. Certain specific values may be envisaged that do justice to young children and youth in sport. Fair sport should take this into account too. With the target perspectives fair play will be considered in a narrower sense. And so the reasoning takes place according to 'the' autonomy of game forms and according to the autonomy of children and youths in sport. The tension between both these perspectives has always been structurally present, youth trainers and coaches will have to learn to deal adequately with this.

7.6 Responsibilities for fair play with organizations

In the previous paragraphs on fair play the main focus was on individual players and how they should behave within sport. When rules are breached many sanctions exist: red/yellow cards and suspensions. Coaches and sports organizations have had much fewer discussions on fair play. This ignorance of coaches and institutions with regard to unfair behavior also becomes manifest in the press – much less is known about this than about the alleged unfair behavior of individual players. A number of examples may explain this.

First of all, the behavior of trainers and coaches should be mentioned. According to Eitzen (1999, p.47) coaches are important role models for their athletes, so several coaches take this responsibility seriously, insisting on fair play, respect for opponents and humane treatment of their athletes. The contrary also occurs, when coaches do not only provoke violence by their players, but they are even trained to play in a violent way (and therefore unfair). Eitzen exemplifies this by following the words of the 'well-known' Green Bay Packers coach Vince Lombardi: 'To play this game, you have to have that fire within you, and nothing stokes that fire like hate'. Behavioral codes for coaches seem to be necessary here. Hence, it is realistic to question which sport associations have drawn up such a behavioral code and monitor its implementation and observation.

Not only the coach, but also a sports team as a whole has a responsibility to behave in a fair way and can be held accountable for this. At present the situation exists that in some ball sports such as football and handball the responsibility for fair play is sometimes passed too easily to the referee. The referee declares, it is often said, what the limits are of what is allowed and what is not. If several players seriously violate the rules, it is possible that the whole team is held accountable. Sanctions are certainly possible in this case. Teams that misbehave grossly in a game, or who have committed too many serious fouls over a certain period may, for example, lose competition points. This seems to be a reasonably effective means, which nonetheless only few organizations have the courage to apply.

A competition arrangement based on the strength of the players is more a responsibility for sports organizations than for individual players. If there are, for example, differences in strength in a certain class of youth sport, leading to results such as 18-1, the organizers have clearly failed. People should know that in youth sport the playing strength of teams may vary enormously, because every year about half of the team moves on to a higher age group, and the team is supplemented by younger children again. With team sports it would be possible to play a few trial matches every year. After three or four matches it should be possible to make a definitive line-up for the team. The responsibility for fair play is therefore clearly with sports organizations. It concerns an institutional responsibility.

This also applies to the principle 'of creating equal chances in the competition'. The factor 'chance' should be neutralized as much as possible. On the basis of the principle of fair play it is difficult to accept that skaters on an outside lane who start in the first group have a clear advantage above those who are the last to start when the skating rink has become less fast. This factor may be (and often is) neutralized to a certain degree by letting the likely candidates for medals start in the same group. And in sports such as rowing and canoeing an honest contest may be impossible because of buoy advantages with a certain wind direction.

Sports organizations should also try to stimulate a certain standardization of sports material and sports facilities, implying that it involves a sportive contest and not a contest between technicians. After all, it is often the case that the more money you have, the greater your chance of winning. For example, rich football clubs can buy the best players, who often end up on the reserve's bench or even in the grand stand. It is assumed that too little action is undertaken to counter these unfair sports practices and this is not very compatible with the idea of 'pursuing equal chances'. This also concerns an institutional responsibility with regard to fair play that transcends the individual responsibility to behave fairly.

We can finish with one summarizing and concluding question: Is it not the case that too few questions are asked of sports organizations about fair play within their own branch of sport? With regard to the commercial influence on American football Chandler & Chandler Fox (1984, p.87) pointed out critically that:

> The game changed when the competition to play professional football became more intense. So much more money was being thrown around and individual players had the terrible pressure of whether or not they were going to make it. So these players started doing things that they hadn't normally done. As the equipment got better, many guys started using their head as a battering ram because the helmets were so fail-proof. Slowly, the feeling surfaced with players no longer respecting the other man's well-being on the opposing team.

It appears that the organizers do not only allow this development, but even stimulate it. On the one hand they introduce more protective clothing, but on the other hand this stimulates the violence in sport. This seem to be incomprehensible contradictions, but according to Eitzen (1999) competitive sport is full of it. Considering Eitzen (ibid) 'sport is fair and sport is foul', 'sport is healthy and destructive' and 'sport is expressive and controlled'. Generally speaking it is advisable to draw a sharp distinction between the individual responsibility of athletes and the responsibility of sports organizations with regard to their responsibility for fair play. The different responsibilities are visualized in the following diagram, which can be supplemented by

other important principles. A distinction is made between aspects
related to a competitive sport, which are typical of a competitive sport,
and aspects that transcend sport which, however, are not less
important for 'good sport', but which also apply to other social fields.

	Sport-specific values which belong to 'the' autonomy of competitive sport	Sport extrinsic values which transcends 'the' autonomy of competitive sport
Individual responsibility	- commitment for a good result - observing the rules	- good clothes - honesty - respect for one's fellow man - focus on health
Responsibility of Clubs/associations	- good game rules - similar playing strength - equal chances	- focus on health - creating a sportive atmosphere - good reception opponent

By comparing individual and organizational responsibilities with
sport-intrinsic tasks and tasks that transcend sport, you can obtain a
better overview with regard to the policy to be pursued, whereby
policy priorities may be determined in a balanced way.

Conclusion

Conceptually speaking it is probably better to distinguish clearly between sport-specific and sport-transcending values, and to reserve fair play for the first category of values (therefore excluding the pedagogical values). Otherwise there could be a lack of distinction regarding the specific values that are discussed. It is surely defensible (and often done in policy) and sometimes more strategic, to give a 'strokeable' and pleasant concept such as fair play as many suitable meanings as possible. But from a conceptual perspective this broader meaning may create a confusion. The meaning of fair play might become less communicable. Besides, a valuable perspective, such as a pedagogical perspective, may be easily overlooked when it has to 'share' its place with all other values, combined in one concept.

From the preceding one should not conclude that it is not important to broaden the moral perspective on sport. On the contrary, such a perspective is so important for good sport – for example as children and youth are involved - that every chance of a confusion of tongues should be prevented. Therefore it is useful to distinguish between 'Fair play in the narrow sense' from 'Fair play in a broader sense', and give pedagogical questions a central   place within the latter (Grupe, 1985).

So it seems that the answer to the question if we should handle educational values separately is 'yes'. But on the other hand it is impossible to leave it out when we are talking about sport for young children and youth sport. In many ways it is impossible and unfruitful to compare sport for children with adult sport practices (see chapter 10). What is, or what is not, a fair sport also depends strongly on the specific age and context. Within professional sports it is not a problem, even a logic of the practice itself, to select only the best players in the team. When valuing the first contact with a sport for children, or the introduction to a differentiated culture in sports and movement, it is certainly not unproblematic to adapt the same kind of selection criteria.

It is clear that values stemming form a child-perspective lead to another understanding of fair play, as is the case with fair play in sport for adults. Especially with respect to sport for the youngsters it is important that organizations take their responsibility to stimulate and create a fair sport for all. And so it is advisable to (1) distinguish between sport-specific and sport-transcendental values, (2) make a clear distinction between fair play in a narrow sense and fair play in a broader sense, and (3) distinguish between individual and institutional responsibilities with respect to fair play. These distinctions can preserve us for one-sided and unfruitful perspectives on fair play so that the specific values can be placed precisely and clearly within a discussion about values and norms in sport.

References

d'Agostino, F. (1981). The Ethos of Games. *Journal of the Philosophy of Sport*, VIII, pp. 7-18.

Buisman, A.J. (1987). *Youthsport and Fair Play*. Haarlem: Vrieseborch. (in Dutch).

Buisman, A., Cleymans, R. & Essen, S. van (1989). *About Fairness und Unfairness: The stories of of individuals*. Berchem: Sporta. (in Dutch).

Chandler, B. & Chandler Fox, N. (1984). *Violent Sundays*. New York: Simon and Schuster.

Delattre, E.J. (1975). Some Reflections on Success and Failure in Competitive Athletics. *Journal of the Philosophy of Sport*, II, pp. 131-139.

Eitzen, D.S. (1999). *Fair and Foul. Beyond the myths and paradoxes of sport*. Lanham, Maryland: Rowman and Littlefield.

Gabler, H. (1990). Fair play Firstly – Sport between Aggression and Fairness. In: O. Grupe (Ed.), *Kulturgut oder Körperkult* (pp. 172-194)? Tübingen: Attempto. (in German)

Grupe, O. (1985). Top-Level Sports for Children from an Educational Viewpoint. *The International Journal of Physical Education*, 22, pp.9-15.

Lenk, H. (1964). *Values, Goals and Reality of the Modern Olympic Games*. Schorndorf: Hofmann. (in German).

Lenk, H. & Pilz, A. (1989). *The Fair Play-Principle*. Zürich: Interfrom.

Loland, S. (1990). Fair Play in Sports Contests – A Moral Norm system. *Sportwissenschaft*, 20, pp. 146-160.

Loland, S. (1998). Fair play: Historical Anachronism or Topical Ideal? In: M.J. McNamee & S.J. Parry (Eds.), *Ethics and Sport* (pp. 79-103). London: E & FN Spon.

Meinberg, E. (1991). *The Morality in Sport*. Aachen: Meyer & Meyer Verlag. (in German).

Morgan, W. (1987). The Logical Incompatibility Thesis and Rules: A Reconsideration of Formalism as an Account of Games. *Journal of the Philosophy of Sport*, XIV, pp. 1-20.

Pilz, G.A. & Wewer, W. (1987). *Result or Fair play? Sport as mirror of society*. München: Copress Verlag. (in German).

Rawls, J. (1955). Two Concepts of Rules. *Philosophical Review*, 64, pp. 3-32.

Searle, J. (1969). *Speech Acts. An Essay in the Philosophy of Language*. *Cambridge*: Harvard University Press.

Steenbergen, J. & Tamboer, J.W.I. (1998). Ethics and the double character of sport: an attempt to systematize discussion of the ethics of sport. In: M.J. McNamee & S.J. Parry (Eds.), *Ethics and Sport* (pp. 35-53). London: E & FN Spon.

Suits, B.H. (1978). *The Grasshopper: Games, Life and Utopia*. Toronto/Buffalo: University of Toronto Press.

8 THE DUTCH AND OLYMPISM

Ricus Timmers & Paul De Knop

Introduction

There is world-wide hardly any empirical research material about how a society as a whole looks upon Olympism. One exception is the research from Naul of the Willibald Gebhart Institute of the University of Essen as part of an international research project 'Sportive Lifestyle Motor Performance and the Olympic Ideals of Youth in Europe' (Naul, 1998) who has done a survey amongst youngsters in four different countries. The questionnaire was focused on young people in the age-group of 12 until 15 years. The emphasis was on the knowledge of the Olympic symbols and the norms and values behind it. This research had a very broad scope and a strong pedagogical emphasis. Most other research projects on Olympism have been historical, pedagogical and also sociological. But never has there been an empirical (sport)sociological research on how society nowadays looks upon Olympism. So, in 1999 a survey was conducted in the Netherlands about the values and norms concerning Olympism. The central question was: which values and norms do the people in the Netherlands, connect with Olympism? In this chapter an outline is given of the results of this research (Timmers, 2000).

8.1 The Olympic Values

Pierre De Coubertin was the founding father of the modern Olympic Games and also of the Olympic ideals. According to De Coubertin the essence lay in the educational character of sport. Values like 'a sound mind in a healthy body', honesty and sportsmanship were very important. But Pierre De Coubertin also acknowledged the importance of achievement. He was convinced that sports was all about achieving the limits of one's abilities. This was translated into the motto of the Olympics: 'citius, altius, fortius'. When an athlete starts in a competition he must have the will to win. But this will to win, according to De Coubertin (MacAlloon, 1981), should go along with values like sportsmanship, honesty and modesty whenever victory was achieved. Sometimes accepting a defeat makes more of an impression on the other competitors and the audience than winning. Thus, Olympism was introduced.

In 1991 the first real definition of Olympism appeared in the Olympic Charter, stating: "Olympism is a philosophy of life, exalting and combining in a balanced whole the qualities of body, will and mind. Blending sport with culture and education, Olympism seeks to create a way of life based on the joy found in the effort, the educational value of good example and respect for universal fundamental ethical principles." (IOC, 1994). At this moment the IOC Charter of 1996 is officially in order. The goals behind it are made more explicit. Peace plays an important part in it: "The goal of Olympism is to place everywhere sport at the service of the harmonious development of man, with a view to encouraging the establishment of a peaceful society concerned with the preservation of human dignity. To this effect the Olympic Movement engages, alone or in co-operation with other organisations, and within the limits of its means, in actions to promote peace" (IOC, 1997).

8.2 Research method

At the beginning of the research we expected that one survey amongst the Dutch population would be sufficient and planned on doing so in 1999, in between the Games of Nagano and Sydney. At the end of 1998 and the beginning of 1999 the Salt Lake City affair arose, in which the IOC had a substantial part, and we decided to split up the survey into two groups. The first group was asked to answer the questionnaire in may 1999, shortly after the Salt Lake City affair, and the second group later in the year, October 1999, answered the same questionnaire. The two groups where large enough, and taken at random, so each of them could on there own be representative of Dutch society as a whole. The surveys were conducted by CentERdata, an institute of the University of Tilburg specialised in collecting data. Their most important instrument is CentERpanel which exists of 2000 households in the Netherlands. The panel is representative for the Dutch population. There were several pre-tests. The first one involved a group of experts in the field of sports and the Olympic Games. The second group existed of staff members of CentERdata. And finally the questionnaire was tested by a group of 30 people with differentiation in age, sex and sporting activities.

Table 1: The survey sample according to sex and age

Sex	CBS[1]	CentERpanel	May-group	Oct.-group	Total
Male	49%	52%	57%	55%	56%
Female	51%	48%	43%	45%	44%
Age	CBS	CentERpanel	May-group	Oct.-group	Total
15 (16)– 24[2]	17%	12%	6%	8%	7%
25 - 34	21%	17%	15%	18%	16%
35 - 44	19%	21%	22%	22%	22%
45 - 54	16%	22%	24%	18%	22%
55 - 64	12%	15%	18%	19%	18%
65 +	16%	13%	16%	16%	16%
		n=3641	n=1291	n=892	n=21

[1] Central Buro of Statistics of the Netherlands.
[2] CBS uses category 15 – 24 years, CentERpanel 16 –24 years.

First of all we have analysed the differences between the May and October group. The question was can we find significant differences between the two groups which could be explained in relationship to the Salt Lake City affair, e.g., we expected that the May group would be more negative about the IOC than the October group. We also tested for other variables. We found out that there were no significant differences between the May and October group. Of course there are a lot of other variables involved but we have reason to believe that the view on the Olympic Games, at least in Holland, did not change in a relative short period (five months) despite affairs like the Salt Lake City one, and thus that our research results are not much influenced by this affair.

8.3 Research results

In order to get more insight into how the Dutch people look upon Olympism, we tried to get some impression on the Olympic knowledge in the Netherlands. In the research four knowledge questions about the Olympics Games were put forward. The question: in which city the first modern Olympics took place was answered correctly by 68,3% of the people. A majority of the Dutch people knew that the last Winter Olympics were held in Nagano. And 54,8% knew the name of the president of the IOC; Juan Antonio Samaranch. Less than one third of the Dutch population knows about Pierre De Coubertin. In the analysis of the average knowledge of the Dutch people these four question were put together. Almost 10% of the Dutch population had no knowledge of the Olympic Games (zero out of four) and 15% knew all the answers.

Variation-analyses showed that the most important variables in relationship towards Olympic knowledge were age, watching sports on television and the interest in sports events. The age-group of 16-24 years had an average of 1.67 correct answers while the age-group of 45 years and older had an average of more than 2 good answers. The same goes for the number of channels one watches sports. If somebody didn't watch sports at all the average knowledge about the Olympics was 1.68 correct answers. With the group who watch sports at one or two channels the average was 2.14, and those who watch sports on more than six channels the average score was 2.56 correct answers. For people who had not been following any sports events lately the average score was 1.42 and those who followed a lot of sports events the average score was 2.67 correct answers. Calculations showed that just 1.7% of the variable Olympic knowledge can be explained by age. The variables age, sex, watching sports and following sport events together explain 5.7% of the variation on the knowledge questions.

8.4 Olympic values and norms

From a historical point of view it is clear that a lot of values and norms have played an important role in connection with Olympism. De Coubertin expressed the importance of values and norms like: honour, a better world, competing is more important than winning, a sound mind in a healthy body, "citius, altius, fortius", sportsmanship and brotherhood. The IOC has translated the heritage of De Coubertin into a definition of Olympism as to be found in the Olympic Charter. Important values and norms within this definition are: peace, solidarity, joy of the game, giving a good example and equal rights for everybody. However, the history of 100 years Olympic Games has shown us other examples of values and norms, like: the use of dope, commercialisation, media-attention, political influence and going for gold, all of which can be seen as the other side of the coin. We have put forward in the questionnaire as many Olympic values and norms as possible.

The Olympic values have been split according to the ideas of Beckers & Nauta (1983) into two groups:
1. The values which are personal, in this case from the point of view of the Olympian who will participate in the Games of Sydney in 2000, and can be matched with needs and motives.
2. The institutional values which focus on particular goals like the Olympic Games in general.

First of all the respondents were given a list of Olympic values and norms and where asked which of these motives, according to them, is the most important for an Olympian who will participate in the Olympic Games. The next question was to select the second most important value. This process continued until the five most important motives where selected. Then the respondents were asked what, according to them, would be the least and the second least important motive of an Olympian who will participate in the Olympic Games. Before making a choice the people were asked to look at the list as a whole and then make a decision.

Table 2: The most important motive to compete in the Olympic Games

	Perc.
1 Winning a gold medal	27.6
2 Joy in the game	15,3
3 Competing is more important than winning	13.9
4 Achieving	9.0
5 Money	7.0
6 Honour	6.8
7 Going to limits of one's abilities	5.0
8 To excel	3.5
9 Sportsmanship	3.1
10 Ambition	2.7
11 Raise their own market value	2.4
12 Citius, altius, fortius	1.8
13 Sound mind in a healthy body	1.0
14 Giving a good example	0.7
15 Discipline	0.3
Total	100.0

'Winning Olympic gold' was the number one motive (see table 2) in all categories: men or women, young or old, high or low educational level and sporting or non-sporting. To get a closer look into what people see as the most important motives we have made calculations taking into account the position of importance: first, second, third, fourth and fifth place. From this we made a top 5 of most important motives of why a Olympian takes part in the Olympic Games.

Table 3: Top 5 of most important motives to compete in the Olympic Games

1. Winning a gold medal	5809 points
2. Achieving	3620
3. Competing is more important than winning	3144
4. Honour	3078
5. Joy in the game	2733

In the top five of most important motives 'winning a gold medal' is also the number one (see table 3) and again in all categories: sex, age, education and sporting or not. It shows clearly that according to the Dutch population the winning of a gold medal is the most important reason why an Olympian would compete in the Olympic Games.

In the top 5 of motives, all together, 'achieving' came in second place, while if asked which is the number one of the most important motive, 'achieving' is found to be in fourth place. Both men and women placed 'achieving' at the number two spot in the top 5 motives.

But if we look at the different age groups then 'achieving' scores high with young people and lower with the elderly. Within the age-group 55 to 64 and 65+ 'competing is more important than winning' takes the second place. This value scores a fourth place within the age-groups 16 to 24, 25 to 34 and 35 to 44. The value 'honour' scores higher with men (3rd) than with women (5th). For women 'joy in the game' is more important than 'money'; while with men it is the opposite. Young men see as most important values: 'going for gold', 'achieving' and 'money'. With older people also 'winning gold' is the number one motive, but also classical Olympic values like 'competing is more important than winning' and 'honour' are important values to them.

The following question was which motives, according to the Dutch people, is the least important if one competes at the Olympics. The respondents could make a choice from the same list as shown before. 'Giving the good example' was found to be the least important motive to compete at the Olympics. A quarter (25.8%) of the people in the

Netherlands placed it at the last spot. According to the Olympic Charter, this value has to be seen as a very important one.

Table 4: Top 5 least important motives to compete at the Olympics

1. Giving a good example	1574 points
2. Money	970
3. Sound mind in a healthy body	951
4. Raise their own market value	725
5. Competing is more important then winning	557

Also in the top 5 'giving a good example' was the least important value (see table 4) with men as well as with women and in all age categories. With men 'sound mind in a healthy body' was number two as least important motive, while with women 'money' took the second position.

Not all Olympic values are on an individual level. A group of values, so called institutional values, focus on particular goals like the Olympic Games in general. The respondents were asked first to look at the whole list of institutional values and make a choice. The most important value in relation to the Olympic Games as a whole, according to the Dutch population, is 'brotherhood' (see table 6). In this case the top 5 shows a different number one (see table 5).

Table 5: Top 5 of most important values viewing the Olympics in general

1. Respect for each other	2432 points
2. Brotherhood	2222
3. World-wide exposure	2044
4. Sports for all	1938
5. Competing	1648

Table 6: Which of the following values is, according to you, the most important if you look at the Games in general?

	Perc.
1 Brotherhood	20.1
2 Respect for each other	13.5
3 Sport for all	13.4
4 World-wide exposure	9.5
5 Competing	8.4
6 Peace	6.0
7 Equal rights	5.0
8 Commercialisation	4.8
9 Solidarity	3.9
10 Media attention	3.9
11 Amusement value	2.5
12 Money	2.3
13 National feelings (Orange/Dutch)	2.2
14 A better world	1.8
15 Anti-discrimination	1.7
16 Gathering of the youth	0.8
17 Nationalism	0.8
18 Dope	0.2
19 Political influence	0.2
Total	100.0

Women find 'respect for each other' the most important value while men place 'brotherhood' in the number one spot. The positions three and five switch in the categories sex and age. With men 'sports for all' takes the fifth place and women put it third.

Here also the question is asked which value is the least important and the second least important. 'Dope' was seen as the least important value in relationship with the Olympic Games in general. Second was 'political influence' and third 'national feelings'. The top 5 shows the same values on the first, second and third places (see table 7).

Table 7: Top 5 of least important values viewing the Olympics in general

1. Dope	562 points
2. Political influence	485
3. National feelings	334
4. Commercialisation	315
5. Media attention	301

Analysis showed that there where differences. 'Dope' is the number one in most categories but in the age-groups 35-44, 55-64 and 65+ 'political influence' was viewed as the least important value in relationship with the Olympic Games in general. 'National feelings' had the third position according to men but with the women this value does not show up in the top 5 of least important values. On the other hand 'media attention' scores high with women and lower with men.

8.5 Second Analysis

In this research we have tried to find out how people in the Netherlands look upon the Olympic ideals. Differentiation was believed to play an important role. If possible we have therefore tried to make a distinction between the views of different categories of Dutch people according to age, sex or their attraction towards sport. Although we found some differences between certain groups with different questions, we could not make real groups according to their specific view on Olympism. There is no proof that young sporting Dutch men have a totally different view about the Olympic Ideals than, e.g., elderly non-sporting Dutch women. It seems as if there is a general consensus amongst the Dutch as far as Olympism is concerned.

The most clear example of it is the answer on the question: what is, according to you, the most important motive for an Olympian to participate in the Olympic Games. In the top 5 as well as the most important motive 'winning the gold medal' was the number one choice according to men and women, young and old, sporting or non-sporting. Clearly the Dutch population see 'winning the gold medal' as the most important value for an Olympian to participate in the Olympic Games.

It can thus be concluded that there seems to be a common view in the Netherlands on how to look upon the Olympic ideals. To test this theory we made six groups based on their involvement in sport. The profiles were constructed from two variables: if one participates in sport or not and watching sports on television. The relationship between the variables is significant, and the correlation coefficient is 0.237. The six profiles can be distinguished from one another through statistical characteristics of the different groups:

Non-Sporting (15.2%)
This group exists of people who do not practise sports themselves and do not watch sport on television. They show no interest in sport.
Characteristics: relatively more women (61.8%), age between 25-44 years and an average of 1.63 correct answers on the Olympic knowledge questions.

Only Active Sporting (7.6%)
These people are only active in sport but do not watch sport on television. Characteristics: mainly women (71.9%), age between 16-44 years and an average of 1.73 correct answers on the Olympic knowledge questions.

Watching Passively Sporting (23.8%)
People in this group watch sports less than one hour a week but do not practise sports themselves.
Characteristics: more women than men (57,3% - 42.7%), mainly 45 years and older and an average of 2.05 correct answers on the Olympic knowledge questions.

Watching and Active Sport (20.8%)
This group of active sportsmen and women do watch sports on television less than one hour a week.

Characteristics: more women than men (55.5% - 44.5%), mainly between 25 – 44 years old, an average of 2.2 correct answers of the Olympic knowledge questions.

Television sporting (12.2%)
People in this group do not practise sports themselves but spend a lot of hours, more than two hours a week, watching sport on television. They are sporting with the distance-control in their hand.
Characteristics: relatively more men (60.9%), mainly 45 years and older, an average of 2.55 correct answers on the Olympic knowledge questions.

Sportsfans (20.3%)
The last group exists of real sportsfans. They practise sports themselves and watch a lot of sport on television.
Characteristics: mainly men (70.2), in the age of 16- 34 years, an average of 2.52 correct answers on the Olympic knowledge questions.

Conclusion

According to our findings there is a general opinion in the Dutch society about Olympism. 'Winning a gold medal' is the number one motive for Olympians to participate at the Olympics in all profiles. The same goes for brotherhood as a goal for the Olympics in general; in all profiles this was the number one value. Not only the number one position is clear but also the relationship with other values and norms are almost similar. The non-sporting type thinks almost the same way about the Olympic ideals as does the sports fan or the passively watching person. They do it despite their differences in knowledge of the Olympics and interest in sport. The conclusion is that the way the Dutch think about Olympism belongs to the cultural heritage of their society. This general view doesn't seem to be influenced in a short period of time or through news facts. According to our tests the May group reacts the same way on Olympism as the October group did, although the May group was closer to the Salt Lake City affair. The results were that there were no significant differences between the May and October group on variables concerning the Olympic values and norms.

The question that still remains to be answered is: does the opinion of Dutch society differ from that of the International Olympic Committee as proclaimed in the Olympic Charter? The IOC-values peace, solidarity, joy in the game, giving a good example and equal rights for everybody, score very low in Dutch society with one exception; joy in the game. 'Giving the good example' is called the least important value for an Olympian to participate at the Olympics. The IOC-values have a strong extrinsic character oriented on motives and goals outside the world of sport. Peace, solidarity and equal rights are more general accepted ideals. These values one can find within political parties, religions or the universal rights of Helsinki. People in the Netherlands do not make a connection between the IOC-values and an organisation, which in their eyes, is responsible for organising a world-wide elite sports event.

References

Becker, J.B. & Nauta, A.P.W. (1983). *Values and Norms*. Den Haag: Vuga. (in Dutch).

IOC (1994). *The Centennial Olympic Congress, Texts, Summaries or Plans of Papers*. Lausanne: IOC.

IOC (1997). *The Olympic Movement*. Lausanne: IOC.

MacAlloon, J. J. (1981). *This Great Symbol, Pierre De Coubertin and the Origins of the Modern Olympic Games*. Chicago: The University of Chicago Press.

Naul, R. (1998). Physical activity and active lifestyle of children and youth. *Sport Science*, 10, Schorndorf: Hofmann Verlag.

Timmers, R. (2000). *The Dutch and the Olympic Games*. Arnhem: NOC*NSF. (in Dutch).

9 ORGANIZING MASCULINITIES AND FEMININITIES: THE GENDERED SPORTING BODY

Annelies Knoppers & Agnes Elling

Introduction

Western competitive sport is a cultural practice that is formally organized along gender lines and also on the basis of performance. Participation can sometimes be gender mixed at the recreational and leisure levels, but most competitive sports are organized by gender at the various competitive levels: women's sport, men's sport and relatively few mixed sports (e.g. korfball and equestrian sports). Even in events such as marathons where men and women run together, performances are assigned value and meanings based on gender since women and men are ranked within their group.[1]

Schaapman (1995) and Acker (1992) argue that we assign meanings to cultural practices at three levels: the symbolic, the structural and the individual levels. The symbolic level consists of the creation of images and metaphors that reinforce and/or challenge cultural practices as well as the practices themselves These practices include sport and its intersection with social relations such as gender and race/ ethnicity (Acker, 1992). Images have an extensive impact because structures (or the structural level) are (re) created based on these images and vice versa. Individuals (individual level) may internalize these images, use them to (re) create structures or (re)construct images.

In this chapter we look at the meanings given to the sporting body at the symbolic level and their implications for social relations such as gender, race/ethnicity and sexuality and their interaction. We

---

[1] Age and ability are also formal organizing categories but we will confine this discussion to categorization by gender.

use Connell's (1987, 1993, 1995, 1998) theory about the multi-dimensionality of gender to frame the summary and discussion of results from various projects which place emphasis on gender and were conducted within the Values and Norms in Sport program: the culture and structures of coaching (Knoppers & Bouman, 1996; 1998), (re)presentation, selection and interpretation processes in and by the sport media (Knoppers & Elling, 1999a; Knoppers & Elling, 2001) and practices and meanings given to social integration (Elling & De Knop, 1999; Elling, 2001).

9.1 Changing ways of looking at gender

Before introducing Connell's gender theory, we begin by looking at the ways researchers in the past and present have looked at gender (Cahn, 1994; Coakley, 1998; Griffin, 1998; Hall, 1996; Hargreaves, 1994; Knoppers, 1992; Messner & Sabo, 1990; Pfister, 1999; Pronger, 1990).

A traditional and still common way of discussing gender is to assume that it is an essential characteristic tied into bipolarity related only to 'male' and 'female'. This assumption of bipolarity means that males are/should be masculine and woman are/should be feminine and that there is a universal form of masculinity and feminity. Consequently when we use these two words it is assumed that everyone will know what we are talking about. These words are supposed to have universality, that is, the words 'masculine' and 'feminine' supposedly conjure up similar images in our minds.

The theorizing about the social meanings of gender has however 'slowly' moved away from this bipolarity because it was seen as essentialist and deficient. First, came the contention in the 1970s that what we call 'sex' is in part a social construction. Consequently the word 'sex' then began to be used primarily to designate a person's biological category of male or female. Gender came to be used to describe the meanings we assign to being male and female, that is, masculinity and femininity. Gender was defined as a social construction; in other words, men learn to be men and women learn to be women instead of such behavior being innate. The learning of sex roles was assumed to occur through a process of (sex role) socialization, that is, people learn the role that fits with their gender and internalize that role. Sport was assumed to play a large part in this socialization process for boys. Boys learned to be masculine in part, through their participation and involvement in sport. Girls learned nurturing skills by playing with dolls and taking care of younger siblings. Fears of 'masculinization' or 'feminization' arose when girls or boys respectively, participated in an activity associated with the other sex. Gender researchers pointed out that these fears implicitly meant a fear of males 'becoming' gay and of women becoming lesbian.

The move toward 'equal opportunity' in the 1970s and 1980s included the idea that everyone should have (equal) opportunities to engage in sport. Since sport participation is assumed to build character and develop leadership skills, it was tacitly acknowledged that girls should participate in sport too but with the caveat that their femininity would not be 'damaged'. Since masculinity and femininity obviously were layered by sexuality and the most common forms of top sport were associated with heterosexual masculinity, woman athletes who participated in traditional male-identified sports were often stigmatized as lesbians. An apologetic discourse dominated in the 1970s in which women athletes and coaches 'apologized' for their participation in male identified sports by showing they were still heterosexual; they did this primarily by their choice of apparel off the court, by distancing themselves from lesbians and by wearing make-up and other accoutrements associated with heterosexual femininity.

The role power played in the construction of gender also began to receive attention from those interested in the social dimensions of gender. Not only were 'masculine' and 'feminine' defined as bipolar concepts tied into biological sex but so was power. Most men were assumed to have power and women were generally assumed to be powerless. Sport participation was assumed to give men power in society because through it they learned skills necessary for acquiring power in the marketplace, that is, for acquiring leadership positions. Part of this power was assumed to come from knowing how to be mentally tough, to be able to work as a team player and to enjoy and rely on one's physicality.

Questions began to be asked however, about the meaning this acquisition of power through sport meant for black men. Although black men were visible participants in top media sports such as football and basketball in the 1980s, they were largely absent from positions of power in society and in sport. They were and are often described in images bordering on the hyper-masculine; their performances are often ascribed to genetic/essentialist attributes. Although sport participation may have allowed some black men to benefit from a capitalist economy, in general sport participation and their hyper-masculine image did not seem to translate into acquiring leadership positions in sport, in the media and in other parts of society. In addition, gay (and lesbian) athletes encountered a great deal of heterosexism and homophobia in sport. Obviously the privileges of power that sport involvement was supposed to bestow on men excluded certain groups of men.

Similarly not all sports were seen as helping women to acquire the skills and benefits attributed to sport involvement. Body building, for example, became an area where judges and organizations wrestled with the question of what is feminine. If a woman bulks up, develops muscles and eliminates most body fat (including breasts) is she still 'feminine'? Another issue related to women's sport participation concerned the topic of 'role-conflict' between 'being an athlete' and 'being feminine': do young women really experience such a conflict or are such conflicts constructed as a way of limiting women in sport? Do the perceived conflicts between being 'feminine' and performance in 'masculine' sports relate to all women? Or primarily to heterosexual white women? Black female athletes for example, tend to be partly excluded from these norms of 'femininity'. In an article about the changes in the images about women in sport, Solomon (2000, p.2) writes that black women athletes are:

> characterized according to a long racist tradition that figures the black woman's body as nonfeminine and laboring . . . Thus, like black male athletes, they're more often praised for their 'natural' abilities than for their intense training and strategizing. The Williams sisters are constantly being described as having raw, soaring physicality - when, that is, commentators aren't obsessed about their hair.

These exclusions from the privileges sport involvement supposedly bestows on its participants, and the absence of women and minorities from positions of power in sport, led to other ideas about looking at gender in the 1990s.

The different examples, mainly based on sexuality and on race, suggested that there are meanings within meanings when we use the words 'masculine' and 'feminine' with respect to sport and male and female bodies.[2] Gender scholars came to the conclusion that the words 'masculine' and 'feminine' are not strict bipolar concepts associated with one sex or the other but that they are multi-layered, multi-dimensional and hierarchical concepts. Gender research began to focus on the meanings given to gender. This is not to say that biological and socializing components/processes were totally discounted but they were seen as incomplete explanations of the way gender is embedded in society and societal processes.

9.2 Connell's theory about the structure of gender

The layered meanings and possible contradictions within the meanings assigned to gender indicate that other ways of looking at gender are needed that do not assume homogeneity and that are not bipolar. Connell (1987, 1995) in his theory about the structure of gender argues that gender is primarily relational, that is, how different social groups are situated in relationship to each other and to a specific type of masculinity. He contends that there are several forms of masculinity and femininity. One form of masculinity that Connell calls hegemonic masculinity, is most desired. It is what most men, individually and collectively want to be like or associate/ identify with. Connell (1993) estimates that only about 5% of Western males actually exemplify all the characteristics associated with hegemonic masculinity. Many males are 'wanna be's.'

---

[2] We could of course make similar arguments on the basis of social class and other social factors. Certain sports, for example, are associated more with the working class (e.g., soccer in the Netherlands) and others more with the economically privileged (e.g., golf in the Netherlands). Yet it is the latter group that holds most of the positions of power in sport and benefits from it collectively.

Hegemonic masculinity cannot be narrowly defined because the definition is time and context bound. Men who are economically successful, white and visibly heterosexual, are seen as representing this form of masculinity in the Western world. Connell defines other forms of masculinity such as that of black or gay men, as subordinate or marginalized masculinities.

Hegemonic masculinity is not a stable structure nor an identity but a dynamic socially relational form associated with a great deal of cultural power. Those who identify with it or support it can be privileged or receive advantages. When we make heroes out of male athletes or business tycoons, or when we value stoicity above emotionality, heterosexuality above homosexuality, white above black, we support characteristics currently associated with hegemonic masculinity and often inscribe them as 'natural' and self evident. Connell calls this support for hegemonic masculinity 'complicity'.

According to Connell there is no hegemonic femininity but an emphasized femininity that is associated with white middle to upper class women who 'accommodate the interests and desires of men'.

There are also marginalized femininities in Western society consisting of lesbians, black women, working class women, etc. Connell argues that the dominant form of masculinity determines to a great deal which aspects of femininity are thought to be desirable at a given time in a given context. If for example, intelligence is a characteristic ascribed to hegemonic masculinity, emphasized femininity is likely to be associated with an intelligence that is less valued in society in general. An important contention is that hegemony is dynamic and contradictory, constantly challenged and reinforced. Consequently, we assume that the construction of hegemonic masculinity is dynamic, often contradictory and is constantly reconstructed in relationship to emphasized femininity, marginalized masculinities and femininities. Hierarchical and exclusionary processes are subsequently essential to maintaining the current gender order.

Connell's theory is especially applicable to sport for two reasons. First, sport organizations tend to define themselves using metaphors of hegemonic masculinity, that is, using a form of masculinity associated with competition and hierarchy that is goal driven and instrumental in its pursuit of success (Connell, 1995;

Kerfoot & Knights, 1998; Knoppers & Anthonissen, 2001;). This makes the concept of hegemonic masculinity as explained by Connell especially pertinent to discussions about gender in sport and sport organizations. Second, his theory is useful for looking at sport because he argues that the current gender order is supported through meanings given to the body. The body plays a large role in the construction of hegemonic masculinity since what the sporting body can do and does are often constructed as 'natural.' Meanings given to sport and the male body are synonymous in many ways. The male body is extremely valuable and glorified in the sport context, especially in national sports. This construction and valuation of the male sporting body are in contradiction to a dominant notion in western culture that tends to associate women with bodies/nature/emotion/privacy, and men with more valued mind/culture/reason/public (Hall, 1996; Kane, 1995; Lorber, 1993). The fact that meanings given to the (male) sporting body seem to place these dominant notions about the body/mind in the background, and instead emphasise the male sporting body, suggests the uniqueness and importance of sport as a social practice. In the following paragraphs we will further explore the importance of the sporting body to gender and of gender to sport.

9.3 The male sporting body and hegemonic masculinity

Connell and others (see for example, Hall, 1996; Hargreaves, 1994; Messner, 1988) argue that the portrayal and images of the male sporting body as naturally strong, muscular and powerful have become increasingly important since the beginning of the twentieth century. This association gives many men privileges in sport and in society, since modern sport is often seen as one of the few practices in which men can (still) out-perform women. Men's bodies tend to be taller, faster and stronger than women's bodies and the emphasis in most contests in popular modern sports is placed on physical characteristics like strength and speed (instead of other facets such as strategy, technique and teamwork). Our research among athletes, coaches and journalists shows that men are assumed to be better athletes, coaches and to know more about sport, simply because they are men (see also chapter 4, 13 and 14 of this book).

The Dutch media play a large role in constructing and reinforcing this association. The best performances in absolute terms are defined as most interesting and most valuable. Male athletes are often represented as physically and mentally strong, as unemotional (unless they lost or won), and as highly skilled. Women athletes are barely visible within the 'regular' sport media, with the exception of specific mixed gender sporting events like the Olympics. These results are comparable to those of researchers who examined the American sport media (Messner, Dunbar & Hunt, 2000; Wilson, 1999). They found that the dominant image presented of a 'real' man/ male athlete is someone who is "tough, strong, aggressive, and above all, a winner in what is still a Man's World . . . " (p. 390). It is this idolized [sporting] male body that is the norm in discourse about the body by the participants in the various studies explicitly dealing with gender and ethnicity cited at the beginning of this chapter. This example of congruency between the American and Dutch sport media investigation results reflects a possible trend towards a globalized hegemonic masculinity that Connell (1998) describes. This globalization of a certain type of sport-related masculinity (and the ability of the sport media to create heroes in sport) is reinforced by the finding that the top sports hero of Dutch youth is Michael Jordan, a black American basketball star (Knoppers & Elling, 2001).[3] These globalisation processes of hegemonic masculinity are often incomplete and contradictory. This is illustrated by the popularity of the Dutch darts player and Embassy winner 'Barney' as a sport hero who came in second after Michael Jordan. 'Barney', does not visibly represent the typical qualities associated with a sporting masculinity.

---

[3] Although Michael Jordan is black, Andrews (1998) and Wilson & Sparks (1996) argue that he is above all presented as an transcendent (all American) hero for white and black males and females.

9.4 Meanings given to the female body and emphasized femininity

Connell's theory about the gender order suggests that gender is relational and multi-dimensional. The results of the various studies conducted under the auspices of the Values and Norms Research Program show that women's sports (and therefore women's sporting bodies) were part of the dominant discourse only in relationship to how they differ from attributes assigned to males, that is, in relationship to characteristics associated to hegemonic masculinity.

Women were largely absent in the two weeks sport coverage we investigated in November 1997; they received 2% of the television time devoted to sport and 6% of the newspaper coverage. In the media coverage of the 1996 Olympics, women's sport received a third of the total amount of time and space. As Kellner (1995) states: 'It is often the exclusions and the silences that reveal the ideological project of the text' (p.113). The relative invisibility of (black and white) women's sporting bodies on daily television and in national newspapers means women and their performances are defined as relatively insignificant (Kane & Greendorfer, 1994).

Not only are women largely under-represented in the sport media, when they are presented they are often (re)presented differently than men are. Like male athletes they are presented as strong and powerful performers, but they also are more likely to be presented as athletes who lack mental toughness and who frequently depend on a male figure such as a father, boyfriend or coach for their success. In other words, they cannot do it alone (like male athletes do). When young people, athletes, coaches or journalists give meanings to the women's bodies, they mostly do so in a negative, comparative sense. In general women athletes are collectively constructed as being weaker and slower than men and this is given a negative valuation.

At times the emphasis in the (re)presentation of women sports and athletes lies in 'aesthetics', often ignoring the necessary strength required to perform in this manner. In our study of the media's representation of the media, for example, the strength women [girl] gymnasts needed to do their various routines was rarely mentioned. When strength and power are made visible in other women's sports, the accomplishments of women athletes are often compared to their male counterpart. In tennis for example, it is not uncommon to hear an announcer say 'she hits as hard as a male tennis player', or 'her serve is as fast as a male tennis player'. The reverse never happens. This tendency to compare where women fall short is also used by sport journalists to defend their neglect of women's sport.

When women are able to do something men cannot, such as getting pregnant and bearing children, that is not defined as an asset in sport. Ironically, men's inability to bear or nurse children does not mean that men's bodies are defined as being deficient which they might be if women were the norm. Instead (the possibility of) pregnancy is defined as a liability for women in the world of sport. Women who are married or have a boyfriend are often seen as less desirable candidates for top coaching positions or as sport journalists, because they might get pregnant (Knoppers & Bouman, 1996, 1998; Knoppers & Elling, 2001). Leaves of absence from coaching or journalist duties due to pregnancy or household responsibilities tend to be viewed negatively. In contrast, (periodic) absences from such duties due to participation in top or Olympic events are praised and accepted as 'normal.' Obviously what the body is doing during periodic absences (bearing a child or competing internationally) is valued differently in the sport organization context. Yet the consequences for the sport teams are similar, that is, both type of absences mean that replacements have to be found.

Coaches not only often tend to use male bodies as the norm for performance, but also want women's bodies to become, paradoxically, more like those of men and young girls. They want women's bodies to become more muscular (like men) and also thinner/smaller (like girls), especially in male identified sports such as cycling and female-identified sports like gymnastics and figure skating (Knoppers & Bouman, 1998; Rose, 1991; Ryan, 1995). The latter two are evaluated according to acrobatic and aesthetic norms. Lenskyj (1987) convincingly argues that these aesthetic norms require a heterosexual appearing femininity, what Connell would call emphasized femininity.

Even women athletes in other sports (who are not formally judged on their aesthetic qualities) are often reminded by coaches, media and sponsors to align themselves with a heterosexual femininity because extremely muscular women are regarded as 'masculine' and 'ugly', that is, as lesbian (Cahn, 1994; Elling, 2001; Hargreaves, 1994;

Kolnes, 1995; Lenskyj, 1987). This example illustrates the relational nature of gender. If male athletes are marked by their (desired) 'bigness' then women have to be smaller.

Bodies not only have gender but they also have markers of race/ethnicity and other social relations inscribed on them. All the participants in the research on the culture of coaching (see chapter 13 of this book) were white; they referred to and assumed only a white male body. The young people who were involved in the social integration study, (see chapter 14 of this book) and who described 'natural' differences between black and white athletes, referred to both black and white male bodies. Cheng (1999) argues that masculinities and femininities can be marginalized on the basis of a social marker such as skin color or gender but individuals who belong to those social groups are not necessarily always marginalized on the basis of their gender performance. In other words, the performance of black athletes may be accepted and celebrated but their skin color still marks them as 'different.' This becomes readily apparent when they perform poorly. Then they tend to be identified as [black] athletes from Surinam or elsewhere (as the chants of the fans indicate) instead of as Dutch athletes like white athletes are (Van Dijk, 1993; Tudor, 1992). When white male athletes perform poorly they are rarely greeted with remarks about their whiteness.

9.5 Gender performance

Those who belong to marginalized social groups but who do 'gender' in a way associated with hegemonic masculinity are often valued in that context. Some coaches said that they appreciated lesbian athletes because of their high levels of performance and described them as having a 'male mentality' (Knoppers & Bouman, 1996). They were defined as being like men and assumed to be stronger and mentally tougher than straight women. This does not mean however, that they are accepted in general in sport. The gender order is after all, filled with contradictions. Research on the sport media showed that the overwhelming images of female athletes are still those in which female athletes are portrayed in a way that makes them desirable to straight men (Knoppers & Elling, 1999b, 2001). Research with teenagers indicated that many young people do not like the gender performance of very muscular female athletes and female athletes performing male identified sports: They tend to describe these female athletes negatively using words such as 'masculine' or 'ugly' in the pejorative sense (Elling, 2001). Female black athletes were largely absent from the discourses of the coaches and young people involved in our studies and were almost invisible in the sport media, especially in regular sport programming (see chapter 14 of this book). They tend to be marginalized and have little or no power in Dutch sport.

Although in general women athletes are expected to perform in a (heterosexual) feminine manner to be accepted, women coaches and sport journalists have to prove their support of hegemonic masculinity to be accepted as 'good' coaches and journalists. This means they have to 'do' gender in the way white, straight men do it (cf. Cheng, 1999). This means for example, seeing gender as not being relevant to sport practices. A common discourse used by both women and men to explain the shortage of women in managerial and leading positions in sport organizations is that of 'blaming the victim', that is holding women responsible for the shortage. Women are described as not making an effort to meet the 'standards', that is, they do not behave or perform like good coaches, that is, like men. A woman coach who performed gender successfully by hegemonic masculinist standards, recounted proudly how she was a man among men when she coached a senior male team. *"They told such awful jokes that they never would have told if there had been women present"* (Knoppers & Bouman, 1996, p.94). Although in general the selection criteria for a 'good' coach/manager or journalist in sport are perceived to be objective and gender neutral, some people recognize the implicit (white) male standards that are used. A sport editor of a national newspaper says about a female journalist: *"She is very good, but maybe in the classical sense that she does what men do."* (Knoppers & Elling, 2001).

As we indicated earlier, performing gender in a way that is associated with hegemonic masculinity may mean an individual is accepted in a particular context but it does not necessarily mean she or he acquires the social power associated with it. Black men can be assigned characteristics of hegemonic masculinity and still not have collective power. Black male athletes wear the 'coat of hegemonic masculinity', but it contains contradictions for them (Sabo & Jansen, 1998). They tend to be defined as 'naturally' better athletes in sports like basketball and track and field (see chapter 4 of this book). The (Dutch) sport media reflect this colonialist image of black men as 'naturally' physically strong by at times portraying them as hyper-masculine, and at times, as being almost 'animal-like' (Knoppers & Elling, 1999; Scheerder, 1996). Collectively, blacks hold few positions of power in Dutch sport. This is true not only for Dutch sport, but in other Western countries where blacks are in the minority as well. This does not mean black male athletes are powerless or accept this construction passively. Hegemony is never complete. Resistance is always a factor.

Black male athletes, have for example, created a form of black masculinity within a few sports that Majors (1990) calls 'cool pose.' It emphasizes an emotional expressivity and celebrates a hyper masculinity. Segal (1993) argues that these expressions of black masculinity overlap with expressions of emphasized femininity. On the basis of our research of the Dutch sport media, we conclude that there is a tendency to portray some black male athletes as emotional and expressive in a way similar to the presentation of female athletes (Knoppers & Elling, 1999a). Is this 'feminization' of black athletes a way of reinforcing the hierarchy in the gender order? Or do the dominant stereotypes about the hyper-sexuality of black men give them more room to express their emotions? To what extent do black male athletes engage in agency/resistance in this manner? Possibly all of these play a role. In addition, it is possible that black athletes may empower each other and other (young) black people through the use of an expressive 'cool pose' behavior in a society dominated by 'white' people. Simultaneously however, these media images may reinforce stereotypes about black male athletes for black and white viewers, and give 'false evidence' of the possibilities for social mobility and gaining social power for black people in society in general. Thus resistance and reinforcement of hegemonic masculinity can be practiced simultaneously.

This dynamic nature of the gender order is also sustained by the construction of sexuality in sport. Gay and lesbian athletes often perform gender by being silent and 'passing' as heterosexual (Griffin, 1998; Hekma, 1994; Pronger, 1990). Heterosexuality is an important component of the gender order that needs to be constantly reinforced as we will show in the next section.

9.6 Heterosexuality

Connell (1987, 1995) sees heterosexuality as one of the key aspects of hegemonic masculinity. This sexual aspect increases the importance of sport for the gender order. Modern sport was initially structured for white middle to upper class men/boys to counter the fear of feminization (Hargreaves, 1994; Cahn, 1994). If boys were primarily under the influence of mothers and women teachers they would grow up 'feminized.' The so-called 'feminization' of boys/men was equated with homosexuality. Boys and men who participated in sport were assumed to learn to be 'real' men, that is, to be heterosexual men through their participation in sport and by being with other 'real' men, that is, competing in a homosocial male sport world (Hargreaves, 1994; Messner & Sabo, 1994). This association between male heterosexuality and sport was perceived to be 'natural' and self evident because heterosexuality was associated with the 'natural' (sporting) body. Ironically it was the male homosociality of this sport world that contributed to this perception of sport as a place of heterosexuality because women were largely absent. Other areas of society in which physicality is assigned an important role such as the military and police were seen in similar ways.

This association between (male) sport and heterosexuality still exists in Dutch sport implicitly and explicitly (see chapter 4 and 13 of this book). When boys between 14-20 are asked why they don't want to perform female-identified- sports like ice skating or gymnastics, they do not only argue that the specific sport is 'feminine' but use words such as 'gay' or 'sissy' (Elling, 2001). Coaches often think it is cute when boys and girl swimmers 'fall ' for each other, but regard it as a nuisance when two female athletes do the same (Knoppers & Bouman, 1998).

According to Connell (1987; 1995) heterosexuality is a key component of hegemonic masculinity and therefore of sport. Perhaps it is an essential component of male sport in part because sport is structured as a homosocial environment in which men compete with and against men. Their sport involvement allows men to be 'affectionate' with men on the field in ways that deviate from heterosexual norms for behavior outside sport. As we indicated earlier, the link between heterosexuality and male sport is constructed as natural. Thus it is of vital importance to the maintenance of hegemonic masculinity that this link be self evident. Consequently there is little room for homosexuality, especially in the popular men's media sports like soccer[4] in the Netherlands and for example American football and basketball in the United States and ice hockey in Canada.[5] Male athletes are assumed to be heterosexual men because of their (superior) physicality. When they play poorly or lack motivation they are exhorted not to play like sissies or a bunch of women (Griffin, 1998; Hargreaves, 1994; Hekma, 1994). Gender and sexuality become conflated with each other.

Of course most males do not participate in the media sports. Through their support for and involvement with media sport they can however, demonstrate their heterosexuality. In other words, boys who are not interested in these sports and/or avoid physical aggression are often viewed with suspicion regarding their heterosexuality (Cahn, 1994; Pronger, 1990). Physical aggression and bodily contact are key component of all the men's media team sports. By identifying with it, boys/men can 'prove' they are heterosexual; by disliking it or being physically fearful, they may be labelled as gay. In itself this identification might matter much if hierarchy was not a part of the gender order. Certain forms of masculinity and femininity such as gay masculinities are marginalized.

---

[4] The fact that soccer is not perceived as a 'masculine' sport in all counties - in the United States more girls/women than boys/men are currently involved (e.g. Wilson, 1999) – already shows the social construction of these gendered images.
[5] See Knoppers, 1999 for an extensive discussion of this point.

Alternative initiatives like the Gay Games can partly challenge existing norms of hegemonic masculinity, but as media presentations of the 1998 Amsterdam Gay Games have shown, they can also be used to strengthen dominant images of gender, race/ethnicity sexuality and sport (Elling & De Knop, 1999; Woldendorp, 1998).

9.7 Athletes as sex objects

Many women as well as men support the form of heterosexual masculinity emphasized in male media sport. Connell calls this support 'complicity'. It is not surprising then that some girls have male sport idols and idolize them because of their heterosexuality. In part this is one way the media may construct the male athletes for their female viewers. In 1998, Newsweek, an American news magazine, featured an article 'Soccer gets sexy' (Dickey & Power, 1998). The authors describe how those who stimulate interest in men's soccer in the USA have begun to do so by promoting several players as 'sex objects'. Similarly our study among Dutch teenagers indicated that some girls sexualize male athletes, especially in soccer (Knoppers & Elling, 2001).[6] The extent to which this sexualization of male sport stars is part of a media or promotion/commercialisation construction, or an audience interpretation, requires further research. Ironically the efforts to promote male athletes as sex objects may also implicitly pose a challenge to the heterosexual construction of male athletes. Pronger (1990) argues that the current construction of hegemonic masculinity requires the construction of the male athlete as subject instead of object. A sexualization of male athletes by the media may stimulate males to see the athletes as sex objects instead of sexual subjects. According to Pronger the emphasis on male athletes as objects instead of subjects keeps the homo-erotic attraction of male sports and athletes a well-kept secret. Consequently if commercial interests would require an emphasis on male athletes as sex objects it may have a profound impact on the dyamics of gender in sport. This

---

6 Among approximately 1000 young boys and girls, soccer player Dani ranked third as their sport hero, after basketball player Michael Jordan and darts player 'Barney'; he was mostly chosen by (white) girls because of his 'sexy looks'.

discussion about male sexuality and sport is obviously full of contradictions many of which have yet to be named and explored.

The sexualization of females in and out of sport has a much longer public history (see Cahn, 1994 and Griffin, 1998, for a detailed account). Within the structure of gender as Connell describes it, the sexualization of men in sport is a different dynamic than men sexualizing women in sport. The sexualization of women occurs systematically within the context of a gender order in sport and in many parts of society. The sexualization of male athletes is more an individual than a structural part of the discourse about men and men's sport. In contrast, the sexualization of female athletes is embedded in the discourse of women in general and women's sport specifically (McKay, 1999). Although our research among sports journalists (Knoppers & Elling, 2001) indicates that explicit sexualisation of female athletes within the work environment has decreased over the last ten years, it is still more common than sexualisation of male athletes. A female sport journalist says: "When we [female journalists] nowadays comment about a good-looking tennis player like, for example 'you can send him to my room this evening', some men react very surprised, whereas they make similar jokes all the time which is perceived as normal." The connections made between sexuality and women athletes is however not just in the form of sexualisation but takes on other forms as well.

Women's participation in the popular media sports that were once associated only with men has posed a challenge to the role sport plays in supporting hegemonic masculinity. Whereas men who participate in popular media sports are assumed to be heterosexual, the involvement of women in these sports has been viewed with suspicion regarding their heterosexuality. The underlying assumption is that since it takes a (heterosexual) man to do well in these sports, a woman who does well must be 'manly' and therefore lesbian (Cahn, 1994). Once again gender and sexuality are conflated with each other, but in a somewhat different way than it is for male athletes. This homophobia has resulted in the active promotion of heterosexual images of athletes by individuals, teams, clubs and/or federations which in its turn, fuels homophobia even more (Elling, 1999; Griffin, 1998; Kolnes, 1995). Solomon (2000, p.1), in an article about women's bodies in sport, argues that "the increasing acceptance of powerful women's bodies has been matched by a frantic attempt at containment . . . We see more images of strong women in action than we've ever seen before. That is a very big change. But the more we see those images, the more we see the same athletes off the court dolled up in prom dresses - or in no clothes at all . . . The contradictions between hard fighting champion and soft core cheese cake are widely felt."

As we indicated earlier, this (hetero)sexualization is part of the structure of the current gender order. Women can do a lot, even compete and excel in sports, as long as they are (heterosexually) attractive and remain accessible to men (Cahn, 1994, p. 268). Of course not everyone constructs male and female athletes in terms of sexuality but these constructions are part of the dominant discourse.

9.8 Consequences

In this section we will briefly discuss some of the consequences of the current construction of hegemonic masculinity. We will attempt to show that its hegemonic nature enables those involved in our research studies to assert that 'gender' does not play a role in sport any more and that sport is a place of equal opportunity. Within the hierarchy of the current gender structure in Western sport, women's bodies are often defined as inferior to men's bodies; consequently, men's events/sports are defined as more interesting and exciting. This definition of men's sport as more interesting is seen as gender neutral although it is often used to women's exclusion from media sport and from holding leadership positions in sport (see chapter 13 in this book for a further discussion about the perception of gender neutrality in sport).

Another consequence of these hierarchical (relational) definitions of white, black, women's and men's bodies in sport pertains to subsequent expectations. The manner in which Dutch athletes, parents and coaches give meanings to the body determines their expectations and daily actions. For example, black men may be more challenged and more motivated to become good athletes compared to white men which may have a long term negative impact on many male black athletes. Only a miniscule number of black men make it to the professional ranks in sport; the odds for black young men to become lawyers or doctors are better than becoming a professional athlete (Coakley, 1998). In contrast, the hierarchical expectations in sport may mean that women may be less challenged and motivated to become good athletes compared to men. Women comprise half the population and half the number of athletes in the Netherlands and yet only a third of the competitive athletes (CBS, 1996; NOC*NSF, 1999). Consequently a great deal of potential may never be developed.

Another consequence of the association between hegemonic masculinity and sport is that the aggressive and competitive aspects of sport are highlighted. The emphasis is often on physical aggression and (absolute) performance (product). The process of performance and the cooperative, dependent, and non-violent aspects of sport are largely ignored (Hall, 1996). If sport were more defined in these latter terms within the context of the process of performance, instead of only in relationship to the end result (the product), then perhaps sport could be a place where equal opportunity would be a reality.

Conclusion

In the foregoing we have attempted to summarize and discuss the literature and empirical research conducted within the Values and Norms Research Program, that explicitly focused on gender and ethnicity. We contend that all the other research studies that are part of this program are about gender and ethnicity as well, although implicitly. In this chapter we have tried to explain these results within the framework of Connell's theory of gender structure We have used the word gender with the assumption that it is broader than male-female relations but encompasses ethnic relations, race relations and other social relations. The meanings given to gender (in the context of sport) are always in the context of ethnicity, race, social class, sexuality, age and ability for example. The visibility of certain athletes and the public nature of sport may often help to reinforce and simultaneously challenge existing stereotypes. As we have pointed out repeatedly, hegemony is dynamic and can be challenged. What is needed then to bring about change, in addition to the constant challenge that the (visible) presence of marginalized social groups provides, is an emphasis on, and openness to, diversity: a diversity of people (social groups) and a diversity of ideas about what can be emphasized in sport (Knoppers, 2000). Instead of hegemonic masculinity and emphasized feminity there would be masculinities and femininities, none of which would be marginalized in sport or elsewhere.

References

Acker, J. (1992). Gendering organizational theory. In: A. J. Mills & P. Tancred (Eds.), *Gendering organizational analysis* (pp. 248-262). Newbury Park, CA: Sage.

Andrews, D.L. (1996). The fact(s) of Michael Jordan's Blackness: Excavating a floating racial signifier. *Sociology of Sport Journal*, 13, pp. 125-158.

Cahn, S. (1994). *Coming on strong: Gender and sexuality in twentieth century women's sport*. New York: Free Press.

CBS (1996). Sport participation 1995. *Socio-cultural tidings* 96/16. Heerlen. (in Dutch)

Cheng, C. (1999). Marginalized masculinities and hegemonic masculinity: an introduction. *The Journal of Men's Studies*, 7, pp. 295 - 315.

Coakley. J.J. (1998). *Sport in society: issues and controversies*. (6th ed.). St. Louis: Mosby.

Connell, R.W. (1987). *Gender & power*. Stanford, California: Stanford University Press.

Connell, R. W. (1993). The big picture: Masculinity in recent world history. *Theory and Society*, 22, pp. 576 - 623.

Connell, R. W. (1995). *Masculinities*. Berkeley: University of California Press.

Connell, R. W. (1998). Masculinities and globalization. *Men and Masculinities*, 1, pp. 3 -23.

Dickey, C. & Power, C. (1998). Soccer gets sexy. *Newsweek*, 134, pp. 72/73.

Dijk, T. van (1993). *Elite discourse and racism*. Sage: Newbury Park, CA.

Elling, A. (1999). A little rough, I like that': About the images of and experiences in women's soccer. *Tijdschrift voor Genderstudies*, 2, pp. 25-35. (in Dutch).

Elling, A. (2001). *Sport fraternizes: practise or myth?: Social networks and images about sport among youth*. Arnhem: NOC*NSF. (in Dutch).

Elling, A. & Knop, P. De (1999). *According to one's own wishes and possibilities*. Arnhem: NOC*NSF. (in Dutch).

Griffin, P. (1998). *Strong women, deep closets: Lesbians and homophobia in sport*. Champaign, IL. : Human Kinetics.

Hall, M.A. (1996). *Feminism and sporting bodies: Essays on theory and practice*. Champaign, IL: Human Kinetics.

Hargreaves, J. (1994). *Sporting females: Critical issues in the history and sociology of women's sports*. London: Routledge.

Hekma, G. (1994). *As long as they do not provoke: Discrimination of gay men and lesbians in organized sport*. Amsterdam: Het Spinhuis. (in Dutch).

Kane, M.J. (1995). Resistance/transformation of the oppositional binary: Exposing sport as a continuum. *Journal of Sport and Social Issues*, 19, pp. 191-218.

Kane, M.J. & Greendorfer, S. (1994). The media's role in accommodating and resisting stereotyped images of women in sport. In: P. Creedon (Ed.), *Women, media and sport: Challenging gender values* (pp. 28-44). Thousand Oaks, CA: Sage Publications.

Kellner, D. (1995). *Media culture: Cultural studies, identity and politics between the modern and the postmodern*. London: Routledge.

Kerfoot, D. & Knights, D. (1998). Managing masculinity in contemporary organizational life: A 'man'agerial project. *Organization*, 5, pp. 7-25.

Knoppers, A. (1992). Explaining male dominance and sex segregation in coaching: Three perspectives, *Quest*, 44, pp. 210-227.

Knoppers, A. (1999). Offense of Ajax plays girls football: gender and football. *Tijdschrift voor Genderstudies*, 2 (4), pp. 16-24. (in Dutch).

Knoppers, A. (2000). Gender and (sport) organizations. In: A. Knoppers (Ed.), *The construction of meaning in sport organizations: Management of diversity* (pp. 43–60). Maastricht: Shaker.

Knoppers, A. & Anthonissen, A. (2001/in press). Meanings given to performance in Dutch sport organizations: Gender and racial/ethnic subtexts. *Sociology of Sport Journal*.

Knoppers, A. & Bouman, Y. (1996). *Trainers/coaches: A question of quality?* Arnhem: NOC*NSF. (in Dutch).

Knoppers, A. & Bouman, Y. (1998). *Always better than my athletes*. Arnhem: NOC*NSF. (in Dutch).

Knoppers, A. & Elling, A. (1999a). *Gender, ethnicity and the sport media: An inventory*. Utrecht/Tilburg: Center for Policy and Management, University of Utrecht/ Leisure Studies, University of Brabant. (in Dutch).

Knoppers, A. & Elling, A. (1999b). *It is more fun to play than to coach: Images of football coaches*. Zeist: KNVB. (in Dutch).

Knoppers, A. & Elling, A. (2001). *Gender, ethnicity and the sport media: Selection and interpretation processes*. Arnhem: NOCNSF (in Dutch).

Kolnes, L.J. (1995). Heterosexuality as an organizing principle in women's sport. *International Review for Sociology of Sport*, 30, pp. 61-77.

Lenskyj, H. (1987). *Out of bounds: Women, sport & sexuality*. Toronto, Canada: The Women's Press.

Lorber, J. (1993). Believing is seeing: Biology as ideology. *Gender & Society*, 7, pp. 568-581.

Majors, R. (1990). Cool pose: Black masculinity and sports. In M.A. Messner & D.F. Sabo (Eds.), *Sport, men and the gender order* (pp. 109–114). Champaign, IL: Human Kinetics.

McKay, J. (1999). Gender and organizational power in Canadian sport. In: P. White & K. Young (Eds.), *Sport and gender in Canada* (pp. 197–213). Oxford: University Press.

Messner, M. (1988). Sport and male domination: The female athlete as contested ideological terrain. *Sociology of Sport Journal*, 5, pp. 197-211.

Messner, M., Dunbar, M. & Hunt, D. (2000). The televised sports manhood formula. *Journal of Sport and Social issues*, 24, pp. 380-394.

Messner, M.A. & Sabo, D.F. (Eds.) (1990). *Sport, men and the gender order: critical feminist perspectives*. Champaign, Ill: Human Kinetics.

Messner, M. & Sabo, D. (1994). *Sex, violence and power in sports: Rethinking masculinity*. Freedom, CA: Crossing Press.

NOC*NSF (1999). *Membership NOC*NSF 1998*. Arnhem: NOC*NSF. (in Dutch).

Pfister, G. (1999). *Sport in the daily live of women*. Schorndorf: Karl Hofmann. (in German).

Pronger, B. (1990). *The arena of masculinity. Sports, homosexuality and the meaning of sex*. New York: St. Martin.

Rose, L. (1991). *The drama of talented girls: Biographies of young gymnasts*. Weinheim/München: Juventa. (in German).

Ryan, J (1995). *Little girls in pretty boxes: The making and breaking of elite gymnasts and figure skating*. New York: Doubleday.

Sabo, D. & Jansen, S. C. (1992). Images of men in sport media: The social reproduction of gender order. In: S. Craig (Ed.), *Men, masculinity, and the media* (pp. 169- 184). Newbury Park, CA: Sage Publications.

Sabo, D. & Jansen, S.C. (1998). Prometheus unbound: Constructions of masculinity in the sports media. In: L. Wenner (Ed.), *Media Sport* (pp. 203-217). London: Routledge.

Schaapman, M. (1995). *Unseen difference: An analysis of the hidden power processes of gender*. Den Haag: VUGA. (in Dutch).

Scheerder, J. (1998). The myth of the black super athlete: Images through sport. *Lichamelijke opvoeding*, 14, pp. 616-620 (in Dutch).

Segal, L. (1993). Changing men: Masculinities in context. *Theory and Society*, 22, pp. 625-641.

Solomon, (2000). *Our bodies, ourselves: The mainstream embraces the athletic Amazon.* Http://www.villagevoice.com/issues/0016/solomon2.shtml

Tudor, A. (1992). 'Them and us": Story and stereotype in TV World Cup coverage. *European Journal of Communication,* 7, pp. 319-413.

Wilson, W. (Ed. 1999). *Children and the sports media.* Los Angeles: Amateur Athletic Foundation of Los Angeles.

Wilson, B. & Sparks, R. (1996). 'It's gotta be the shoes': Youth, race and sneaker commercials. *Sociology of Sport Journal,* 13, pp. 398-427.

Woldendorp, J. (1998). Gay Games and jamborees do not belong in the sports section. *Trouw,* 11 July . (in Dutch).

PART THREE

VALUES IN STRUCTURES AND ORGANISATIONS

10 DUTCH AMATEUR SPORTS ORGANISATIONS IN TRANSITION: ORGANISING DIVERSITY

Anton Anthonissen

Introduction

Competitive amateur sports clubs in the Netherlands are facing new challenges. Social changes and their own internal dynamics are producing various areas of tension within and between the clubs. The increasing emphasis on economic growth, for example, would seem to conflict with voluntary commitment to these clubs, and the multi-cultural nature of present-day Dutch society is leading to a confrontation between historically-determined club cultures and the demands of various sportsmen and women. Sports clubs have a tendency to only deal with these tensions when the problems become so pressing that they cannot avoid doing so (Anthonissen & Boessenkool, 1996, 1998; Ibsen 1997). Their reactions are often of a rational and instrumental nature, tinged by economic considerations: greater focus on top performance, an increasing need for professionalisation, and an increased emphasis on the financial side of things. Socio-cultural processes are only dealt with on an incidental basis, although the actual practice in Dutch sports and sports organisations shows that it is precisely in that context that tensions exist (Anthonissen, 2000; Janssens, 1999; Knoppers & Elling, 1999).

Where socio-cultural processes in the world of amateur sport are concerned, discussion focuses on the lowering of standards: within the organisation complaints are voiced of lack of involvement in voluntary work for the club, lack of respect for other members, or neglecting to pay one's membership fee. On the field there is a lack of fair play, of honesty (drug enhancing performances, a failure to accept differences (discrimination) etc. The underlying question, however, is just whose norms and values are involved. In the world of Dutch amateur sport reference is usually made to values and norms which are the result of the way club organisation has developed historically (on the basis of voluntary commitment) in relation to competition and top performance. Social scientists link these norms and values to the dominance of white heterosexual masculinity in sport and sports organisations (Burstyn, 1999; Coakley, 1998; Donelly, 1996; Knoppers & Anthonissen, 2001; Taylor & Toohey, 1999).

In the world of organised amateur competitive sport in the Netherlands this relationship is hardly recognised, if at all. Discussions focus mainly on the question of how the various different target groups (women, minorities, young people, the disabled, gays etc.) can contribute to the prevailing norm and thus to the present organisational method. At the same time diversity is the basic principle of policy and action within sports organisations (NOC*NSF, 1999, p. 9). There is a recognition of the fact that in a multi-cultural and individualist society, people who differ with regard to age, cultural background, gender and sexual orientation, and who express a variety of different demands, wish to participate in organised sport in some way or another. Despite the fact that involvement in sport via a sports club is still the most obvious way of participating, it is coming to be realised that the traditional structure and closed nature of sports clubs are not adequately attuned to the changing and varied demands expressed by (potential) sportsmen and sportswomen (Anthonissen, 2000). It is partly for this reason that recent sports policy has focused on a more demand-driven sport structure, one in which the requirements expressed by sportsmen and sportswomen and by clubs must be the guiding principle (Arends, Egdom, Lucassen & Prent, 2000). This means that in future the amateur sports sector will need to be organised with a view both to the type of sports involved and to diversity.

In this chapter I will focus on the concept of diversity and show the limitations (and possibilities) in this concept for the amateur sport sector. I will explore the question how diversity can be used as (one of the) basic principle(s) for organizing the Dutch amateur sportclubs.

10.1 Diversity in and between Dutch amateur sports organisations

Diversity within and between sports organisations has for a long time been interpreted in a different manner to that described above. Diversity was organised in terms of social compartmentalisation on religious or ideological grounds. Amateur competitive sports organisations were all built up on the basis of identical ideas: a broad base involving a large number of (young) members produced the skills supporting a small number of top players delivering top performances: in other towards a pyramidal structure (Anthonissen, 1997; Crum, 1991). Originally, physical education at school and top-class sport were part of the same system. The ties between school sport and broad-based sport were later broken and those between broad-based sport and top-class sport were reinforced. Sports clubs were run by voluntary officials. In this approach to organisation, it were values such as self-motivation and solidarity which dominated. Members were aware of the club's mission, felt that they had taken on obligations to the club by joining it, and were prepared to devote themselves to it. Shared identity based on membership, participation and performance were inextricably bound up with one another as a norm.

By the mid-1990s, it had became clear that this image was no longer in tune with reality. Like other organisations, the speed of social change led to sports organisations becoming more complex and dynamic (Anthonissen, 1997). The number and type of sports have increased and although the total number of participants in sport has remained the same, the average age of club members has risen (Van der Heuvel & Van der Poel, 1999). As a result of mergers, the number of clubs is decreasing (Makkinga, 2000) and the image of the sports club as the dominant organisational form is beginning to disintegrate. Traditional sports clubs are being eroded from within: the membership is changing (more varied, but older), members are sometimes less performance-oriented and/or wish to play at times they choose for themselves (more individual). There is also a tendency for members not to always want to play with people who are "different". There are, for example, signs of a "flight of the minorities", whereby members of "minorities" are leaving "Dutch" clubs to engage in sports within the confines of their own culture. In this connection the negative aspects of the clubs they leave behind (not feeling accepted, discrimination etc.) are mentioned most alongside the positive aspects (more pleasant social contacts) of the new club (Janssens, 1999, p.38). In addition, there is also a "flight of the whites", with "Dutch" club members leaving "their" club because it is becoming more multi-racial; "they" are less committed and therefore more prepared to switch to other clubs where the "Dutch" club culture still exists (Janssens, 1999, p.48).

In clubs which are actually ethnically diverse (or are becoming so) – generally in socially disadvantaged neighbourhoods in large urban areas – tensions sometimes run high: little involvement, problems arranging transport, insufficient organisers, membership fees not paid, feelings of discrimination and vandalism (Anthonissen & Van Eekeren, 2000). Some originally "Dutch" clubs apply an admissions policy, with a quota for members of minorities, both for the club as a whole and for its teams. Nevertheless, there are also positive examples of sports clubs which promote internal ethnic diversity, emphasising that there is strength in such diversity, the basis for which would seem to lie in social commitment. As yet, it is the negative examples which are most frequently discussed, both by people in general and in the media.

Besides of diversity within organisations, the diversity between them is also increasing. It is becoming more difficult to provide clear definitions of amateur competitive sports organisations because the belief that a single type of organisation is the basis for all organised amateur competitive sport no longer fits in with what happens in actual practice. As a result of "the flight of the minorities" which we referred to above, an increasing number of sports clubs are being set up (if the premises and funds are available) to cater for specific target groups.

In the context of government policy and sports policy, withdrawal into such clubs is seen, on the one hand, as constituting an emancipation process which will eventually lead –via a transitional phase– to full integration. On the other hand, efforts are being made to get members of minorities to join traditional sports clubs (Lagendijk & Van der Gugten, 1996, p.12). Women, gays and disabled people have certainly gone through the same emancipation process in the past, but one cannot say that they are fully integrated. There are, after all, still separate clubs for women, gays and the disabled. This is, on the one hand, a natural process and is often the result of a free decision on the part of the individual sportsman or woman involved, but at the same time there would also appear to be barriers in the way sports clubs are organised internally. These barriers are rarely considered and when they are it is only in general terms: the introverted club culture (Hoogendam & Meys, 1998; Ibsen, 1997). Hardly any attention is paid to the wishes and ideas of various "minorities" (in the broad sense), which may or may not fit in with the way clubs are currently organised. The closed culture of traditional amateur sports clubs makes gaining access no easy matter.

Besides a shift towards clubs which cater for specific target groups, we can also identify a more fragmented picture. Within the existing categorisation by target group, we also find that people's "own" clubs can vary considerably. There are for example clubs for members of "minorities" which cater only for adult members, "Dutch" clubs which focus only on juveniles, and clubs exclusively for the elderly (Anthonissen & Boessenkool, 1996, 1998). There are also various types of "umbrella" clubs where all sorts of different sports take place under one roof; there are groups of clubs which co-operate with one another, the municipality, schools and welfare organisations, to develop activities in their neighbourhood (Makkinga, 2000), and there are also examples of collaboration between clubs and commercial organisations (sports schools, companies, medical centres etc.) to organise sport. Within these organisational types there is great diversity in the extent of involvement on the part of members (and their parents). Involvement is no longer automatically linked to the sports on offer as was the case with traditional "Dutch" clubs. That is possible because in a number of cases the rules are less restrictive than normal amateur clubs. Increasingly it is the requirements expressed by sportsmen and women which determine the nature of the club, and diversity within and between organisations is being taken more and more for granted.

10.2 Diversity as the basis for organisation

The diversity frame begins with the readiness to recognise and accept that there are differences in the way in which people assign meaning to their sport and in which they and the other members of the organisation assign meaning to the method of organisation. "The critical implication of diversity is not simply differences in personal characteristics such as age, gender, ethnic background, (in)validity, but rather the cultural diversity that can be associated with those differences. Cultural diversity reflects the unique sets of values, beliefs attitudes and expectations, as well as language, symbols, customs, and behaviours that individuals possess by virtue of sharing some common characteristics with others" (Doherty & Chelladurai 1999, p. 281). This still says little about the way in which people deal with the differences in relationships between individuals and groups and the way in which personal characteristics play –or are allowed to play– a role. One is dealing here with the question of which differences are significant and the way in which power imbalances, resulting from differing social positions, play a role and colour those differences.

Embracing the concept of diversity demands an attitude and behaviour which go further than merely tolerating differences; it involves being prepared to discuss power factors and access to sources and funds. If diversity is to become the principle on which sports clubs are organised, those occupying positions of power must be convinced of the added value diversity can have for the effectiveness of the organisation (Fink & Pastore, 1999, p.314). Research has shown that ethnically diverse groups are more creative and produce better results (Ling, 1990). This applies not only to ethnically varied groups but also when all kinds of other differences are involved. It is, however, a process which requires a long time to take effect and this is often a reason for organisations to abandon it prior to or during the course of the process (Thomas, 1990). If the process is in fact given the chance to develop, group members can share common experiences with one another. Sharing characteristics and sharing experiences can than interfere with one another. This provides the scope and opportunities to actually engage in the "management of diversity".

Golembieuwski (1995) shows that in the course of the process a number of approaches to diversity succeed another (or fail to do so). There is first the phase of "diversity under duress" in which demands are made for assimilation and in which discrimination is often present. The second phase is based on "equal opportunity", with the basic assumption being that equal opportunity will lead to equality at all levels of the organisation. In the case of Dutch sports clubs, this basic assumption would appear to be valid, but as yet it often has little effect in practice. In the third phase, that of "augmented affirmative action", attention focuses more on the statistics which will demonstrate that equality. In this phase there is usually a major discrepancy within sports clubs between the reality and the basic assumption: only 9% of managers and 11-18% of team sport coaches are women (Emancipatieraad, 1997). Fewer than 1% of managers and coaches are from "minorities" (this percentage is not an exact one because sports organisations do not record the necessary data – Knoppers & Anthonissen, 2001).

Whereas the emphasis in the first three phases is on acceptance of the concept, which may or may not be borne out in the statistics, in the fourth and fifth phases it is the process by which diversity is endowed with significance as the central value within organisations which plays the main role. In the fourth phase it is "valuing diversity", the attitude element, which is central to the day-to-day practice of the organisation. This phase involves genuine openness to differences between individuals. In the fifth phase, the management of the organisation takes a pro-active approach to implementing "management of diversity", the element of behaviour in which attention focuses on strategies which an organisation can implement in order to capitalise on the diversity of its members (Fink & Pastore 1999, p.320). The emphasis on the process in the final two phases focuses on the socio-cultural aspects of organisations.

Up to now attention in the world of sport has focused mainly on equal opportunity, integration, and the percentage of different categories of sportsmen and women. Less attention appears to be given to the process whereby attention is paid to attitude and behaviour.

In the view of sports federations and umbrella organisations (NOC*NSF, 1999), the notion that clubs must deal with matters by themselves means that it is their responsibility to deal with these aspects.

Diversity implies examining social relationships within organisations and making the differences which play a role within those relationships into a productive factor. The traditional basic principles in the world of amateur sport – such as teamwork as regards both performance and pleasure, contributions (voluntary) by individual members to furthering the aims of the club, fair play and social commitment – are basically favourable preconditions for focusing on the behavioural aspects of the development of social relationships. From the point of view of social relationships sport is often considered to be the social cement that transcends differences of age, culture, language, class, sexual orientation and (in)validity. The everyday reality within sports clubs shows that there are various barriers to putting that dream into actual practice. We will deal with three of those barriers here. Firstly, there is the prevailing ideology and image of the sports pyramid in which specific norms and values and images of performance in competitive amateur sport are emphasised. The supply-driven nature of sports clubs (but also of other organisations in the world of sport) constitutes a second barrier, influencing the way volunteers and professional support workers collaborate with one another. Thirdly, the scope of social involvement in sports clubs is unclear.

10.3 Limitations for diversity

10.3.1 The concept of the sports pyramid

The pyramidal structure of sports clubs is the dominant structure whereby they are organised and performance is embedded. This approach assumes that the club needs to have a broad base consisting of a large number of members (particularly juveniles) in order to ensure optimum performance by the best individual players or the top team. The longer they have been active in the club, the more strongly organisers and other club members believe in this idea. Ibsen (1997) also shows that the longer a club has been in existence, the greater the efforts that are made to implement the concept of the sports pyramid.

Ingham, Blismmer & Wells-Davidson (1999) have argued that the pyramid has its roots in the wish to achieve the best possible performance, which at the moment automatically refers to a professionalisation frame. This frame originates from a development in the sports sector which took place several decades ago and which now determines much of management policy. For a long time the starting point for participation was amateurism. Later, as a result of the influence of commercial organisations, high achievers were rewarded with the possibility of earning money with their sport. As a result a different attitude to participation in sport developed, one in which participation and achievement or competition came together under a single denominator (Coakley, 1998). A dominant discourse arose in which the best type of sport was defined as the best performance. The professional athlete soon became the best type of athlete and the word amateur slowly became synonymous with beginner and less-skilled (Knoppers, 2000).

The original clearly-defined boundary between amateur and professional became more fluid and made it possible for Olympic sport (initially meant for the best amateurs) and professional sport to become part of a single monoculture, in which the professionalisation of top-performance plays a central role (Ingham, Blissmer & Well Davidson, 1999). The pyramid was designated as the ideal type of structure to ensure optimum performance and the best basis for organising the single-sport culture.

The use of the image of the pyramid to structure Dutch sports organisations, as part of the effort to achieve highly-valued top performance, has a gender and ethnic subtext (Knoppers & Anthonissen, 2001). Organisers of "Dutch" sports clubs see mergers with "minority" clubs – usually playing at a lower level – as problematical because they would weaken the pyramidal structure. It is therefore unsurprising that members of "minorities" who play in the lower teams of traditional "Dutch" clubs frequently leave. Despite the fact that the number of "minority" clubs is increasing (Janssens, 1999), fewer members of "minorities" engaged in sport in the period from 1991 to 1995 (Van der Heuvel & Van der Werff, 1998).

The question is whether all this has to do with the prevailing monoculture in which the norms and values involved in performance (particularly at top level) are dominate. After all, "minorities" are less concerned with (top) performance, and when deciding on a club to join consider social enjoyment to be more important. Within the prevailing monoculture, social enjoyment is not the primary goal and it is highly likely that members of minorities will feel less at home there (Anthonissen & Van Eekeren, 2000; Duyvendak, Krouwel, Kraaijkamp & Boonstra, 1998).

Traditional sports clubs also believe that women are less able to contribute to achieving top performance within and for the club. Reference is then generally made to biological differences and the effect they have on performance. From this point of view, women are seen as less strongly built and less performance and competition-oriented than men, thus making them less suitable for competitive sport - particularly at top level (Hargreaves, 1994, Knoppers & Elling, 1999). The more dominant this idea is within clubs, the less women's sport is given a chance within the club (Knoppers & Bouman, 1996). It is striking that an increasing number of women are deciding not to participate in traditional competitive sport within the context of sports clubs but are choosing newer sports (fitness training and aerobics) in which the main consideration is health rather than performance (Van der Heuvel & Van der Werff, 1998). Besides the fact that these sports allow one to decide for oneself when one engages in them, and are subject to few hard-and-fast rules, one may wonder whether these choices are not also related to the unmistakable monoculture of sports clubs.

Dutch amateur sports organisations tend to define themselves using the metaphors of the pyramid and white masculinity, which is associated with competition and hierarchy and which is goal-driven and instrumental in its pursuit of success (e.g. Kerfoots & Knights, 1998). It fits in with the dominant values in society in which instrumental action and economic thinking (effectiveness and efficiency) and (top) performance are dominant. Because they focus on these values the officials who run amateur sports organisations have a tendency to define the criteria for allocating funds and facilities in terms of top performance (Anthonissen & Boessenkool, 1998). Such criteria as gender, ethnicity and other significant differences are considered to be irrelevant. This norm not only influences the way sport is played but also the way in which competitive sport is organised. Virtually all amateur football clubs, for example, state that they wish to be promoted as soon as possible to the first division (men) of the Royal Netherlands Football Association, and they are prepared to devote the greater proportion of the club's general funds to achieving this.

10.3.2 The emphasis on supply-driven competitive sport

Sports clubs in the amateur sector, operating from the dominant ideology, are used to working in a supply-driven manner. People join a club because they wish to make use of what it has on offer. In various branches of sport, steps towards differentiation have begun, with cautious account being taken of changing demands. What clubs offer is to a great extent determined by volunteers within the clubs, who thus contribute to organising competitive sport. The success or otherwise of a more demand-oriented approach depends on the involvement of volunteers and their readiness to organise the club's activities differently. Doing so also needs to benefit the volunteers and the club. The idea is still prevalent that volunteer sports club officials are in a position to experiment with socially valuable skills, thus increasing their career prospects (Van Bottenburg & Schuyt, 1996). On the other hand, making use of the services of volunteers benefits sports clubs because it reduces organisation costs. Profit motives are absent, meaning that sport can be kept cheap enough for people to pay for it.

The extent to which sports clubs run themselves is very considerable, with 96% of the work being done on a voluntary basis. Only a restricted number of paid officials (24%) work for clubs, usually as trainers and/or coaches (NOC*NSF, 1997, p.28). There is little diversity: less than 1% of the 10,000 qualified football coaches in the Netherlands are women (Stol, 1995) and these generally coach juvenile, women's or lower league teams (Knoppers & Elling, 1999). Management tasks and committee work are primarily carried out by volunteers. Virtually all clubs find it difficult to recruit and hang on to competent officials and committee members. As a result of tendencies towards decentralisation and privatisation and also because of the wave of mergers, the number and complexity of tasks within sports clubs are increasing, demanding greater availability and expertise on the part of voluntary officials (NOC*NSF, 1997). Increasingly people with the relevant training and experience are recruited from outside the club so as to guide it through these turbulent developments (Anthonissen & Boessenkool, 1998). The question is therefore whether career opportunities still exist for members or whether that is nowadays an outmoded idea. The great majority of management and community work is carried out by middle-aged white males. Members of this group indicate that other club members hardly contribute to organising the club and that they feel compelled to recruit officials and committee members in the same way, meaning that they always end up recruiting men of the same type (Anthonissen & Boessenkool, 1998).

Sports federations and umbrella organisations are attempting to provide support for clubs in dealing with these issues. The solution is sought in further professionalisation and restructuring of the sport sector, combined with quality improvements and demand-driven work (NOC*NSF, 1999). There is scope for differences: "differentiation in the form, content, intensity and financing of professionalisation is desirable" (Meeuwsen, 1999, p.9). Up to now clubs have received little or no support from the existing infrastructure. There are a large number of organisations which provide support for the sport sector with a large number of products, but they are not always attuned to the demands expressed by sports clubs and their members (Van Eekeren, Anthonissen & Boessenkool, 1998). However, the clubs themselves do not always know how to formulate their demands effectively, or how to communicate them to the support organisations, because they reason on the basis of existing supply-driven ideas. Little or no attention is paid to diversity. The national umbrella organisation NOC*NSF is therefore attempting to restructure the sport infrastructure "towards a demand-driven sport infra-structure" (Arends et al. 2000). The support provided must become transparent for the sports clubs and for their members (openness and clear tasks), efficient (optimum scale) and effective (demand-driven). Local "sports front offices" have therefore been set up where clubs can submit requests for support. The "back offices" are where the various support organisations operate and to which the clubs are then referred. It is noticeable that in this proposal the primary process in which sports clubs engage, namely the sport itself and volunteer-based work, is seen as a focus but do not constitute the actual basic principle. Expectations are that clubs will shift from dealing with everything themselves to further professionalisation in the shape of a club manager or club co-ordinator (Meeuwsen, 1999). The proposal for restructuring the sports sector would seem to focus primarily on the effects at the intermediate level (in other words the support organisations) and not on the primary process and thus the demands expressed by sportsmen and women. It is precisely the demands expressed in the primary process which make visible the increasing diversity of sports clubs. Attention needs to be given to the diversity of types of sport and the different socio-cultural processes required to arrive at a different working method focusing both on demand and on support for volunteers. The fact that volunteers do not have enough time, and the restricted availability of the relevant professionals, mean that socio-cultural processes within clubs receive little or no attention and often give rise to miscommunication. Communication takes place from within different frames which hardly overlap one another, if at all.

10.3.3 Lack of clarity as to social involvement

Focusing on the demand side of sport and on the concept of diversity can have consequences for the social legitimacy of sport and sports clubs. The way in which sports clubs view their own legitimacy has to do with the meanings which they assign to sport and to society. Kearny (1992) and Van Bottenburg & Schuyt (1996) have surveyed the many different significances which sport and society can have. Whereas sport can be meaningful for individuals in the sense of recreation, performance and/or pleasure, in social contexts such as sports clubs and other organisations it also has a social significance. This is called "the double character of sport" (Steenbergen, De Vos & Tamboer, 1992; Steenbergen & Tamboer, 1998), whereby sport is assigned both intrinsic value (sport as an end in itself) and external value (sport as a means or as an instrument). Sports federations and umbrella organisations have a tendency to hold clubs accountable to the concept of sport as an aim in itself (often in terms of participation and performance), whereas national and local government bodies emphasise primarily the social significance (for example the aspect of integration). This policy distinction has been the subject of discussion for many years. The proposals put forward for restructuring the sports sector also seem to foresee these two lines being organised as separate types of support. (Arends et al., 2000).

The document on growth produced by the NOC*NSF (1999), the national umbrella organisation for sport, takes "the double character of sport" as a basic principle but at the same time restricts it. It chooses "sport as the cement binding together the local or regional community" (NOC*NSF, 1999, p.9), referring to the principle of self-organisation of sports clubs. The emphasis here is indeed on the social aspects of clubs, but little is said about any relationship to other social issues. The national sports organisation does however distance itself from the approach adopted by the present government, namely "sport as an instrument to solve problems in other fields of policy" (NOC*NSF, 1999, p.9). The dispute as to the social function of sport is conducted primarily at macro level. "Investment in sport is investment in society" is the slogan often heard in this context (Van Bottenburg & Schuyt, 1996).

At local level, in the everyday reality of sports clubs, this link is put into practice to a greater or lesser extent. There is a realisation in deprived areas of major cities, for example, that after-school activities and counselling need to be organised in order to encourage young people to do well at school and to prevent them becoming involved in criminal activity. At the same time, however, a small club in a new residential district may admit only "Dutch" children in order to be certain of a reasonable supply of parents to act as volunteer officials. The extent to which a club is socially committed is determined by the members themselves. Different clubs deal with this in various different ways. Taking these differences as the basis of policy is more in tune with reality, and such an approach takes sport and society seriously as forces which impinge on one another. "Sport has no (eternal) essence because it is a social practice and material forces shape social practices that conflict, and consensus can exist simultaneously, that consensus is never permanent and that sport and society are continually changing as historical, economic and social forces change" (Coakley, 1998, p.124). The manner in which sports clubs assign meaning to sport and to the society of which it forms part expresses the level of commitment and responsibility which they have. This can differ very considerably from club to club and from time to time. Making this diversity within and between clubs one's basic principle is a way of bringing aims and reality closer together.

Conclusion: diversity as a serious business

We often hear it said that the decision to participate in sport is a matter of free will and is made on the basis of equality. "Sport has been labelled as the great equaliser" (Taylor & Toohey, 1999, p.2). This is also expressed in the way in which amateur sport is organised, namely on the basis of uniformity. Sports clubs are constructed according to the ideology of the sports pyramid in which performance is clearly a uniform concept. Nevertheless, diversity in performance is an essential element in the choice of whether or not to play a sport. It demonstrates the individual qualities of sportsmen and sportswomen in relation to others. Within the sport itself, in the relationship to others, the individual meanings assigned to participation in sport are becoming more important. Such individual meanings are coloured by different experience in social relationships in which personal qualities play (or can play) an essential role, and they may express themselves in other requirements as a basis for people wishing to participate in competitive sport. The need for a demand-driven approach is therefore an issue raised from within clubs.

The social reality around (in the form of potential members), within and between sports clubs, is characterised by increasing diversity which can be meaningful, in a demand-driven organisational method. Making diversity meaningful and making it a serious basic principle, mean accepting differences which focus on variety in the membership, in social relationships, types of sport, rules, and types of organisation, and where the management approach makes these differences in behaviour productive. Organising sport is therefore becoming paradoxical. On the one hand it assumes that when people become members of a club they support its aims and are invited to apply its shared norms and values. On the other hand the unique values and norms of individuals, with all their personal qualities, must be valued and made productive. "The shared values and expectations inherent in an organisational culture of diversity continue to facilitate the direction and co-ordination of members: a culture of diversity does not support random, disorganised behaviour. Rather, in this organisational culture it is acknowledged that individuals bring their personal cultures to the club, and those differences are capitalised on to the benefit of the individual, the group and the organisation" (Doherty & Chelladurai, 1999, p.289).

The manner in which the tension between shared values and personal cultures is made productive is an indicator of the way in which sports clubs are able or wish to create commitment to the organisation and to society. It means that clubs are encouraged and enabled (by support organisations and umbrella organisations) to define this commitment, and to seek their own new types of organisation in which socio-cultural processes are central. Taking diversity seriously thus becomes a shared responsibility within the sport sector, something which is by no means a simple challenge.

References

Anthonissen, A. (1997). *Between beercoaster and floppy-disk.* Arnhem: NOC*NSF. (in Dutch).

Anthonissen, A. & Boessenkool, J. (1996). *The Sport club between tradition and commerce.* Arnhem: NOC*NSF. (in Dutch).

Anthonissen, A. & Boessenkool, J. (1998). *Meanings of Management: Diversity of Managerial Performances in Amateur Sport Organisations.* Utrecht: ISOR. (in Dutch).

Anthonissen, A. & Eekeren, F. van (2000). *New Chances in Sports.* Utrecht: Services Sport and Recreation of the Municipality Utrecht, (in Dutch).

Anthonissen, A. (2000). Professionalization: Sportclubs and the reinforcement of the pyramid Structure. In: A. Knoppers (Ed.), *The construction of meaning in sport organizations: management of diversity* (pp. 61-76), Maastricht: Shaker.

Arends, H., Egdom, H. Van, Lucassen, J. & Prent, A. (2000). *Towards a Demand-Oriented Sport Infrastructure. A Sketch account on the Future of the Dutch Sport Infrastructure.* Arnhem: NOC*NSF. (in Dutch).

Bottenburg, M. & Schuyt, K. (1996). *The Social Meaning of Sport.* Arnhem: NOC*NSF. (in Dutch).

Burstyn, V. (1998). *The rites of men. Manhood, Politics and the Culture of Sport.* Toronto/London: University of Toronto Press.

Coakley, J. (1998). *Sport in Society: Issues and controversies* (6th ed.). London: McGrawHill.

Crum, B. (1991). *About the sportification of Society.* Rijswijk: WVC. (in Dutch).

Doherty, A. & Chelladurai, P. (1999). Managing Cultural Diversity in Sport Organizations: A theoretical Perspective. *Journal of Sport Management,* 13, pp. 280-297.

Donnely, P. (1996). The local and the global: globalization in the sociology of sport. *Journal of Sport & Social Issues,* 3, pp. 239-257.

Duyvendak, J.W., Krouwel, A.P.M., Kraaijkamp, R.E. & N.G.J. Boonstra, (1998). *Integration true Sports. A research on mixed and unmixed participation of immigrant and native sportsmen and sportswomen.* Rotterdam: Managerial office Rotterdam. (in Dutch).

Eekeren, F. van, Anthonissen, A. & J. Boessenkool (1998). *SPIN Organisation Research.* Arnhem: NOC*NSF. (in Dutch).

Emancipatieraad (1997). *Sport & Gender: Women in the picture.* The Hague: Department of Social Affairs, Consulting and research. (in Dutch).

Fink, J.S. & Pastrore, D.L. (1999). Diversity in Sport? Utilizing the Business Literature to Devise a Comprehensive Framework of Diversity Iniatives. *Quest,* 51, pp.310-327.

Golembieuwski, R. (1995). *Managing Diversity in Organizations.* Alabama: The University of Alabama Press.

Hargreaves, J. (1994). *Sporting Females: Critical issues in the history and sociology of womens's sports*. London: Routledge.

Heuvel, M. van der & Poel, H. van der (1999). *Sports in the Netherlands: a policy oriented sketch*. Tilburg: KUB. (in Dutch).

Heuvel, M. van der & Werff, H. Van der (1998). *Trend analysis of Sport: Development, Sports participation and Degree of Organization in the period 1975-1995*. Tilburg: KUB. (in Dutch).

Hoogendam, A. & Meys, L. (1998). *Volunteers in sport clubs. Organizing Involvement*. Utrecht: NOV. (in Dutch).

Ibsen, B. (1997). *Change in the Voluntary Sector in Sport*. Paper presented at the ISSA symposium, Oslo.

Ingham, A., Blismmer, B. & Wells-Davidson, K. (1999), The Expendable Prolympic Self: Going Beyond the Boundaries of the Sociology and Psychology of Sport. *Sociology of Sport Journal* 16, pp. 236-268.

Janssen, J. (1999). *Ethnic Dichotomy in Sports*. Den Bosch: Diopter (in Dutch).

Kearny, A.T. (1992). *Sports as Source of Inspiriation for Society*. Arnhem: NOC*NSF. (in Dutch).

Kerfoots, D. & Knights, D. (1998). Managing Masculinity un Contempory Organizational Life: A 'man'agerial project. *Organization*, 5, pp.7-25.

Knoppers, A. & Bouman,Y. (1996). *Trainers/coaches: a question of quality?* Arnhem: NOC*NSF. (in Dutch).

Knoppers, A. & Elling, A. (1999). *It is more Fun to Play: Images about Football Coaches*. Zeist: KNVB. (in Dutch).

Knoppers, A. (2000). *The construction of Meaning in Sport Organisations: Management of Diversity*. Maastricht: Shaker.

Knoppers, A. & Anthonissen, A. (2001/in press). Meanings given to Performance in Dutch Sport Organisations: Gender and Racial/Ethnic Subtexts. *Sociology of Sport Journal*.

Lagendijk, E. & Gugten, M. Van der (1996). *Sport and Ethnic Minorities: Facts, Development and Policy (1986-1995)*. Rijswijk: Ministerie VWS. (in Dutch).

Ling, S.C. (1990). *The effects of group cultural composition and cultural attitudes on performance*. Unpublished doct. dissertation. London: University of Western Ontario.

Makkinga, R. (2000). *Utrecht in Motion*. Utrecht: Municipality Utrecht. (in Dutch).

Meeuwsen, S. (1999). *Professionalization of Managerial Tasks in Sport clubs, Job planning in sports*. Arnhem: NOC*NSF. (in Dutch).

NOC*NSF (1997). *Space for development*. Arnhem: NOC*NSF.

NOC*NSF (1999). *A Vision of Vital Sport clubs in 2015. An Integral Frame for the Content of the Sport sector (concept)*. Arnhem: NOC*NSF. (in Dutch).

Steenbergen, J., Vos, N.J. de & J. Tamboer (1992). The Double Character of Sport. In: *Lichamelijke opvoeding*, 14, pp. 638-641. (in Dutch).

Steenbergen, J. & Tamboer, J.W.I. (1998). The Double Character of Sport: Conceptual Dynamics. In: J. Steenbergen et. al. *Values and Norms in Sports: Analysis and Perspective of Policy*. Houten/Diegem: Bohn, Stafleu Van Loghum. (in Dutch).

Stol, P. (1995). *A Search is Needed: Woman Coaches!* Utrecht: Universiteit Utrecht. (in Dutch).

Taylor, T. & Toohey, K. (1999). Sport, Gender and Cultural Diversity: Exploring the Nexus. *Journal of Sport Management*, 13, pp.1-17.

Thomas, R. (1990). From affirmative action to affirming diversity. *Harvard Business Review*, 68, pp. 107-117.

11 CONSTRUCTING VIABLE SPORTS CLUBS

Jan Boessenkool

Introduction

From a historical point of view, the process of managing and organising sports clubs is a by-product of people's wish to engage in sport. One important variant is sport in a school context, leading to participation in a competitive setting. In the Netherlands, organised sport takes place almost exclusively within voluntary clubs, and the same applies in the Nordic countries (Ibsen, 1997). In recent years, organising and managing sport has become an independent policy topic both for club administrators and local and national government, a topic which is the subject of considerable interest.

As voluntary associations, sports clubs are under pressure. Club committees – i.e. voluntary administrators or club managers – encounter dilemmas, tensions and problems all of which have their origin not only in individual members' perception of the relevant sport and all sorts of social changes, but also in the committees' own actions. Ibsen (1997) points out that in the Scandinavian countries, too, sports clubs are under increasing pressure, leading to various changes.

As a result of all kinds of social changes, the structure of clubs has for the first time become a topic for discussion in amateur sport too. In professional sport organisations are now set up like businesses, and the "club" character has virtually disappeared. But in the world of amateur sport too things are no longer organised "on the back of an envelope" (cf. Anthonissen, 1997).

Previous studies focused on the consequences of social change for amateur sports clubs (cf. Anthonissen & Boessenkool, 1996, 1997, 1998). Although the level of diversity has increased on both the supply and the demand sides, a number of characteristic features of the way in which sports administrators respond to changes have proved to be extremely stubborn (See chapter 10 of this book). Pyramid and integration thinking are a favoured reaction to problems, tensions and dilemmas. The question, however, is whether other scenarios can be envisaged and whether these have already been made concrete both theoretically and/or empirically. That is the subject of the present contribution. To that end, a literature study has been carried out, along with empirical research, on a number of popular branches of sport in the Netherlands: football, volleyball, basketball, gymnastics and road cycling.[1] The basic assumption is that the significances, values and norms that are intrinsic to sport are related to developments and pre-conditions outside the field of sport. Internal and external significances have a dialectical relationship with one another.

The question of what viable (or vigorous) clubs are, whether now or in the near future, can be answered primarily on the basis of the concept of vitalisation. A definition of that concept will enable us to focus our empirical and theoretical search. Vitalisation is the process whereby sports clubs and their managers consciously deal with social changes, and/or changes in the way sport is perceived by their members (Anthonissen, 1997). To what extent do managers consider the social context of their club? Are they capable of properly analysing the internal processes of the club – e.g. finances, number of members, club officials, achievements, culture, identity, communication? An overall analysis of internal and external developments can enable the club to make targeted, well-considered choices for the immediate future.

Crum (1991) identifies a shift (starting in the sixties) in value orientation, with competitiveness and values taken from the work ethic (discipline, standardisation, devotion to duty) being replaced by values related to leisure, quality of life, and self-realisation (Steenbergen & Tamboer, 1998).

In this contribution we will seek to identify significant values. However, we first need to say something about the features of sports clubs. We will then go on to place them in their social context and to indicate the consequences that position has. Using the results of

---

[1] The empirical data presented in this paper is based on a qualitative study carried out in 1999-2000 of what a large number of high-quality sports clubs consider to be the good practices on which clubs should be based. This study was carried out by Arjan de Jong and myself. We interviewed approximately 50 managers at 15 sports clubs, and representatives of sports federations, local authorities and the media. The results are presented in a research report (NOC*NSF, 2001).

empirical research and comparisons with the literature, we will discuss a number of relevant topics on the basis of which we can draw conclusions as to what we can and wish to understand by "viable" (or "vigorous") sports clubs.

11.1 Features of sports clubs

Sports clubs are social practices and have characteristic social structures. In their interaction with their environment (or environments) these structures –in this case social and cultural relationships and features– continue or change. Sports clubs, just like other organisations, are both systems and parties.

In our view there are four crucial topics which characterise contemporary sports clubs (and the changes taking place within them) in the Netherlands: their voluntary nature, their legitimacy, the primary process and their structure and management.

Voluntary nature

The voluntary nature of sports clubs is a dominant organisational feature. The members have joined on a voluntary basis and undertake –or may not in fact undertake– tasks on behalf of the other members of the club. This voluntary character is striking when compared to other types of organisation. In definitions of voluntary associations there are two recurring aspects: in the first place social ties which do not belong to the state, and in which the core is to be found in the private lives of individuals and not in the formal economy. Secondly, they do not focus primarily on material interests and are not linked to primary relationships such as the family or religion (SCR, 1994, p.582). Voluntary associations are sometimes an exception. Sills speaks of "making a living associations" (for example cartels) as types of voluntary association in which material interests are indeed the basic principle (Sills, 1968, p.363).

Theories of voluntary associations often take the aims of the organisation as their starting point (Gordon & Babchuk, 1959; Handy 1988; Knoke & Prensky, 1984; Laporte, Bollaert, De Knop & Taks,

1997; Sills 1968). Each author produces a different categorisation, but in all cases two types of voluntary organisation are central. The various different types are given different designations. There are "expressive" variants in which the aims are to be found within the organisation itself. The volunteers are involved with the other members (mutual support organisation) or with the people whom the organisation wishes to assist. The latter are referred to as "service delivery organisations" (Handy, 1988, p.12). These types of voluntary organisation traditionally have a highly internal focus. In addition, there are instrumental variants in which the aim lies outside the organisation. These wish to influence society (or parts of it). In the literature, various designations are applied: social movements, pressure groups, campaigning organisations (Handy, 1988; Klandermans, 1983; Visser & Smid, 1979).

Amateur sports clubs belong to the expressive variant. A mutual support organisation is an organisation "of, by and for" its members (Handy, 1988, p.12). The significance of organising within this club construction is rooted in value orientations and common interests which bind people to one another (Kruithof, 1973). Between the 1920s and the 1950s, associations (including sports clubs) in the Netherlands were compartmentalised on denominational lines (referred to in Dutch as verzuiling, or "pilarisation"). Catholics, Protestants and socialists set up an extensive network of organisations with a strong ideological basis (Van Munster, Van den Berg & Van der Veen, 1996, p.16). Since then, there has been a breaking down of traditional religious and ideological barriers, but that process is certainly not at an end. Various influences of these networks can currently still be identified, for example in symbols, rituals (prayers at the start of the annual members' meeting) or in the name of the club. This does not detract from the fact that in recent years there has been greater diversity in the way members assign significance to their membership. The values based on the old denominational system have become less homogeneous. Involvement in a sports club does not mean the same thing for everybody. The principle of "of, by and for the members" is no longer taken for granted, as many have testified both orally and in print. Nevertheless, the instrumentalisation of membership is only apparent to a limited extent. Identification and involvement on the basis of a clearly defined (denominational) background is still expressed in the way in which clubs wish to legitimise themselves.

Legitimacy

The legitimacy of sports clubs is to be found in generalised social expectations which those involved subscribe to as belonging to the club: "Why are we here?" Gastelaars speaks of the frame of reference of the organisation (Gastelaars, 1997). As a result of the distinction between work and private life, the domain of "leisure" has been created, within which sports clubs justify their existence. Voluntary involvement is the central value and the guideline for action. Members are active within the club on the basis of a feeling of identification and involvement with it. That involvement sometimes has a number of supplementary ideological aspects which are apparent in the structure of the organisation, its aims and/or its constitution, (for example a Christian basis) or the name of the club, for example. These historical, involving ideological components in the social values of clubs, are becoming less important (e.g. Van Munster, et al., 1996, p.16).

Sports clubs are attempting to hang on to their ideological principles. On the one hand, they sometimes cling desperately to their denominational identity, but, on the other, this restricts them when it comes to broadening their outlook. The question of identity is creating difficulties for clubs. How, for example, should they deal with multi-culturalism?

The primary process

The primary process consists of the core activities carried out by staff in interaction with customers or members. Core activities are given shape according to central values (Hasenfeld, 1983, p.143) and aim to ensure involvement on the part of members and to make possible selection with a view to competition. Training sessions and social activities are therefore organised in order to carry out club tasks collectively. It is striking that mobilisation activities are associated with increased "personal attention".

Core activities are carried out by volunteers. These are people who fulfil an unpaid and voluntary function within and for the club (Laporte, et al., 1997, pp. 38-40; Lucassen, 1987, p.14). In the past it was only out-of-pocket expenses that were reimbursed. Currently, however, salaries for technical officials and payment for support tasks are widely accepted, and are important points for negotiation when club managers are being appointed.

The position and the role of club members are the subject of lively discussion. Are members in fact customers? Membership is voluntary, and beyond paying their membership fee members have no explicit obligations. Nevertheless, they are implicitly expected to carry out club tasks. Core volunteers, in particular, give priority to their commitment and expect others to do the same (Meys, 1997, p.57). In actual fact the results are disappointing: and there is a great deal of "membership apathy" (Sills, 1968, p.369). Do members wish to be (merely) consumers of services? Pearce points out that little is known about the motives of volunteers within voluntary organisations (Pearce, 1993, p.3).

Structure and management

The structure and management are to a large extent determined by the democratic principles of the club structure. This is a flat, broad structure. There are few formal hierarchical relationships between the general meeting of members, the executive committee and the other committees. In many clubs committee members are also members of the executive committee on the basis of the "linking pin" principle (Terp, 1983). Decision-making formally takes place at the general meeting, which is open to all members. Each member can help decide on the course the club is to follow. The meeting appoints managers and can also dismiss them. The formal democratic structure of the club often differs radically from the actual informal practice, with club administrators constituting a power factor that is more dominant than the general meeting. Michels (1959) speaks in this connection of the "iron law of oligarchy" (quoted in Sills, 1968, p.369). Within every organisation there is a tendency for a small group to decide matters. The small group of members who hold power in the everyday course of events are difficult for the other members to control. Membership apathy means that administrators tend to bring club processes into line with their own personal aims. In the organisation of sports clubs administrators in fact play a managerial role.

11.2 Sports clubs in context

Like other sectors, sport is confronted by relatively influential changes. They are affected by social processes of individualisation, commercialisation, bureaucratisation and the retreat from ideology. Various authors have pointed out the consequences of these processes for the dynamics of sports clubs (e.g. Beckers & Serail, 1991, Crum 1991, Rubingh & Westerbeek, 1992; Van Bottenburg, 't Hof & Oldenboom, 1997). The internal focus of traditional organised sport means that for a long time it has been able to distance itself in a certain sense from general tendencies, but it is now subject to these influences to a greater extent. Hasenfeld (1983) makes a distinction: on the one hand there is the general environment, namely the social developments confronting every organiser. One might mention individualisation, decreasing involvement on the part of members and changes in government policy on the provision of subsidies. On the other hand there is the direct environment with which there is a direct relationship and in which resources and services are exchanged, for example local government, other sports clubs in the immediate vicinity, and federations or umbrella organisations.

The unpredictable nature of social processes has to do with the increasing pluriformity of society. Accepted management concepts do not work (or do not work any longer), although many attempt to hold on to the ancient planning and control thinking, in which the belief that society can be "created" plays a major role.

Beck (1994) views present-day society as developing towards a "risk society", in which the increasing volume and pace of change mean that people need to learn how to deal with uncertainty and its associated risks. Some (Beck) plead for greater continuity while others (e.g. Huls, 1992) argue in favour of learning to deal with discontinuity and change. In the world of sport, which is rather conservative, the idea of continuity is popular. In the past the continued existence of the club was seldom a matter for discussion, but survival and vitalisation are now defined as among the main aims of the organisation, or are at least the subject of regular discussion.

The increasing complex and interconnected nature of developments make it difficult for those involved to distinguish between the various different influences affecting the sports sector in general and sports clubs in particular. This is all the more so because these influences operate directly (through interactions between the members within the club itself) and indirectly (in the interaction with actors in the direct environment). The boundaries between clubs and their contexts, or between social systems in general, are vague and permeable. Understanding the situation requires first unravelling the various different developments and then relating them to one another. We will restrict ourselves here to mentioning the social processes confronting clubs: political and economic developments, social developments, the use people make of their leisure time, demographic changes, changes within sport itself (e.g. Anthonissen & Boessenkool 1998; Van den Heuvel & Van der Poel, 1999). The most important consequences manifest themselves in a number of areas of tension.

Areas of tension

Although we can assume that the structural behaviour of people in the field of sport does not differ essentially from their behaviour outside it, clubs do have their own dynamics. This is the result, on the one hand, of the nature and history of (sports) clubs and, on the other, of the unique position they hold. The general developments referred to intermingle with these internal dynamics in such a way as to throw up a number of specific questions. For many clubs, the most pressing question is that of how to survive. The problems associated with this issue are: insufficient (young) members, more assertive members, pluriformity in the assignment of significance and in demands, problems with finding people to run the club, financial shortages, pressure on facilities, increasingly complex regulations, etc.

Falling membership and the problem –both a quantitative and qualitative one– of finding people to run the club have been the subject of discussion since as far back as the eighties (e.g. Verstegen, Andriessen & Begeer, 1983; Dekkers, Mandemaker, Stoppelenburg & Van de Ven, 1989). The problems vary with the type of voluntary work involved, with it being particularly difficult to find capable administrators. It is also difficult to find referees, trainers, people to carry out maintenance and cleaning and to man the canteen, or to do secretarial work (Janssens, 1996). Not every club is confronted by staffing problems to the same extent. From the qualitative point of view, there is great pressure on the knowledge and skills of volunteers. The demands expressed by the context in which sports clubs operate (federations, municipalities, competing clubs, etc.) are becoming greater. Many authors see increased professionalisation as a solution to shortages of people to run the club and to the lack of involvement on the part of members (e.g. Dekkers et al. 1989; Laporte et al. 1997; Rubingh & Westerbeek 1992; Van Bottenburg et al. 1997; Verstegen et al., 1983). Professionalisation is taken to mean various different things: payment for club work, training for volunteers, having club positions filled by persons with a higher education, hiring in experts from outside the club, appointing managers, etc.

From the financial point of view sports clubs are dealing with a national government which is adopting a "hands-off" approach, and which is transferring tasks to local government. This would not be a problem were it not that many municipalities, in their turn, are expecting more and more from sports clubs. Cost is applied as a basic principle. There is pressure on subsidies and they have sometimes been withdrawn or made subject to more stringent requirements. Government spending has fallen in the course of the nineties (cf. Oldenboom, Hopstaken & Van der Meer, 1996). In addition, a wide range of costs paid by clubs have increased: water rates, energy costs, property tax, environmental costs, wage tax and turnover tax (Janssens, 1996). There are also major differences between municipalities: the extent to which costs are passed on depends on the priority given to the sports sector in municipal policy.

Another area of tension has to do with formal as opposed to informal decision-making. Sports clubs are so-called "minimal" organisations (Verstegen et al., 1983). As a rule their tasks and powers are hardly made explicit, if at all. The general meeting of members is actually the highest decision-making body, but in practice it is the executive committee which is the most powerful body within the club. There is a high level of informal consensus about this situation. In a way the general meeting of members is a survival from the past. A number of clubs are considering introducing alternative decision-making bodies, for example a members' council. Increases in scale make it necessary to consider more formal approaches to organisation and far-reaching differentiation of tasks (Verstegen et al., 1983). The gap between administrators and members is becoming wider and the supply of information more diffuse. The choice between performance-oriented and recreational sport is a thorny issue within many clubs. The majority, whether consciously or unconsciously, apply the pyramid model (see chapter 10 of this book). Even when the pyramidal structure is threatened by social trends –for example demographic changes (fewer young people), socio-cultural developments (different interests and far more options), educational changes (different demands on children) and market-oriented thinking (image of sports)– the same pyramid continues to be the basic principle of administrative operations.

Orientations

The various areas of tension are forcing sports clubs, and their administrators in particular, to consider the future. How can they survive, and preferably remain as viable and vigorous as possible? What choices need to be made? What choices do sports clubs make in actual practice? Theoretically speaking, we can distinguish four possible orientations.

Firstly, there is the missionary orientation, with a strong and explicit ideological approach which profiles the club's identity. Central to this are such values as self-motivation and solidarity. Members are aware of the club's mission, are prepared to work to promote it, and have entered into obligations by becoming a member. Members genuinely participate in the life of the club. Involvement is a central feature and is taken for granted. Financing is provided primarily through membership fees and member recruitment drives.

The second orientation is the professional one. Professionalisation is generally associated with payment for facilities. Quality standards are the central values. Trainers, themselves well-trained, work for club teams according to specific codes for example. They and other professionals have certain knowledge and skills which make them the new internal power factor. The traditional democratic decision-making structure in which all members have a say is disappearing. Members, and certainly club officials, are increasingly acquiring the status of employees, although there are the usual tensions between voluntary work and paid work. The customers in this context are the spectators who attend competitions. Internally there is a focus on the conditions which can guarantee professional quality. The usual sources of funding, such as membership fees, admission charges and perhaps subsidies, are insufficient to guarantee this. Other types of funding, such as sponsoring and television fees, are supplementary and have not infrequently become the main source of funds. This implies a far-reaching level of external dependence and therefore constant uncertainty as to the continued existence of the club.

Thirdly, there is the commercial orientation. Many see this as a trend which is unavoidable given the increasing influence of market-oriented thinking. The actions taken by administrators are influenced primarily by expectations of profit and loss. Central values are hardly involved any longer in the actual practice of the sport concerned. Efficiency, a business-like approach and effectiveness have become the dominant values, from the perspective of maximum profit. Members are potential "customers" for the products and services provided. Supporting services, such as administrative work and the supply of materials, are acquiring a greater say because it is important that products and services are effective, customer-friendly and efficient

The fourth and final orientation is that aimed at individual customers. Members, as customers, are central. The central value is customer-friendliness, whereas within the commercial orientation it is profitability. Quality is seen primarily in complying with the wishes and needs of the members, in providing tailor-made work. This is the basis for the particular type of professionalism (for example of trainers). Members are participants in the process of providing a service. Their involvement is largely dependent on the quality of the tailor-made work.

We have now considered a number of (future) directions –in the form of theoretical constructs– which sports clubs can choose in order to cope with various changes in the social context. Our theoretical principle, however, is that clubs and club administrators do not merely need to adapt to changes.

According to this line of reasoning, we would argue that alternative orientations for sports clubs can only succeed if the main actors themselves provide the basis of support. Increased variety is necessarily an inherent part of this. Failing to recognise that variety, and to make the necessary choices unavoidably lead to an impoverishment of club life in general.

In saying all this, we do not wish to suggest that those involved can determine what the future of their club will be entirely of their own free will. That would be a case of naive humanism (Hall, 1991, p.56). People can indeed make their own history –to a certain extent– but they always do so on the basis of circumstances which they have not chosen for themselves. Those circumstances restrict the options for choice and influence the perspective of the actors.

11.3 Viable sports clubs

In recent years, there has been a major increase in the attention paid to sport and to sports clubs, including in the form of criticism. Sports clubs are frequently said to be (too) traditional and internally focused and to fail to fulfil their social tasks effectively. Their administrators are insufficiently aware of social developments and are too much involved with their own successes, particularly by increasing the scale of the club, integration thinking and the pyramid model. Even so, sports clubs still play an important and extremely central role in the area of public society and they are assigned countless tasks and functions, not least by politicians and policy-makers. There are seemingly also a great number of positive aspects to sports clubs and their administrators, and the world of sport does not merely need to try to catch up with developments; its social significance can in fact even be extended.

Our empirical investigation and a comparison of the results and recent publications result in a number of themes according to which we can analyse the situation within present-day sports clubs: the changing social context; social function; diversity and identity; context and networking; structure and the basic principles of the type of organisation; the quality of leadership and the organisation; the future: vitalisation.

Many of these themes are closely related to one another. The quality of the organisation as a whole, for instance (expressed, for example, in effective volunteer policy), will be highly dependent on the quality of the leadership, and the latter will be related to the networking ability of the administrators etc.

The changing social context

The question is to what extent the main figures involved, namely club administrators, consciously recognise and reflect on social changes so as not merely to react to them but to continually form part of a dialectical relationship with them: that they pro-actively form part of the same developments and share responsibility for them.

Van den Heuvel & Van der Poel (1999, p.69) say that "in various divisions of sport, social trends have led to the existing organisational structure being called into question and to consideration of what changes are necessary." Van Bottenburg et al. (1997) even speak of a cultural turn-around confronting sport, given the far-reaching differentiation of supply and demand in this sector. In 1997, the umbrella organisation of sport in the Netherlands, the NOC*NSF, instigated a discussion on the infrastructure of sport (SPIN) in order to be able to respond in a more demand-driven way to the wishes expressed by the rank and file (sport participants and clubs).

At club level the majority of administrators would seem to hardly concern themselves with social developments, and not at all with what these mean for their own club. In general they are already satisfied if they have things relatively well under control, and can keep them so. Actually – and actively – taking account of these developments is more an ideal for policy-makers and (academic) researchers who see the sport sector as confronted by a whole range of changes.

Nevertheless, it is important that the consequences of such changes are realised and that they are the subject of constant attention. Participation in organised sports activities is increasing, including elderly people and immigrants. Differentiation in sport and physical activity is continuing: they are more individual and more multicultural, young people spend their time "zapping", there is decreasing identification with the club (problems finding club officials), competition with sport as a leisure activity, and new types of organisation including the need for collaboration and/or mergers (Van den Heuvel & Van der Poel, 1999). Sport is now an economically and technologically important sector, involving vast sums of money, in both professional and amateur sport.

The struggle for space in urban areas and in recreation areas outside urban areas is intensifying. Larger numbers of people wish to use the restricted amount of space available in a greater variety of different ways. From a political and administrative perspective the sport sector will be called to account with respect to its social responsibility, as recompense for continuing support from the public purse.

Sport does not stand outside the context of social developments but is an integral part of them and contributes to determining them. Sport is more than a binding element of society. It does not suffice to define sport solely in terms of functions and aims. It also serves to shape and reinforce identity. It brings people together but at the same time excludes others.

The dilemmas and choices to be made come together in the issue of the identity of each club: who or what do we wish to be and why are we here (Gastelaars, 1997)?

Social function: diversity and identity

In their policy-oriented survey of predicted trends, Van den Heuvel & Van der Poel (1999, p.102) point out a number of policy themes that impinge directly on clubs. They too ask to what extent clubs are strong, viable and change-oriented enough to face up to the issue of whether they will remain the central framework for sports activities, or whether new arrangements for sport are necessary, ones which are more consumer-oriented. Do sports clubs (already) target these specific groups or are they all fishing in the same waters? As yet, there is little reason for optimism as regards the discernment of sports administrators. Compelled by pyramid and uniformity thinking, they focus primarily on how to further improve the performance achieved by elite participants.

In our investigation of good practices at viable sports clubs, it has become clear that a large number do in fact make more or less clear choices as to what they wish to "stand for". The question is whether their identity and the image at which they aim are in line with one another. Gymnastics, for example, has a "stuffy", provincial image and is also seen as a sport for girls. There is hardly any need for it to create a profile for itself any more. There is little direct competition within this branch of sport, unless it is with commercial providers (sports schools). Many gymnastics clubs, however, are continually engaged in expanding their horizons by offering new types of (exercise) activities. In the case of football clubs, it is vital that they should have a clear understanding of their target groups. The clubs we investigated do indeed have such an understanding, although it is extremely diverse: people who search for (technical) quality, performance-oriented juniors, and election replaced by self-selection.

Within these clubs, image and identity are not greatly divorced from one another. The same goes for other branches of sport, but this has more to do with the actual nature of the sport. Volleyball, for example, is a sport for the better educated and attracts people who prefer to avoid physical contact while still engaging in team sport and for whom the atmosphere and identification with the club are essential. Basketball has a more trendy image and, partly because of this, attracts young people. At one of the clubs studied, discussion of the mission, aims and identity of the club are in fact quite central. For road cycling clubs, the issue of young members (or actually the lack of them) is the greatest concern. Road cycling is seen as a sport for middle-aged men (with pot bellies). Clubs are confronted by the problem of ageing and are consequently concerned about their future. One club chairman wishes to tackle things in a more businesslike manner and focuses on the provision of a service: selling a good product. This conflicts somewhat with the wish to retain the character of the club and the consequent appeal to members to perform voluntary club duties. Another cycling club attaches a great deal of importance to club life and even has its own clubhouse. The attention paid to people aged over 55 is noticeable.

There is increasing social pressure on clubs to collaborate with parties from other sectors (health care, education, welfare). The clubs studied show hardly any desire to actually do this, although they recognise the value of (future) collaboration, especially with schools. Volleyball and basketball are school sports par excellence. Road cycling is hardly appropriate to a school context at all. A study carried out in a number of neighbourhoods in the Netherlands (VWS/CBM/DSP, 2001) shows that the level of collaboration between the education, sport and welfare sectors is far from good –indeed it is almost non-existent. Besides the fact that they have their work cut out just dealing with their own problems, there is a lack of central guidance, co-ordination and responsibility.

The same basically applies to collaboration between sports clubs, whether or not within the same branch of sport. Cultural differences are generally too great a stumbling block. Mergers are too difficult to set up and often take place only when other options are no longer feasible (Boessenkool, Van der Spek & Anthonissen, 1997). For most of those questioned, multi-functional or all-embracing sports clubs offer no solution either because the target groups are too diverse.

The question of whether viable sports clubs understand their social function in the sense of providing sports facilities to various different target groups can be answered, very cautiously, in the affirmative – very cautiously because relatively weak target groups are only served to a limited extent and sometimes only of necessity and in an instrumental manner. "Dutch" clubs are hardly accessible to ethnic minorities, who are therefore increasingly joining clubs of their own. Only a few clubs, because of a perceived social responsibility, welcome handicapped people or the elderly.

Context and networking

The literature shows that sports clubs have long had an extremely internal focus. Lucassen & Hoogendam (1998, p.57) speak of "typical clubs, whose functioning is to a great extent determined by the culture of 'with and for one another." (e.g. Meijs, 1997). For a long time, there was no great need for them to look beyond their own boundaries. The monopoly position of the traditional sports club has now been breached. Countless other sports providers have entered the market which are "far better able to respond to the capricious requirements of sports consumers" (Lucassen & Hoogendam, 1998, p.57).

As with other organisations, the boundaries between "inside" and "outside" have become extremely blurred. Competition between sports clubs is no longer merely on the field of play but is increasingly becoming competition in terms of survival, of strategic management: the optimum mix of external environmental factors and internal structuring, between supply and demand, etc. An internal focus still seems to be an important feature of clubs which are defined as viable or vigorous. Administrators realise, however, that good contacts with politicians and civil servants can make a contribution (a major one) to achieving the aims of the club. It should be mentioned, however, that this takes place largely on an individual basis. Hardly any coalitions are formed (for example in the form of a lobby group) in order to increase the clubs' position of strength within the direct environment, for example with respect to the local authorities. It has become clear on a number of occasions that not all municipal authorities are sports-minded to the same extent, while civil servants dealing with sport also have their own preferences as regards the tasks of sport and/or clubs. These facts certainly play a role in decision-making. At the same time, they mean that decision-making is also open to being influenced.

Hasenfeld (1983, p.63) gives a striking example of the direct environment of an organisation. When applied to sports clubs, his example produces the following six main stakeholders which need to be incorporated into any analysis:

- Providers of complementary services – welfare work, schools etc., insofar as focusing on sport;
- Recipients and consumers –members, spectators, sponsors, parents;
- Competing organisations –other sports clubs, especially within the particular branch of sport concerned;
- Providers of authority and legitimacy –government regulations, the law applying to associations, federations;
- Providers of fiscal resources –(local) government;
- Providers of clients –neighbourhood, district, village, town, or specific target groups.

Anthonissen & Boessenkool (1998) argue that it is necessary to identify not only the actors (the stakeholders) in the direct environment but also the nature of the relationship with them. In other words, what are the features of the interaction with the context? There is an awareness, for example, of other cultural differences, social relationships (including power relationships), conflicting interests, emotional relationships, varying perspectives on reality, situational dependencies, identity issues, layers of reality, restricted rational predictability.

Structure and basic organisational principles

As already mentioned in section 2 of this chapter, amateur sports clubs belong to the "expressive" variant of voluntary organisations: the aims are to be found within the organisation itself and the volunteers are involved with the other members. A mutual support organisation is an organisation "of, by and for" its members. Administering the club "for" the members is in actual practice often interpreted as management of the members, however.

Because of what the literature refers to as "membership apathy", one might expect viable clubs to have found alternatives in order to deal with the reduced involvement of their members. One of the most striking results of our study is precisely the emphasis on the principle of the mutual support organisation. Practically all the administrators we questioned indicated that this feature is the core and the strength of their club, and they emphasise that this must remain so in the future. They are, incidentally, not opposed to further professionalisation in the form of payment for club duties or a minimum level of reimbursement for expenses. This applies particularly to less attractive jobs such as running the club bar, cleaning, maintenance and secretarial work.

Many consider that a more businesslike approach is necessary in addition to professionalisation. In practice, however there is a great deal of ambivalence. People cling to the "for and by the members" principle, which is simply not compatible with a businesslike approach. One may also wonder whether a choice is made to supply a product, service or performance, with a different type of organisation and organisational structure perhaps being more suitable, or to make the most of club life, with atmosphere and identification becoming primary. The availability of a sufficient number of high-quality club officials is directly related to this. However, clubs sometimes find themselves facing a dilemma. They wish to hold on to the club's structure because of their basic principles and responsibility but at the same time they want to make the club more like a business. The latter aim is frequently achieved by placing constituent interests in separate organisations, which may or may not be dominated by external interests such as sponsors. Choices are seldom unequivocal. The pressure to professionalise, to commercialise and to improve performance is constantly present (internally), and is resisted because of the importance attached to the dominant club principle, that of "of, by and for the members".

Van den Hcuvcl & Van den Poel (1999) also point out that the traditional organisational principles of sports clubs are under pressure. How can they meet the needs and demands of (individual) sports participants? Do collaboration and/or mergers provide solutions? Do sports clubs need to present themselves more as businesses? It is obvious that the direction in which clubs are moving (or have to move) is far from clear. In practice, the orientations listed in section 3 are found in a wide variety of hybrid forms. At the moment there is a great level of diversity, partly because of the changing stakeholders, and also because of the somewhat vague idea we have of social trends. Much, if not all, depends on the quality of the leadership, specifically on how the executive committee is able to organise the club.

Quality of leadership and the organisation

The literature on sport deals only sporadically with the topic of leadership. In contrast the dissertation by Anthonissen & Boessenkool (1998) focuses almost exclusively on the construction of significance amongst administrators and the action they take. The authors distinguish between three types of administrators: "Handymen", "engineers" and "directors". "Handymen" wish to maintain the status quo as much as possible and react to impending changes and threats by displaying a nostalgia for the harmony of the past. They are constantly repairing what has gone wrong, acting on the basis of their high level of involvement. "Engineers" wish to innovate, with an eye to the future, but do this primarily in a technical-instrumental manner, preferably applying management models taken from business and industry. "Directors", finally, enter into a dialogue with the membership and are aware of social changes and of diversity within the club. They are prepared to learn, but they also want their administrative work for the club to be enjoyable.

The success of sports clubs is closely associated with the strength of the leadership, mainly in the person of the chairman. It is striking that these strong leaders are at the top of the club pyramid, carry out a lot of work and are also able to control virtually everything in the manner they see fit. Our impression is that hardly anything takes place within the club that they are not aware of. In terms of the typology referred to above, most of the chairmen of the "good" clubs interviewed are "handymen" with "director" tendencies. They take customer service into account, value participation (within the limits they set) and communicate a great deal, although often top-down. They are also to a certain extent externally focused. They are excellent organisers and are able to constantly mobilise others and foster commitment among them. Their quality is to be found particularly in their ability to "keep an eye on the shop" and to keep things going. They are the linchpins of their clubs. This is simultaneously their strength and their weakness. After all, the club constantly has to worry about what would happen if they were no longer there. The danger of a major gap opening up if the chairman should suddenly disappear is always present and strikes fear into the hearts of the other club administrators.

The quality of an amateur sports club is ultimately a combination of many factors. There is, for example, a direct interaction between quality and the leadership of the club. A good club executive committee is, almost by definition, one which has managed to effectively regulate the structure and staffing at various levels. Volunteer policy is attuned to what is going on within the club and is in agreement with the club's identity. There is a good mix of paid and voluntary club duties. There is sufficient support within the club as a whole for the level of professionalisation chosen and for the extent of the businesslike approach adopted.

Meijs (1997) speaks of a "type of organisation managed by volunteers" as being essential for a voluntary club. The core volunteers still display commitment but membership apathy is a threat. Volunteer work is changing, whether or not of necessity, from being entirely unpaid, via reimbursement of expenses, towards a salary system. In the literature too, this shift is not infrequently presented in a normative sense as the sole chance many clubs have of surviving: professionalisation is often interpreted as being more businesslike, including having more paid positions, including for those who are intended to actually deliver the sporting performance. The question is to what extent this development clashes with the voluntary nature of sports clubs and whether this course of action is the only viable one. The question is to what extent an equilibrium can be found between the pleasures of the "good old sports club" and the many, greater demands currently made on it both internally and externally. Van den Heuvel & Van der Poel (1999, p.102) remark: "In order to maintain or reinforce their position on the sports market, clubs can engage in product innovation, product differentiation and in providing a greater level of service and customer orientation. The question is whether this can be achieved by a voluntary organisation or whether professionalisation is necessary." This is an extremely pertinent question. The clubs studied have, to a reasonable extent, been able to match their ambitions to the possibilities open to them. Viable clubs are realistic and can to a great extent meet the targets set –with the necessary nuances, it is true (such as a central chairman who occupies too central a position). In other words, the quality of the organisation as a whole fits in with the existing opportunities and restrictions and expresses itself in a certain stability.

Viable clubs at least have their finances in order and do not depend on (casual) external sources of funding. They have co-ordinated any constituent interests with those of the club as a whole and these are accepted by the majority of the members (for example by setting up separate foundations). Most of all, they take account of their members (and the diversity of their members) and have selected the target group and quality (technical, service, social) which they wish to represent. They are generally able to mobilise enough club officials, even though it takes some effort, probably precisely because they value voluntary work and not least because they recognise the strength of identification (with the organisation). Moreover, not everything or everybody is a part of the pyramid: performance (by selected teams) is important but not at all costs. Personal attention and funding are distributed equally across the whole membership.

A recurring topic of discussion, including in viable clubs, is the distribution of work between volunteers and professionals. Meijs (1997, p.47) has produced the following system of categories:
1. An organisation run by volunteers is one in which the aims are drawn up by the volunteers who form the executive committee of the club but with policy-making and policy implementation being in the hands of professionals;
2. In a volunteer-support organisation, aims and policy are formulated primarily by professionals and only a restricted number of executive tasks are carried out by volunteers;

3. In voluntary organisations the aims of the organisation are set and achieved by volunteers, who may be assisted in this by professionals.

Amateur sports clubs belong to the third category, although according to Meijs (1997) many clubs can already be placed in the first category. The question arises of whether the perceived shift towards greater influence on the part of professionals will continue and whether there is or will be a different type of organisation. Applying the terms used by Handy (1988), there is a shift from "mutual support" to "service delivery". In the latter type the accent is more on organisation and organising, and one is dealing with managed organisations (Meijs, 1997, p.49)

What do we find in actual practice? We find a variety of systems ranging from exclusively volunteers to exclusively professionals. In the field of amateur sport we can identify a large number of hybrid types (Meijs, 1997, p.61). What is essential, however, is whether the professionals are contracted to provide support for volunteers or whether they decide what goes on and make use of volunteers as "helpers". This in turn depends to a great extent on what the actual primary process of the club is: does this mainly involve participating in sport in a club context with the accent being on commitment, involvement and identification? Or is it primarily a matter of performance-oriented sport in which the club (whichever one it happens to be) is simply a means, and could just as well be a different club or organisation. To put it in simple terms: is it primarily a question of atmosphere or of performance? One does not need to exclude the other, but there is often a tension – performance versus recreation– within which choices need to be made which directly affect the identity of the club.

Viable clubs, it would seem, are devoted to voluntary work and only make use of professionals when this is essential. The professionals therefore also need to provide support for the volunteers and not vice versa.

11.4 Future: vitalisation

The question of what viable sports clubs are (and will be in the future) is not easy to answer, either on the basis of empirical investigation or a reading of the literature, at least not at a concrete level. Social differentiation, and thus the variety of types of club, is too great. It used to be a relatively simple matter to define a traditional sports club, but "modern" sports clubs are found in a variety of forms, ranging from extremely businesslike and commercial to closed, highly internalised clubs for and belonging only to their "own" members. At some clubs it is sport itself and performance which are central while at others the main thing is in fact socialising, with sport being no more than a means to that end. In addition, in an attempt to differentiate the club from other clubs, the question of the identity and thus of the associated target group or groups will come to play a greater role.

As already indicated, one of the chairmen interviewed stated that the continuity of a club depends on three things: the finances being in good order, recruiting good club officials and identification with the club. The main thing is seemingly maintaining the status quo. Where the clubs studied are concerned, this generally means maintaining the current level. An acknowledgement of the need for more reflection on developments and the need to make choices, as emphasised in the above literature, is seemingly still far off. In any case it does not take place very explicitly. The approach is primarily reactive, adaptive and focused on preservation. There is hardly any sign of a more pro-active attitude, with a vision of the club's future.

It is striking, in contrast to what we might expect on the basis of previous studies and the literature, that in the clubs studied there is no talk of better performance and also not of increases in scale. Quite the contrary: they are in fact more concerned with the core principles of clubs: "of, by and for" the members! They do not aim at implementing a more commercial approach, do not wish to earn money, and do not primarily use club funds to achieve better performance. They are not against better performance but only if it can be achieved on a break-even basis by tapping into other sources of funds. They do not wish to be dependent on sponsors. There is therefore hardly any commercialisation in the case of the clubs studied, and professionalisation (in the sense of appointing paid professionals) is also not very common.

Professionalisation is being implemented, it is true, but not very enthusiastically. It involves mainly secretarial and financial work for which no volunteers can be found any longer. However, many of those interviewed indicate that the club appoints such professionals only if it has been unable to find someone to carry out the work on a voluntary basis.

Where professionalisation is concerned, clubs do expect adequate support from their federation or umbrella organisation. Individual clubs seem at present to have their hands full when it comes to keeping things going. It is perhaps the case that the external demands made on sports clubs are too high, even much too high. Carrying out extensive analysis of the direct environment and the general environment, and the role which sports clubs can and should fulfil in processes of social integration are matters, it would seem, that can only be dealt with by bringing in the assistance of (external) experts from umbrella organisations, federations and (local) authorities. The functions envisaged for sports clubs exceed their capacity. It may well be that society cannot require any more of them.

It is probably already quite an achievement for clubs to adopt a more service-oriented attitude (or wish to do so), to be more aware of the wishes of their members (and of the diversity of those wishes) and to be reasonably able to distribute personal attention and funds across the breadth of their membership. In addition, involvement and identification are still important values for the clubs concerned. With reference to the orientations dealt with in section 2, we can conclude that good clubs are hybrids with features of all the directions mentioned. Besides concerning themselves with identification, they attempt to manage the club more professionally by reinforcing the organisation and improving the service provided. We can identify missionary, professional and more individual customer-oriented features. It is striking that it is still the commercial orientation which is found least frequently.

Conclusion

If we take a general look at the clubs studied and at the literature, we can soon identify a number of themes which are seemingly important for the vitality of a sports club. In the first place everyone agrees that it is more than necessary for sports clubs to see themselves as part of a continually changing context. The continued existence of (traditional) clubs is by no means taken for granted any longer, as a result of social complexity and dynamics, which express themselves as a greater variety of significances in the desire to participate in sport in a certain way, and in more stringent demands made on clubs by the authorities in particular. Even though clubs may in fact wish to remain as closed as possible, they cannot escape analysing their social position. However, it is clear that individual sports clubs are not capable, or are insufficiently capable, of carrying out such analyses. Professionalisation in sport will need to come precisely through the provision of support by external experts. This means that club managers, on the one hand, and associations/umbrella organisations and local authorities on the other, will need to act far more as allies than as ancient enemies who make life difficult for one another. The common interest which they share is, and remains, that of involving as many people as possible in sport in the most pleasurable manner possible. It is no more and no less than that. Lobby groups and centres of expertise can make significant contributions to achieving this.

Secondly, it is necessary to engage in discussion, and ultimately to make choices, with respect to the issue of identity, at both management and club level. The most appropriate way of doing this is probably to engage in open dialogue without the result already being determined beforehand to a large extent. It is essential to recognise that existing power relationships and conflicts of interest within the club may play a major role. The guideline for discussion should be the question of the primary process or the tension between performance and recreation, including the choice of the (specific) target groups which are to be reached. The majority of viable clubs have a clear identity. The necessary choices have been made and/or there is internal discussion of the future direction of the club. The variety of choices both presented and made is great, but the core remains club life and the ability to find enough voluntary club officers.

Thirdly, there is the question –one in fact arising from the previous point– of the optimum type of organisation and structure (in other words, the extent to which the approach is a businesslike one) and the associated policy on volunteer work: the best possible relationship between volunteers (and voluntary tasks) and professionals. It is only after these choices have been made that the issue of financing becomes relevant: dependence on subsidies, sponsoring, the size of the membership fee, payment for club duties and performance, etc. In general viable clubs have decided that their officers should be volunteers as much as possible, precisely in order to continue to emphasise the club character. Any paid staff are brought in to provide support for the volunteers and not to take over from them. It would seem, therefore, that these clubs are wrestling less with their level of dependence on sponsors or with commercialisation in general, than with the area of tension between performance and recreation, including the way personal attention and funds are distributed in particular. If club administrators –acting like true directors– realise that they are not simply dependent upon their context but that they can themselves give active shape to it, sports clubs will benefit considerably.

References

Anthonissen, A. (1997). *Between beercoaster and floppydisk*. Arnhem: NOC*NSF. (in Dutch).

Anthonissen, A. & Boessenkool, A. (1996). *The sport club between tradition and commerce*. Arnhem: NOC*NSF. (in Dutch).

Anthonissen, A. & Boessenkool, J. (1997). Knutselaars en ingenieurs. In: P. Verweel & A. van Dijk (Eds.), *The ladder up downstairs, a psychology of management*. (pp. 82-100). Assen: Van Loghum. (in Dutch)

Anthonissen, A. & J. Boessenkool (1998). *Meanings of Management: Diversity of Managerial Performances in Amateur Sport Organisations*. Utrecht: ISOR. (in Dutch).

Beck,U. (1994). *Risk Society. Towards a new modernity*. London: Sage.

Beckers, T. & Serail, S. (1991). *New relations in sport.* Tilburg: KUB. (in Dutch)

Boessenkool, J. & Jong, A. de (2001). *Sport clubs in the 21st. Century: For and by members?* Arnhem: NOC*NSF. (in Dutch).

Boessenkool, J. Spek, M. van der & Anthonissen, A. (1997). *Soccer clubs and fusions.* Zeist: KNVB. (in Dutch).

Bottenburg, M., Hof, C. van & Oldenboom, E. (1997). *Good, better best: Towards a quality policy in a multiform sport sector.* Amsterdam. Diopter. (in Dutch).

Crum, B. (1991). *About the sportification of society.* Rijswijk: WVC. (in Dutch).

Dekkers, H.T. Mandemaker, P. Stoppelenburg, R. & Ven, R. van de (1989). *Sport clubs in motion.* Tilburg: IVA. (in Dutch).

Gastelaars, M. (1997). *Multiple Human service. A typology of service providing organisations.* Utrecht: SWP. (in Dutch).

Gordon, C. & Babchuk, N. (1959). A Typology of Voluntary Associations. *American Sociological Review,* 24, (1), pp. 22-29.

Hall, S. (1991). *The minimal self and other essays.* Amsterdam: SUA. (in Dutch).

Handy, C. (1988). *Understanding voluntary organizations.* London: Penguin Books.

Hasenfeld, Y. (1983). *Human service organizations.* Englewood Cliffs: Prentice Hall.

Heuvel, M. van den & Poel, H. van der (1999). *Sport in the Netherlands: a policy oriented exploration of the future.* Tilburg: KUB. (in Dutch).

Huls, N. (1992). *Control in the risk society.* Zwolle: Tjeenk Willink. (in Dutch).

Ibsen, B. (1997). *Change in the voluntary sector.* Oslo: ISSA.

Janssens, J. (1996). *The problems of sport clubs.* Arnhem: NOC*NSF. (in Dutch).

Klandermans, D. (1983). *Participation in a social movement. A mobilization campaign.* Amsterdam:VU. (in Dutch).

Knoke, D. & Prensky, E. (1984). What relevance do organizations have for voluntary organizations. *Social Science Quarterly,* (2), pp.

Kruithof, C. (1973). *The collective promotion in a social society.* Brussel: Edition l'Université. (in Dutch).

Laporte, W., Bollaert, L., Knop, P. De & Taks, M. (1997). *Voluntary work in a changing sport world.* Brussel: Vubpress. (in Dutch).

Lucassen, J.M.H. (1987). *Making work of sport.* Rijswerk: WVC. (in Dutch).

Lucassen, J.M.H. & Hoogendam, A. (1998). Time out. In: J. Steenbergen, A.J. Buisman, P. De Knop & J.M.H. Lucassen (Eds), *Waarden en normen in de sport* (pp. 45-66). Houten: Bohn Stafleu Van Loghem. (in Dutch).

Meys, L. (1997). *Management of voluntary organisations.* Utrecht: NOV publicaties. (in Dutch).

Michels, R. (1959). *Political parties. A social study of the oligarchical tendencies of modern democracy.* New York: DOVER.

Munster, O. van, Berg, E. van den & Veen, A. van der (1996). *The future of the midfield.* Den Haag: Delwiel.

Oldenboom, E., Hopstaken, P. & Meer, F. van der (1996). *The national spending in sport.* Amsterdam: SEO-publicatie. (in Dutch).

Pearce, J. (1993). *Volunteers. The organizational behavior of unpaid workers.* London.

Rubingh, B. & H. Westerbeek (1992). *Management of sport clubs. Spel en Sport,* (1), pp. 2-7. (in Dutch).

SCR (1994). *Social Cultural Rapport.* Den Haag: VUGA. (in Dutch).

Sills, D. (1968). *Voluntary Organizations. Instruments and Object of Change Human Organization.*

Steenbergen, J. & Tamboer, J.W.I. (1998). The double character of sport: Conceptual dynamics. In: J. Steenbergen, A.J. Buisman, P. De Knop & J.M.H. Lucassen (Eds.), *Waarden en normen in de sport* (pp. 69-95). Houten: Bohn Stafleu Van Loghum. (in Dutch).

Terp (1983). *Professionalization in sport*. Amersfoort. (in Dutch).

Verstegen, R., Andriessen, J. & Begeer, J. (1983). *Many hands make work light*. Tilburg: IVA. (in Dutch).

Visser, J. & Smid, G. (1979). *Union work must be learned*. Amsterdam: SUA. (in Dutch).

VWS/CBM/DSP (2001). *Sport participation in four districts in the Netherlands* (in press). Den Haag. (in Dutch).

12 SOCIAL CONSTRAINTS IN COMMUNICATION: THE CONNECTION BETWEEN FRAMES AND CUES

Anton Anthonissen, Jeroen Vermeulen & Paul Verweel

Introduction

Amateur sportclubs in the Netherlands increasingly ask for external advice for the problems they are faced with. These problems concern managerial questions such as how to get club members to participate in all kinds of organisational activities, how to deal with professionalisation, how to deal with increasing multi-cultural diversity within the club etc.. In order to help managers of sport clubs to act on these questions, support programs have been set up by, amongst others, sport associations and local government. The advice and/or support that is offered is often seen in an instrumental way, as concrete means to an unambiguous end. In this contribution to the book, however, we will look at the process of giving and receiving advice as a form of communication with its own dynamic of constructing shared meaning about what is seen as problematic for the sport clubs. We will offer analyses of two communicative interactions between a club offical of the footbalclub WIK ("Willen Is Kunnen" – If You Want It Enough, You Can Do It") and a support worker. These interactions will illustrate that the dominant, and highly instrumental, sender-receiver model of communication is inadequate for understanding the complexities of the process. Instead we will propose to study these communicative processes form the perspective of sense-making (Weick, 1995). This perspective will lead us (and hopefully also those involved in the communicative interactions themselves) to reflect on the mutual assumptions and values that guide and constrain the communication between support workers and club officials.

The WIK Football Club would like to involve more parents in its activities. The rapid increase in the number of juvenile members, particularly from ethnic minorities, means that there are not enough club officials to supervise and train the teams and to arrange matches. Various attempts to recruit the parents of the young ethnic minority players have been unsuccessful. Something has to be done about communication, and the club has approached the municipality for support. As an experiment the municipality has called in a social work organisation with expertise and experience in the field of inter-cultural communication. A professional (social) support worker, himself a member of an ethnic minority, has been deployed to assist the club. The Moroccan support worker and the Dutch club official have arranged a number of meetings to discuss the approach they will take. This is an excerpt from one of their discussions (SW = support worker, CO = club official):

SW What do you think of an information evening for everybody? Or perhaps a separate one for Moroccan parents and one for Turkish parents, so as to deliberately correct the image they have of clubs? I mean something on the lines of "Listen, everybody, these are the problems. And this is your club too". The idea would be to formulate a goal and then we would look at how we fill in the details of what we do that evening.

CO We already tried that and nobody turned up ... and if you get people to do something and see that there is no succession [he means follow-up] ... there first has to be somebody who succeeds things [he means follows up things]...

SW OK, but I'd like to hear what you think it could lead to ...

CO Well, when we did it last time there was no succession and it didn't lead to anything ...

SW I'm afraid that you didn't do much then to correct the image they have of clubs ... I'd like to try myself to see whether I can correct that image ... with the club's co-operation, of course ... but if you say you've already done it, then there's no point in trying it again.

CO No, no, that's not how it works ... because even if we've tried it once already we still have to keep trying.

SW I can't guarantee success ... but I do know that we can organise a good information evening ... we'll just phone people and get them to agree to come.

CO You can try to change the image at an evening like that, but if they get enthusiastic about the club then there has to be somebody who keeps an eye on them and if you don't have somebody like that then it'll all just collapse again

SW We'll come back to that later ...

CO Well, I'm looking for priorities ...

SW I know what you mean ... but you seem to be sceptical ... I'll come to your idea in a minute because when we've done something about the image, we can perhaps set up a working party to look into it (succession) ... given that I'm Moroccan, we can also see whether somebody can be made available to run the working party ... that kind of thing ... but I know that the question of the image first has to be corrected ...

CO Well, we have to do both ... we also have to recruit people

SW As regards the capacity ..., I don't have as many hours available as I thought; we can start with the information evening or recruit immediately and see how many then come ...

CO Well, recruiting people is so difficult ... I've got a list and if I write down the people we really need than it comes to about 44 ...

SW Oh, then it's difficult for me to do anything about the problem.

CO Yes, I know that you can't do it by yourself in four hours a week.

SW Well, I don't even have four hours, I've only got 2 _ hours for two clubs.

CO So it's not possible then.

SW Its pretty much the time I spend on discussions like this, the rest needs to happen ... perhaps the expectations are ... but OK, I do want to help ... we will in any case need to see what we can do.

This excerpt indicates the difficult position in which a lot of club officials, who are confontated with the process of inter-culturalisation and individualisation find themselves in the Netherlands. The idea on which Dutch clubs and associations are based is that they run themselves (NOC*NSF, 1999). These clubs were set up on the basis of membership fees and of members doing the work themselves. The favourable system of subsidies compared to those in neighbouring countries, and the low rents for high-quality premises, together with the compartmentalisation of society along religious and ideological lines, led to the setting up of a large number of clubs and associations. However, various changes in society now mean that the existing ties between people are becoming weaker, in other words they are determined less by people's socio-cultural background and they have therefore become less unconditional. Clubs say they are facing problems as regards participation by club members (or their parents). They don't come to meetings. They sometimes don't pay their membership fee. They no longer automatically become the organiser of their child's team (Anthonissen & Boessenkool, 1998). Club officials have long felt that they were on their own in facing these problems, but during the past five years – with initiatives from the NOC*NSF and financing from local and central government – various club support projects have been started. These provide club officials with support by professionals with expertise in sport or financing and the ability to find tailor-made solutions to problems of organisation and management (NOC*NSF, 2000). Support in the area of socio-cultural issues is only provided on an incidental basis because of the basic principle that "clubs will run themselves". The support featuring in the excerpt just quoted does however focus on the socio-cultural side of organising a club.

12.1 The complexity of communication patterns

This excerpt shows two people looking for possible solutions to the club's problem. The club official gives vent to his frustration. He has already made so many efforts and nothing has helped ("nobody turned up", "there is no succession [i.e. follow-up]"). The support worker has a clear idea, namely that the image of clubs amongst minorities must be altered. An information evening needs to be arranged. He doesn't have much time but his intentions are good ("we will in any case need to see what we can do").

The discussion shows that the official's urge to act and the support worker's good will are the basis for communication. There is, however, no real dialogue, and each of those involved only looks at matters from his own perspective. The official is looking for parents ("see if we can recruit people"). He is also in a hurry, because once again he will not have enough team organisers for the impending tournament. The support worker wants a working party to be set up ("see whether somebody can be made available"). so as to create a base of support within the club. The club official ignores the statement of the support worker that he –as a Moroccan– is an expert on minority issues ("given that I'm Moroccan"). The discussion ends inconclusively ("see what we can do").

If we take a literal look at the communication in the excerpt, it becomes clear how complex communication patterns are. That complexity is not only to be found in this excerpt but it also determines what happens in many discussions. The excerpt illustrates that people can be both extremely flexible and at the same time inflexible. On the one hand the support worker – without interrupting – realises that the official has made a slip of the tongue (he uses the Dutch word opvolging [succession] instead of vervolg [follow-up]) and the official, for his part, understands the shaky Dutch grammar of the support worker. On the other hand the two are not able to enter into a true exchange of ideas. Each seems to be imprisoned within his own "story". The story of "establishing an image by means of an information evening" is at odds with the story of "get parents involved by recruiting them". Moreover, both persons are influenced by the context from which they speak. The club official thinks in terms of identification and involvement as the central values of a club, membership of which is voluntary. The members ought to participate and if they do not do so they must be called upon to do so. When he has a problem he takes immediate action and time hardly plays a role. The support worker thinks in terms of social work and looks for the need behind the question. It is not a matter of participation but of image. According to the values and norms which determine professional thinking within social work organisations, wrong images can be combated by providing information, and information is provided at information evenings. He works in terms of hours and not of problems.

This example makes clear that communication relates not only to individuals but also to their contexts, contexts in which frames of reference such as professionalism and voluntary involvement, along with all the associated value judgements and systems of norms, play a dominant role in the way the two men act. Although the deployment of professional expertise seems to promise a functional solution (greater knowledge), the conflict between professional and voluntary frames in fact causes a communication problem. In order to better understand the communication between club officials/members on the one hand and professional support workers (in this case social workers) on the other, we will first deal with the theoretical background.

12.2 Communication and making sense

Watzlawick (1993) believes that communication processes can be understood as two systems. People can communicate both via images and digitally. Language (words) enables us to provide a digital description of what we observe and intend to tell our interlocutor about. It is clear from the excerpt that those involved are able to get one another to share such terms as "recruit" and "information evening" and then to determine in more detail what the specific content of those terms is. But communication also takes place by means of images, such as those of "social worker" and "club official" or "member of a minority" and "native Dutch person", which are general abstractions. The terms are not exact but evoke a system of associations and thus fulfil a general function. This communication makes it possible for people to understand one another in the context of the discussion despite the fact that they use the wrong words ("succession" instead of "follow-up") or produce ungrammatical sentences. The communication between an ethnic minority support worker and a native Dutch club official therefore requires attention to be paid both to the shared digital knowledge and familiarity of words, and to the underlying language of images which are determined by the specific circumstances from which the two men operate.

We can make a second theoretical observation about the manner of communication. The theory of the sender (who says something) and the receiver (who hears something) is part of social science which most researchers have left far behind. Our example shows however that in practice it often dominates the way in which a discussion is organised. We see two senders and at the same time two receivers, who are in fact receiving themselves. In the present excerpt, no interaction or communication takes place. Theory says that communication must be viewed as an interactive system in which information sources, messages, information channels and opportunities for reception, are co-ordinated with one another (Berlo, 1960). We will not deal with all the criticism which can be levelled at this position (Ruler, 1996) but merely point out that in the case of the encounter between the club official and the support worker we need to focus not only on the digital reproduction of the conversation but also specifically on the information channels, information sources, messages and opportunities for reception which have been put forward. In fact, we are not dealing with "worlds" which are familiar with one another. We are dealing with a new encounter (between social work and sports clubs) in which a great deal of use is made of the language of images, and there is little shared experience or familiarity with one another's digital knowledge.

This chapter on values and norms within communication processes focuses primarily on the underlying images which the participants maintain and the inter-personal relationship which occurs in the course of this encounter, which is a new one for both parties (both persons and both types of work). We will deal with the underlying mechanisms dominating the communication between the two types of work, with the way in which the participants are therefore influenced in the course of the communication, and with how the participants are able to achieve results by communicating these underlying images, values and norms.

Before returning to the club manager and the support worker, we wish to associate this theory of communication with theories of sense-making. The communication between the persons involved is, after all, aimed at exchanging meanings and influencing the other's sense-making. Sense-making is a process of communication, while in communication shared meanings are exchanged as language (Watzlawick, 1993).

12.3 Sense-making in organisations

Weick (1995) makes a connection between the meanings which are used and the way in which people communicate within organisations. During the organising process existing meanings are used to "place" new experiences. In the way in which they assign meanings to new experiences, sports clubs and their officials focus on organising people who are of like mind. Martin (1992) refers in this context to the integration perspective of organising. Internationalisation, individualisation and multi-culturalism have led to the breakdown of the compartmentalised system and have thus eroded this concept. Martin (1992) speaks in this case of processes of differentiation (different groups within associations) and fragmentation (individual differences between members). Many officials still operate on the basis of their historically determined integration perspective, in which social cohesion is based on common values and norms which, in the area of sport, mean that the main thing for the club and each individual member is organisation "of, by and for" the members. The assumption that cohesion means agreement on common values and norms can ironically be counter-productive for cohesion. Du Gay (1996) sees this assumption as an ideological projection in which the perspective of the club management is confirmed as the dominant and desirable perspective. The opinions of other people are welcome as long as they reinforce the perspective of the club management. We also find this in a certain sense in the discussion between the club official and the support worker. Everything is fine as long as parents are recruited. We assume, however, that cohesion contains elements of integration, differentiation and fragmentation that are more like forces working alongside and through one another in an organisation and in society than categories that can be used to describe organisations. In order to involve parents in the club, more is therefore necessary than to merely offer them voluntary work from the perspective of the club official and then to say that that is because the club is there for everybody because they are all members! It is precisely this common value approach which has led to the shortage of officials because the differentiated view of parents who come from minorities, and the fragmenting view of native Dutch parents cannot be organised on the basis of this kind of integral ideology of club organisation.

12.4 Frames and communication

Members of organisations try to make sense of their experiences, and that is what our two actors are doing. However, they both live in different organisational settings and hold different beliefs. Verweel & David (1995) point to the creation and existence of cultural regimes in organisations and societies that are based on these beliefs and settings. Cultural (and political) regimes form a frame for interpretation that continually mediates our relationship with reality. The frame includes perceptions of the world outside the organisation, of members' satisfaction, and of the qualities of our own organisation and of ourselves. A frame gives meaning to perceptions and determines communication. Perceptions, communication and the associated actions are therefore mediated by our own frames of meaning. In essence reality consists of a variety of frames people use when making sense of their experiences. Weick (1995) refers to these experiences/events as cues. Frames and cues can be thought of as vocabularies in which words that are relatively abstract (frames) include and point to other less abstract words (cues) that come to make sense in the context created by the more inclusive words. We can see the same relationship here as that between image and digital language (Watzlawick, 1993).

In communication we are dealing, therefore, with the way in which the link between frames and cues, or between image and digital language, is made either explicitly or implicitly, by those involved in relationships. As long as mutual understanding of the way interlocutors make use of this link is missing, there is no communication, as is shown by our example (Gumperz, 1982).

In communication a "connection" is always created between a frame and a cue. (Weick, 1995, p.110). This does not mean that there are no links between the past and the present; on the contrary, they are connected. Frames tend to be moments of past socialisation and cues tend to be the present moment of experience. Meaning is created when individuals can construct a relationship between these two moments. "This means that the content of sense-making is to be found in the frames and categories [regimes] that summarise past experience, in the cues and labels that snare specific present moments of experience, and in the way these two settings of experience are connected" (ibid., p.111). The understanding of new experiences is "pre-structured" by the existing meanings and the existing regimes (e.g. Du Gay 1997).

Weick (1995) argues that meanings are born in interaction; when they are expressed in words they attain the dimension of language and can then be discussed. Words impose labels on subject matters and form part of a discourse. A discourse is everything said, written and conveyed about a particular topic. Although there is a dominant discourse, there are always alternative discourses, most of which are usually marginalised. The dominant discourse reflects or creates a dominant ideology, and is presented as common sense and obvious (hegemonic). Discourses are frames or systems of meanings and are indistinguishable from social practices; in other words, discourses evolve from practices or actions and discourses provide words and images that facilitate practices (Tolson, 1996). Actions or practices, therefore, do not only follow words. Sense-making is an active and continuous process in which words and actions or practices constitute (and reconstitute) each other. Changing practices therefore requires changing the meaning of words. Creating new definitions requires (inter)action.

This theoretical approach provides a framework for looking at communication as a sense-making process and also a strategy which van be involved in communication processes. This means that when we look at communication processes we not only have to listen to individual stories and to the inter-subjective aspects, but we also need to look at the levels of meaning assigned in the (sports) organisation and in society. Frames, cues and connections occur not only at the subjective and interactive level but assume a broader meaningful context in the process of communication, in other words, they assume an actor in context (Anthonissen & Boessenkool 1998). During communication processes, people (actors) frequently make use of suppositions which are significant from the perspective of the wider context in which they function. Taking account of the assumptions of "the other" can make visible a connection between frame and cue, creating room for action. In order to investigate this process further we will use an excerpt from another conversation between the club official and the support worker. By now, things are a few months down the road and there have been a number of discussions, without any action being taken.

Excerpt 2:
SW I mentioned a number of possible reasons why Moroccan and Turkish parents are not involved and I made a number of suggestions for dealing with the problems that [THIS?] creates for the club.
CO Yes, it was clear and the way you explained things made clear that we mustn't set out sights too high.
SW The biggest problem has to do with the involvement on the part of the parents.
CO Yes, that's the point ... what you said last time got me thinking ... your first point in this memo is expectations ... some parents think that people are paid for working within the club ... and that they have to do it too ... well, I think it would already go a long way if we tried to get everybody to understand how the club is organised ... that it's a question of volunteers and that you can't even run the club at all without parents, and that goes for all the parents.
SW Yes, we have to correct that wrong image.

CO And we can do that in both directions, of course ... because perhaps parents from minorities also have perfectly good reasons for not driving children to matches or going to matches at all, whereas we think that they don't give a damn.

SW To correct that image we need to think of something like an information meeting intended to correct ideas about the club ...

CO Yes, and then we can perhaps use audio-visual material to give an idea of a club.

SW Yes, but let's be sure that it then doesn't become a project within a project –let's look at what is possible and feasible in this area.

CO Yes, I agree, let's restrict ourselves to organising an information evening and working out the details of that.

SW If it's going to be an information evening, we can deal with it with a traditional invitation letter, but you can also invite people in a different way ... my suggestion is ... Saturday is always a difficult day for me, but I could be there on a Wednesday, but perhaps that's a problem for the parents ... let's choose a date.

CO You mean a Saturday evening.

SW Well, preferably during the day ... then we can talk to the children too.

CO You mean talk to the children on a Saturday afternoon.

SW Well, talk to the children and give them the letter to take home ... but if you have a different suggestion.

CO Well, I don't know ... because the children are spread out over the course of the day ... you don't get them all in the canteen at the same time and I don't know whether you can reach them all.

SW Well, perhaps per group ... each group has an organiser and you arrange with the children that they have to tell their parents and you give them a letter to take home.

CO Yes, it's a good idea to send a letter too...

SW Yes, and we can get it translated ... you need to tell them that something important is happening ... you have to dramatise it and shock them: "We've got a problem" –that's how it works in some cultures ...

CO (laughs) Yes, we want it to work, so if you think that's what we need to do ... we'll do that.

SW Yes, the end justifies the means ... we'll tell the children on Wednesday and again on Saturday and so on ... but Saturday is sometimes difficult for the parents.

CO   Well, I was thinking more of an evening during the week ... a Friday evening, for example ... that's the best evening ... we had a meeting of members on a Friday recently and that's when the seniors train ... and we never had so many people.

SW   I was thinking more of a Wednesday evening, for example.

CO   The children would be there, yes, but still ... I think Friday evening would be a good idea and then approach it on several fronts, with a letter, an announcement in the club magazine, tell the children during the training sessions, and then have the organisers tell them again on Saturday.

SW   Well then, I think a Friday evening is in fact the best ... on Saturday we usually visit family or go away and on Friday it's like "I don't need to work tomorrow", so it can be Friday.

12.5 Communication about assumptions

Excerpt 2 consists of an entirely different type of discussion between the same two people. Instead of two senders, each sending his own story without regard to whether or not it is being received, what we have here is a dialogue. We might say that the conversation starts to make sense. Why is that?

The two interlocutors are now able not only to absorb information provided by the other into their own frame but also to go in search of the other person's frame. "What you said last time got me thinking" means that the club official is willing and able to put himself into the social worker's frame. He has not just been thinking. He has thought beyond the confines of his own frame and has gone in search of the other person's assumptions. In the first conversation he only raised objections from within his own frame and context, but now he is capable of following the other person. We see the same phenomenon where setting the date is concerned. Arguments presented by the other person are considered on the basis of his experience and interpretation framework. The Moroccan background of the support worker, for example, is now turned into a productive factor. The support worker is able to contribute this knowledge and experience and the club official does not ignore it but confirms it: "We want it to work, so if you think that's the thing to do ... [dramatisation and giving people a shock as part of Moroccan culture] we'll do that ."

Ultimately the time ceases to play a role for the paid professional and he is prepared to discuss giving up his free Friday evening

In terms of our theoretical approach, the point is that the discussion produces concrete action. This is not because there is the same integrated interpretation framework but because of their shared experience during the past few weeks (when nothing happened other than talk), the two interlocutors are now able to go in search of one another's frame, whether or not it is implicit. From that position they are not only better able to communicate with one another, but even dare to investigate their own frame and put it forward for discussion.

What one notices is what is no longer said. The club official is now prepared to set aside his belief in direct recruitment. The professional social worker no longer immediately counts the hours involved and the unfavourable times at which he will need to work. What one also notices is the way they accept one another's knowledge of the situation of the parents and the children. In the first excerpt there was a certain amount of competition as to who was more knowledgeable, but now each contributes his knowledge to complement that of the other. The support worker and the club official each now opens his own social and work horizon and enters into that of the other. Events (in this case the fact that months have gone by without the information evening taken place) are now placed both in one's own interpretation framework and in that of the interlocutor, and questions are even asked about the interpretation framework of the other person rather than simply repeating the same statement, or at most making one's own frame explicit. Not only is there now a worthwhile discussion but seemingly the barriers to taking action have now also been removed.

12.6 Demand-oriented work within sports organisations

The two men in the excerpts represent the increased interaction between clubs and the context in which they operate. The proud but disappointed club official is prepared to seek help from the world outside the club in order to discuss his internal problems regarding volunteers. In the world outside, there is a growing supply of existing and new professional support workers whose job it is to assist club officials and their clubs. Umbrella organisations in the area of sports such as NOC*NSF attempt to convince the support workers that traditional methods of assisting clubs and associations are no longer sufficient. The situation of the clubs demands a tailor-made approach in which the support process, in other words communication, is at least as important as the tangible results. The new professional credo for support is that it should be provided in a demand-oriented manner. The demand expressed by the club official should be the starting point.

The presented excerpts - which is only two among thousands – shows that working in a demand-oriented manner is no easy matter. The club official wants to recruit parents, but from the perspective of his profession the support worker believes that the club's image must first be discussed. The club thinks in terms of problems and the professional thinks in terms of hours. The club wants more people to roll up their sleeves and get down to work and the professional wants reflection on the basic principles. The club has a bureaucratic structure –an eroded one which is no longer effective– of management boards, youth management boards, committees and general meetings of members. The professional must give a bureaucratic account of his work in variables of input, throughput and output. The social work foundation for which he works is required to show the body which funds it (the municipality) that it is effective, and the club official wants only unconditional help from the same funding body. In short, we are dealing with a large number of conflicting processes which do not make communication easy.

The most important mistake made in communication between service providers and organisations is not to discuss these differences. In other words, to discuss them solely from the point of view of what one perceives as being impossible, as we saw in the first excerpt. Another mistake is to think linearly about increasing understanding within the process of communication. One cannot trust that after a number of processes (such as those in excerpt 1) have been discussed that the processes apparent in excerpt 2 will automatically take effect. Research has shown that in a large number of cases the processes apparent in excerpt 1 continue to operate, so that the process of providing support fizzles out (Anthonissen & Van Eekeren, 2000). There is more likelihood of the automatic processes found in excerpt 2 failing to operate than of their operating because there is in most communication no reflection on frames, and the parties think and act even more than before on the assumption that their own frame is "right". We therefore argue that a request for support is primarily a request for communication. Communication cannot however be taken for granted during a conversation; rather, it is a goal –one in which both the parties involved must share their contexts, frames and experience with respect to a given issue.

12.7 Good practices

Communication in the context of support for clubs and associations requires one to consider both functional and social aspects of the club's demand in the relationship with the club's officials. The problems currently facing clubs and associations cannot be solved by introducing new professional recruitment and/or marketing techniques into an existing culture of voluntary work. Above all, the "old social relationships" are not capable (or are no longer capable) of operating without new functional adaptations. Support workers need to realise that in their social relationship with club officials this consciousness must be transformed into communication. They also need to understand that much of their own action is embedded in applications outside volunteer-run sports clubs, and that their own actions must therefore again be questioned and adapted.

We have seen that the communication and the relationship between the club official and the support worker are influenced by the different cultures of the organisations involved, in which different attitudes or values and norms apply over the course of time, and professionalism applies when functionality is concerned. We have also seen that the two sectors have hard technical or instrumental frames where organisational principles are concerned. Finally, there is the issue for which support is to be provided. In fact, all these functional aspects require communication. Besides the influence that organisational context-/culture and professionalism/voluntary approaches have on these aspects they also influence the social relationship between the support worker and the club official. We have indicated that it is important for both the functional result and the social relationship that each party is able to empathise with the frames of the other, and to call its own frames into question without it being necessary to abandon its own views.

The absolute pre-condition for communication is that each partner should work to acquire shared experience on the basis of its own interests, views and context. It is precisely by acquiring shared experience that a foundation can be laid for investigating and sharing one another's assumptions. This requires one to empathise with the points of view and context of the other party, both in one's official or professional capacity and as an individual. Even working together for months to organise an information evening, or to start recruiting, without being successful can produce this kind of shared experience. The dialogue between the professional and the voluntary frame requires time and reflection (Schon, 1983; Vermeulen, 1997). Anyone who believes that it can be done without time and reflection will waste a lot of time and will only achieve superficial results. Organising sports clubs assumes commitment and responsibility. That involvement is not only commitment to the "cause" but also specifically to the individuals concerned. Supporting the cause necessarily also means (critically) supporting the individual. The responsibility for this runs not only from the support worker to the club official but also vice versa. It is ultimately given shape in the communicative relationship. Communication is therefore a social and relational issue rather than a technical and financial one. In order to meet these pre-conditions when providing support for clubs and associations, a considerable amount of work still has to be done – including all the necessary theoretical and empirical knowledge provided by this study – if support workers and club officials wish to get along with one another.

References

Anthonissen, A. & Boessenkool, J. (1998). *Meanings of Management: Diversity of Managerial Performances in Amateur Sport Organisations*. Utrecht: ISOR. (in Dutch).

Anthonissen, A. & Eekeren, F. van (2000). *Inter-culturalisation: New Chances in Sports*. Utrecht: Service Sport and Recreation of the Municipality Utrecht. (in Dutch).

Berlo, D.K. (1960). *The process of Communication*, New York: Holt, Rinehart and Winston.

Du Gay, P.& Hall, S. (Ed/1996). *Question of Cultural Identity*. London Sage,

Du Gay, P. (Ed./1997). *Doing Cultural Studies*. London: Sage.

Gumperz, J.J. (1982). *Discourse Strategies*. Cambridge: Cambridge University Press.

Martin, J. (1992). *Cultures in Organisations: Three Perspectives*. New York: Oxford University Press.

NOC*NSF (1999). *Vision on Healthy Sport clubs in 2015 (concept)*. Arnhem: NOC*NSF, (in Dutch).

NOC*NSF (2000). *Reasearch on the Sport infrastructure (SPIN)*. Arnhem: NOC*NSF (in Dutch).

Ruler, B. van (1996). *Communication management in the Netherlands*. Bohn Stafleu Van Loghum. Houten. (in Dutch).

Schon, D.A. (1983). *The Reflexive Practioner. How Professionals Think in Action*. London: Basic Books.

Tolson, A. (1996). *Mediations: Text and Discourse in Media Studies*. Arnold Publishing Co.

Vermeulen, J. (1997). Professional Practice as Language Practice. In: A. van Dijk & P. Verweel (Eds.), *The Ladder Up Downstairs: A Psychology of Management*. Assen: Van Gorcum. (in Dutch).

Verweel, P. & David, K. (1995). *Hidden Dimensions: Culture and Power in Mergers*. Utrecht: SWP. (in Dutch).

Watzlawick, P. (1993). *Pragmatic Aspects of Human Communication*. Houten: Bohn/Stafleu/van Loghum. (in Dutch).

Weick, K. (1995). *Sense making in Organizations*. London: Sage Publications.

13 'I WAS A MAN AMONG MEN': MEANINGS COACHES GIVE TO GENDER

Annelies Knoppers

Introduction

The construction of gender has changed a great deal in the last thirty years, especially in the paid work force due to the feminist movement and to economic forces. Women have entered all occupations with possibly the only exception that of priest in the Roman Catholic church. In addition, men are entering previously all-female occupations such as nursing and child care. Whereas household and child rearing tasks used to be largely the responsibility of women, the number of hours men devote to these tasks has increased. Thus it may seem that we need to pay little attention to the emancipation of women and subsequently to the topic of gender.

There are however statistics about the emancipation of women and men that reveal a different picture (Emancipation in numbers, 1995; Equality, 1999). Most women still hit a glass ceiling in their attempts to reach the higher positions of leadership. The number of women in top executive positions is still relatively low (Vinnicombe & Harris, 2000). Women still spend almost twice as much time on care-related tasks than men do. Dutch women with paid jobs spend twice (16.4 hours) as much time per week on tasks related to the home than men (8.4 hours) with paid work (Equality, 1999).

The statistics about sport also show progress and stagnation (Emancipatieraad, 1997). Women comprise about half the participants in sport. A third of the athletes involved in competitive sport are women. Women occupy fewer positions of leadership in Dutch sport organizations (10.3%) than in other voluntary organizations (20.4%) including those associated with leisure activities (Emancipatieraad, 1997). Only 9% of the sport managers and 11 - 18% of the certified coaches of women's and men's teams are women (Emancipatieraad, 1997; Stol, 1995). This percentage varies by sport ranging from 50% for swimming and diving to less than 1% in football/soccer. It is obvious, given the number of female athletes, that more women should or could be coaching than are now doing so. Various programs and initiatives have been undertaken by sport organizations and federations and by the government to explore the under-representation of women coaches. One of these was a three-year study that looked at the way coaches give meaning to gender and to the culture in which they coach (Knoppers & Bouman, 1996, 1998). In this chapter I report on some of the findings of this study and explore the extent to which they may be helpful in explaining the gender imbalance in coaching. I do so within the context of Connell's theory about the structure of gender (see chapter 9 of this book).

13.1 The coaching study

Certified coaches who were coaching in one of ten sports (handball, korfball, volleyball, hockey, football/soccer, basketball, swimming, tennis, athletics and cycling) were involved in the study. The sports were chosen based on the gender ratio of the number of registered athletes so that a variation of these ratios could be included in the study. The chosen sports had gender ratios that ranged from high to medium (korfball, handball, swimming, tennis, volleyball, hockey) to low (football/soccer, basketball, athletics, cycling). The samples of coaches in each sport were chosen based on the number of certified women coaches to ensure that the percentage of women and men coaches would be similar. This meant that sample size varied from sport to sport as the number of men that was randomly sampled per sport was based on the number of certified women in that sport.

Questionnaires were sent to 1756 coaches of whom 720 coaches returned usable questionnaires (41%). A little more than half (57.2%) of the respondents were men; 42.8% were women. The questionnaires, consisting of closed and open questions, focused on the background of the respondents, their sport history, and their views on coaching and on gender. Extensive reports on the methodology, the data analyses and the results can be found in Knoppers & Bouman (1996, 1998). In this chapter I will primarily use the responses of the 'majority' to describe the way they constructed gender and sport.

The coaches who participated in the study were on the average 34 years old. Most of the coaches had graduated from a professional school. The majority had received a degree either in education (teaching) or in administration/ management. Most of the coaches involved in this study were volunteer coaches. A third of the men and a quarter of the women received some renumeration for their work because they had acquired a high level certificate. All coaches who returned questionnaires were asked to participate in an interview. Four women and four men (matched on age, household configuration and sport experience) were then chosen from each sport for in-depth interviews. These interviews were used to explore issues that had emerged from the results of the questionnaire.

In this chapter I place some of the findings within the context of Connell's theory about the structure of gender (see chapter 9 in this book). Connell (1987, 1995, 1998) argues that the gender order is dynamic and constantly reinforced and challenged. He cites three (overlapping) sub-structures of cultural practices that reconstruct, challenge and reinforce hegemonic masculinity: emotional relations (patterns of sexuality), power relations (modes of social control), and the division of labor. I will look at each of these sub-structures as they exist in Dutch sport as constructed and construed by the coaches, and the way these substructures sustain and/or challenge the current gender order.

13.2 Emotional relations: Patterns of sexuality

As Knoppers & Elling show elsewhere in this book (chapter 9), Connell views heterosexuality as a key factor in the construction of sport and hegemonic masculinity. It is embedded in the division of labor and in power relations. I will discuss homophobia/heterosexism and sexual harassment as examples of how patterns of sexuality can sustain hegemonic masculinity. In several analyses using Connell's three substructures, sexual harassment is discussed under relations of power (e.g. McKay, 1997; 1999). I however have chosen to place it under patterns of sexuality to emphasize its sexual component. Sexual harassment is not solely an issue of harassment based on power but also of sexuality as the discussion will show.

13.2.1 Homophobia and heterosexism

Patterns of sexuality refer to the presence/absence of homophobia and heterosexism (Connell, 1985, 1995). Although the scholarly literature documents the explicit presence of homophobic behavior in sport (e.g. Cahn, 1994; Griffin, 1998) there was little evidence of it in the comments made by the coaches who participated in this research study. In part this may be a reflection of the position of gays and lesbians in Dutch society. Yet other research (Hekma, 1994) shows that homophobia does occur in Dutch sport, and that the prevailing idea about the visibility of gays and lesbians in sport is 'you can be it but don't show it.' In our study we did not explicitly address this issue with the coaches but waited to see if they would bring it up.

Most of the coaches had a partner of the other sex. The subject of sexuality rarely came up explicitly although lesbians were mentioned several times. Two women came out as lesbian in the interviews by talking about their partner. Gay masculinities were completely invisible in the entire study. In other words, the topic of homosexuality in sport was noticeable due to the silence surrounding it. Possibly too there is a difference in the discursive silence about lesbians and that about gays (Cahn, 1994; Griffin, 1998; Pronger, 1990). Further studies are needed that look at how coaches construct sexuality and sexual relations. At this point it is difficult to make conclusions about the extent to which implicit homophobia existed among the coaches who participated in our study.

In contrast to the lack of comments that might be interpreted as anti-gay, heterosexism was evident in various implicit ways. Sexual harassment was defined by the coaches as a male-female problem excluding the possibility of same- sex sexual harassment. Although some of the comments made by coaches indicated that lesbian athletes were valued because of their 'male-like mentality', the concern was often expressed that having lesbians on a team could wreak havoc if they had romantic relationships with each other. Interestingly, this concern about the possible impact romantic relationships could have on a team did not extend to korfball (men and women) or soccer (mixed at the youth level). Korfball was constantly praised for being a 'family' sport where husband and wife could play on the same team.

13.2.2 Sexual harassment

McKay (1999), in a study of Canadian sport managers, found that sexual harassment is often seen as the 'normal' behavior of men. Women who are associated with emphasized femininity are often assumed to be willing to accommodate men. If women are not willing, they are often held responsible for setting the boundaries. Sexual harassment is often framed as a power issue in the scholarly feminist literature (e.g. McKay, 1997; Tomlinson & Yorganci, 1997; Wise & Stanley, 1987). Those with little or less power are expected to be receptive to sexual overtures and to ignore sexist comments and jokes from those in higher positions. The research on Dutch coaches suggests that the way sexual harassment works in the sport context, varies. Women coaches who actually named and reported sexual harassment said they were harassed by club managers, sponsors, male coaches, fathers, older male athletes and/or by male students (tennis). In other words they were not only harassed by someone who had more power because of his occupational position but also because of his gender. Their status as 'coach' did not protect them.

Most coaches did not classify sexist and misogynist comments as incidents of sexual harassment but considered them 'normal' behavior for the sport setting.[1] A woman coach, for example, reported being hit by a male coach because she told him what to do. He refused to be told what to do by a woman and "decked" her. She did not report this as an incident of sexual harassment but as an aberration of this particular man. Generally women were held responsible by women and men for incident involving unwanted bodily contact and were expected to either ignore these advances, see them as individual aberrations and/or report them. Yet women who did report such incidents to their board usually received little support or understanding. If the incidents continued, then the women were often held responsible because they should have stopped them or taken other actions. The relatively few women coaches who worked with adult male athletes were acutely aware of the possibility of sexual innuendos. They continually monitored their behavior with men in coaching and in social settings. In this way sexuality became a part of social control (power relations).

---

[1] The hegemonic nature of sexual harassment in sport is thoroughly discussed in Brackenridge, 1994; Hall, 1996; Lenskyj, 1992; McKay, 1997; Nelson, 1994.

Obviously then, although the coaches did not express explicit homophobia, implicitly their norm was heterosexuality. Both homophobia and heterosexism however were characterized by silence although of a different sort. Women were expected to get used to and tolerate misogynist remarks because they are part of sport. If they were harassed to the extent that body contact was involved, they were expected to speak up. Alternate sexualities and same sex harassment were rarely talked about by the coaches. Although there was a great deal of resistance by the coaches to the topic of gender and sport (as we shall see in the section about division of labor), possibly the resistance to talking about the role sexuality plays in sport was much greater.

McKay (1999) calls sexual assault and harassment the 'iron fist' in controlling emphasized femininity and marginalized femininities. He goes on to say that the iron fist is "complemented by a "velvet glove" that "persuades" both men and women that the ascendancy of men's values, interests and privileges is both natural and legitimate" (ibid., p. 201). In other words, the subordinate status of women in sport becomes accepted as 'natural' and 'self evident.' Power and hierarchy often go hand in hand.

13.3 Power: modes of social control

The subordinate status of women was evident in the devaluation of women by the coaches involved in the study. Women athletes were described by women and men coaches as weaker/ less skilled than men, as whiners with little mental toughness, as fighting like cats, as holding grudges for a long time, and, as being jealous of each other. That which was associated with emphasized femininity was not valued in athletes. Women coaches engaged in this devaluation as if they were not women themselves. Men were described as being competitive with each other which made them better athletes, as working out disagreements in a physical or verbal manner that cleared the air, and, as doing assigned tasks without whining. This discourse reinforces the hierarchy of the gender order and was the dominant discourse.

There was however a minority discourse that resisted the subordinate status of women. A few women and men coaches thought women athletes were more motivated than men athletes and more eager to learn. A few women had developed successful self-presentation strategies that differed from the male-identified norm. One woman coach used whispering as one of her ways of communicating (as opposed to the yelling and screaming she saw other [male] coaches use). She said that this way her (male) athletes really had to listen to her.

In general, however, in order to be valued as coaches, women coaches had to take on characteristics and behaviors associated with hegemonic masculinity. The higher the level of competition, the less room there seemed to be for behaviors not associated with hegemonic masculinity such as nurturing, cooperation, and interdependency. Women coaches were expected to present themselves as competent coaches, that is, is as being better than their athletes, and as athletes in their own right with an extensive competitive history. It was often assumed that women could not coach top men's teams because women could not out-perform male athletes. The relevance of this performance criterion to coaching expertise was rarely questioned. Simply put, women coaches were expected to act like 'men'. When these coaches presented themselves differently they were criticized as being inadequate. In this way hegemonic masculinity continued to be privileged and was continually reproduced.

13.4 Division of labor

As indicated in the introduction to this chapter, there are divisions of labor along gender lines in Dutch sport organizations. Women are under-represented as coaches and when they do coach, they tend to coach youth sport. There were no national coaches who were women at the time of this study. I will look at the perceptions of coaches about this division of labor with respect to the meanings given by coaches to the work-family relationship and to equity.

13.4.1 Work and family responsibilities

The dominant discourse about the division of labor in which women are assumed to be primarily responsible for household and child rearing was taken as a matter of common sense by most of the coaches, especially the male coaches. The male coaches tended to have female partners who were responsible for the household and child rearing. Relatively speaking men showed little understanding that their sport labor was made possible only by the work of their women partners. Many male coaches expected female colleagues to invest as much time as they themselves were able to put in thanks to their female partners. They tended to see their women colleagues as falling short in their devotion to coaching, yet failed to see that they compared them to themselves.

Most of the men attributed their personal household arrangement to free choice and economic forces. They saw these arrangements as self evident and gender neutral. Interestingly, women who worked in a small part-time jobs mentioned time constraints more often and talked about having to stop doing volunteer work in sport. In contrast one of the forty men interviewed recounted how he was looking forward to becoming a 'house man' next year because then he would have time to coach! Obviously men and women give different meanings to 'household responsibility'. It is in this area of work and family responsibilities that most of the differences between women and men coaches were visible and where the subjects acknowledged these differences. Yet they felt that little could be done to change this.

Interestingly the majority of the women coaches involved in the study held a full-time job in addition to their coaching and sport involvement. In this aspect they differed from the 'average' Dutch woman since only 40% of Dutch women hold full-time jobs (Emancipation in numbers, 1995). Those women (and men) coaches who did not have a paid job were in the minority.The women coaches (who had partners) who had relatively little trouble with time constraints tended to have male partners who were also involved in sport. These women felt that their partner understood and encouraged their participation. Their children tended also to be actively involved in sport. Tentatively we can conclude that the time involvement of a heterosexual woman coach in sport, that is, the division of labor, is dependent on the attitude of her (male) partner. As a whole, the coaches saw the division of labor in sport organizations as gender neutral. This gender neutrality is the subject of the next paragraph.

13.4.2 Perceptions of equity

One pervasive norm that emerges out of studies dealing with gender and sport is the perception that sport is a place of equal opportunity (Hall, 1996; Knoppers & Bouman, 1998; McKay, 1997). Most of the coaches involved in this study saw their sport club, organization or federation as a place that was accessible and offered equal opportunities to all. They tended to believe that the best person is always selected for a (top) coaching position and that gender does not play a role. Most of the women coaches who participated in these studies said that little had stood in their way to achieving their goals in sport. According to them, the fact that they were women had made little or no difference. The primary exceptions to this perception were women in higher (paid) coaching positions. Two-thirds of them thought they had to be better than men to obtain a higher (paid) coaching position. A top woman coach explains: "Women don't get to coach at the top because men do not want them there and have a difficult time accepting them" (Knoppers & Bouman, 1998, p.103). Such coaches were the exception. Most used a discourse of gender equity. Their perceptions were in opposition to the actual practices such as those of the recruitment, selection and promotion of coaches.

Most coaches began coaching because they were asked, not because they responded to an advertisement. Their recruitment was primarily a function of the old boys' network. Several coaches told stories about how, even when an advertisement was placed, the selection was already a foregone conclusion. As Knoppers & Anthonissen (2001) have shown, the ideal coach is one who has characteristics associated with or attributed to hegemonic masculinity. The best coaches are those who are stronger and better skilled than their athletes. Since the prevailing perception of coaches (and sport managers) is that males are stronger and better skilled athletes than women, males are perceived to be better coaches because they are males. Consequently, relatively more men than women tend to be asked for coaching positions and to be sponsored to take certification courses. In response to a hypothetical situation where a male and female coach with similar credentials were both applying for the same job of coaching a men's top team, two-thirds of the respondents replied that the man would probably get the job. Sometimes not having a coach at all for a top team seems more desirable than having a woman coach. A woman coach describes how she was unable to get a job although she was qualified: "A sport manager of Club X let the top men's team go without a coach for half a year while I was available and had the necessary qualifications. He was looking for a male coach" (Knoppers & Bouman, 1998, p.36). Ironically most coaches assert that the 'best' person for the job also gets it and that gender plays no role in recruitment or selection.

Most of the coaches are not concerned about the relatively low number of women coaches although there is a shortage of coaches. They place the responsibility for the gender imbalance on women: women are not motivated enough to put in the required hours, they prioritize household responsibilities over sport, and they apply only for jobs for which they think they will be considered as a serious candidate (in contrast to men who apply for jobs they like whether or not they have the required credentials).

Why do these coaches have the tendency to engage in 'victim blaming' with respect to the shortage of women coaches, even those who recognize that the culture is not always woman-friendly? Why do they persist in portraying sport as an equal opportunity situation when the data show otherwise? Although coaches were not asked directly, I will make several attempts to explain this seeming contradiction.

First, these results are not unique to the Dutch sport context. Similar contradictions have been documented in Canadian, Australian, American, Finnish, and English sport (Hall, Cullen & Slack, 1990; McKay, 1997; 1999; Knoppers, 1992; Raivo, 1986; West & Brackenridge, 1985). The perception that sport is a place of equal opportunity may be part of the dominant way in which sport is constructed and consequently, structured.

Second, the women (and men) coaches who were involved in these studies were all certified. Possibly they thought that if they could obtain a certificate, so could others. They may have taken themselves as the criterion for 'equal access/opportunity.' They may have been grounding their ideology of equity in their own experience.

Third, possibly the increased visibility of women athletes and coaches (although a few) is seen as evidence that women have equal opportunities in sport if they want them. About half the men involved in these studies coached women/girls so they see girls/women being active in sport. These athletes may not have encountered the barriers some women coaches run into or that keep women out. When the coaches involved in the current study were asked why there is a shortage of coaches (in general) they cited similar reasons that they had cited for women: lack of time and ambition. The big difference is that when these 'reasons' pertain to generic people, 'men' may be the implicit norm. Yet then these reasons are not seen as male or gender issues but issues concerning the structure of sport and society itself. Sport and/or society needs to be changed to accommodate those issues. When similar questions are asked concerning the shortage of women coaches, the answers are framed in terms of gender (women) and they (women) need to be changed (instead of the structure of sport and society). Men's problems seem to be structural generic problems; women's issues tend to be seen as personal women's issues.

Fourth, the majority of those involved in this research grew up in, live in and work as coaches in a world in which a great deal of power is in the hands of men. Most of the coaches have been athletes themselves, often at top levels. More women coaches than men coaches had competed in top level sport. This history of sport involvement by women and men coaches means they have been involved in the world of sport for many years. Some are even coaching in the sport organization where they were involved as a young athlete. Consequently there is a good chance that they have internalized the dominant discourse about sport, gender and equal opportunity. They may have internalized the characteristics of hegemonic masculinity valued in the sport world and made them their own. These characteristics have become 'common sense'.

Fifth, complicity with hegemonic masculinity confers privileges and advantages. By supporting hegemonic masculinity, that is, displaying these characteristics in their role as coach, women can be accepted in the sport world although they are women (with women's bodies that deviate from the male norm). In order to succeed in the current Dutch sport world, especially at the top levels, complicity with hegemonic masculinity is almost a prerequisite although there are stories of individual resistance.

Sixth, equity is a desirable goal. It is much easier to say that this desirable goal for sport is a reality then to have to deal with the consequences of inequitable practices and of creating and accepting alternate discourses about sport. In other words, desired values and norms about equity may be equated with current practices. This means that inequitable practices and meanings given to gender are masked and/or made invisible (Benschop, 1996).

Conclusion

Obviously there is overlap among the three substructures of gender discussed here. Issues of power are related to patterns of sexuality and to the division of labor and vice versa. Each reinforces aspects of hegemonic masculinity. Bringing about change in a (sport) culture identified with and used to sustain hegemonic masculinity is extremely difficult. The intersection between gender and economic forces for example, may help to keep hegemonic masculinity firmly entrenched. As long as an absolutized version of 'citius, altius, fortius' remains the motto for sport, true gender equity may be difficult to obtain (Knoppers & Anthonissen, 2001). Yet some change is always possible because hegemony is never complete, and power is never an all or none proposition.

Kanter (1984) talks about the need for change masters to being about changes in the structures in which gender is embedded. Change masters are people in the top of organizations who consciously work for change and use their powers of persuasion to convince people at all levels that this change is a necessity for everyone, not just women. Change masters ensure that people at all levels are involved in bringing about change so that it is not a top down or policy mandate but a multi-layered effort. Change masters who are committed to gender equity in sport can use their power to create conditions under which it is possible. Perhaps they could begin by acknowledging that sport is not gender neutral, and that current sport practices give meaning to gender and that current meanings given to gender define sport.

References

Benschop, Y. (1996). *The coat of equality: Gender in organizations.* Assen: Van Gorcum. (in Dutch).

Brackenridge, C. (1994). Fair play or fair game; Child sexual abuse in sport organizations. *International Review for the Sociology of Sport*, 29, pp. 287 – 299.

Cahn, S. (1994). *Coming on strong: Gender and sexuality in twentieth century women's sport.* New York: Free Press.

Connell, R. W. (1995). *Masculinities.* Berkeley: University of California Press.

Connell, R.W. (1987). *Gender & power.* Stanford, California: Stanford University Press.

Connell, R. W. (1998). Masculinities and globalization. *Men and Masculinities*, 1, pp. 3 -23.

Emancipation in numbers (1995). Department of Social Affairs and Work. The Hague. (in Dutch).

Emancipatieraad (1997). *Sport & gender: Women in the picture.* (In Dutch). Den Haag: Department of Social Affairs, Consulting and research.

Equality (1999). The Netherlands can use Europe as an example. *Equality matters* 1(2), p. 2.

Griffin, P. (1998). *Strong women, deep closets: Lesbians and homophobia in sport.* Champaign, IL. : Human Kinetics.

Hall, M. A., Cullen, D. and Slack, T. (1990). The gender structure of national sport organizations. *Sport Canada: Occasional Papers, volume 2*, (1), Ottawa, Canada: Government of Canada, Fitness and Amateur Sport.

Hall, M.A. (1996). *Feminism and sporting bodies: Essays on theory and practice.* Champaign, IL: Human Kinetics.

Hekma, G. (1994). *As long as they do not provoke: Discrimination of gay men and lesbians in organized sport.* Amsterdam: Het Spinhuis. (in Dutch).

Kanter, R.M. (1984). *The change masters: Corporate entrepreneurs at work.* London: Allen & Unwin.

Knoppers, A. (1992). Explaining male dominance and sex segregation in coaching: Three perspectives. *Quest*, 44, pp. 210-227

Knoppers, A. & Anthonissen, A. (2001/in press). Meanings given to performance in Dutch sport organizations: Gender and racial/ethnic subtexts. *Sociology of Sport Journal.*

Knoppers, A. & Bouman, Y. (1996). *Trainers/coaches: A question of quality?.* Papendal, Arnhem: NOC*NSF. (in Dutch).

Knoppers, A. & Bouman, Y. (1998). *Always better than my athletes.* Papendal, Arnhem: NOC*NSF. (in Dutch).

Lenskyj, H. (1992). Unsafe at home base: Women's experience of sexual harassment in university sport and physical education. *Women in Sport and Physical Activity Journal*, 1, pp. 19-33.

Mc Kay, J. (1997). *MANaging gender.* Albany: State University of New York Press.

McKay, J. (1999). Gender and organizational power in Canadian sport. In: P. White & K. Young (Eds.), *Sport and gender in Canada* (pp. 197-213). Oxford: University Press.

Nelson, M.B. (1994). *The stronger women get, the more men love football.* New York: Harcourt Brace.

Pronger, B. (1990). *The arena of masculinity. Sports, homosexuality and the meaning of sex.* New York: St. Martin.

Raivo, M. (1986). The life and careers of women in leading positions in Finnish sport organizations. In: J. Mangan and R. Small (Eds.), *Sport, culture, society: International perspectives,* pp. 270-280. London: E & F Spon.

Stol, P. (1995). *A search is needed: Women coaches!*. Internship report, Center for Policy and Management, University of Utrecht, Utrecht. (in Dutch).

Tomlinson, A. & Yorganci, I. (1997). Male coach/athlete relations: Gender and power relations in competitive sport. *Journal of Sport & Social Issues,* 21, pp. 134-155.

Vinnicombe, S. & Harris, H. (2000). A gender hidden. *People Management,* 6, pp. 28-30.

West, A. & Brackenridge, C. (1985). Who rules sport? Gender divisions in the power structure of British sport organizations from 1960. *International Review for the Sociology of Sport,* 20, pp. 96-107.

Wise, S. & Stanley, L. (1987) *Georgie Porgie: Sexual harassment in everyday life.* New York: Pandora Press.

14 SPORT AND THE MEDIA: RACE AND GENDER IN THE REPRESENTATION OF ATHLETES AND EVENTS

Annelies Knoppers & Agnes Elling

Introduction

The role that the media play in sport, and that sport plays in the media, has increased significantly in the last 20 years. In fact, media sport is for many people their way of being involved in sport (Stokvis, 2000). Media sport not only consists of live representations of sporting events but also of interviews, analyses, pictures, summaries, etc. of the event. Whatever one sees or hears/reads however, consists of media re-presentations, in other words, the media present or frame an 'event'. They give meaning to it and those participating in it (the athletes). There are three types of research studies that can be conducted on the sport media: content analyses, production process analysis, and, consumer research. In our three-year study on the Dutch sport media we used the three types to examine regular and Olympic sport coverage. The purpose of our research was to explore the way the print and television sport media construct gender and race/ethnicity. The broad scope of our research prohibits us from presenting it totally. Instead therefore we have chosen to report on a small section of this research dealing with gender and race/ethnicity in Dutch television coverage of the Olympics. We use three case studies to explore the ways in which athletes are described (descriptors) and the manner in which the representations of specific events are constructed to appeal to a specific audience (genres). The results of these case studies reflect the major findings of the content analysis. We begin by summarizing some of the existing literature on media sport, with emphasis on Olympic coverage and on the representation of men and women and black and white athletes and different ways of presenting events (genres).

14.1 Olympic coverage

The Olympics provide a setting in which black and white women and men compete at the same site in a variety of sports. This makes it a unique setting for conducting research about the representation of gender and race by the sport media. Because it is so linked to nationalism, Olympic coverage is often more extensive than that of regular broadcasting. Dutch public television, for example, devoted about four times as much time (180 hours in 16 days) to coverage of the 1996 Olympic Games as they do to regular sports broadcasting (45 hours in 16 days) (Knoppers & Elling, 1999a). Rowe, McKay & Miller (1998) argue that television audiences of the Olympics want to see their national athletes, to watch the world's best athletes and to be a part of the international spirit. Nationalism plays an important role in Olympic coverage which means, in part, that women athletes, who are often invisible in regular sport broadcasting, become visible when national identity is at stake. The time (4%; 2 hours) given to women's sports in regular sports broadcasting in the Netherlands jumped to 33% (61 hours) in the broadcasts of the 1996 Olympics (see table 1). These results mirror those of other countries (Higgs & Weiler, 1994; Spears & Seydegart, 1996; Toohey, 1997).

Similarly to the erasure of gender, Van Dijk (1993) and Andrews (1996) found that when national pride is at stake and 'black' athletes win, their ethnic origins are 'temporarily' erased. Whereas when they 'fail', they tend to be more often identified by their place of origin.[1]

---

[1] 'Black' Dutch athletes are mostly from Surinam, or the Dutch Antilles. Although relatively large groups of Indonesian, Turkish and Moroccan minorities also reside in the Netherlands, they are less integrated within the major (elite) sports.

Table 1: The top ten sports in television coverage (% time) [a]

Olympic coverage 1996			'Regular' coverage 1997		
Sport	Total (%) (9584 min)	% women	Sport	Total (%) (2850 min)	% women
1. Track & Field	20.6	36.7	1. Soccer	55.8	-
2. Field Hockey	14.5	54.5	2. Tennis	14.0	0.3
3. Volleyball	10.8	39.5	3. (Speed) Skating	6.2	19.9
4. Gymnastics	9.5	53.7	4. Basketball	4.8	-
5. Swimming	9.0	49.5	5. Billiards	3.7	-
6. Cycling	7.7	21.0	6. Cycling	2.0	-
7. Rowing	5.3	45.3	7. Sailing	1.8	13.7
8. Boxing	3.6	-	8. Volleyball	1.7	14.6
9. Tennis	2.6	53.7	9. Field Hockey	1.3	45.9
10. Weight-lifting	2.2	-	10. Handball	0.9	22.2
Total	100	38.1	Total	100	3.7

a During the Olympics in 1996 (16 days) and 16 'regular' days in 1997 (November) from Blom (1997) and Van der Ven (1998)

Representation of women and men athletes

Most regular and Olympic sport coverage is devoted to male athletes and constructs a masculinity that is congruent with what Connell (1998) describes as hegemonic (see chapter 9 of this book). The American sport media tend to portray male athletes as independent, muscular and technically strong individualists (e.g. Duncan, 1990; Duncan, Messner, 1998; Duncan, Messner, Williams & Jensen, 1990; Sabo & Jansen, 1992). This counts not only for the descriptors used to describe their success but also for attributions about failure, mistakes and the opponents. Duncan & Messner (1998) found that the success of male basketball players in television broadcasts of NCAA championships was attributed largely to their strength and skill; when they lost/erred, it was because of the greater strength and skill of the opponent and/or because they tried too hard, took an impossible shot, etc.. We know very little about the representation of male athletes and the construction of masculinity by the sport media in other countries.

If hegemonic masculinity is time and context bound we would expect its portrayal to vary by culture. Connell (1998) argues however, that the ideals associated with hegemonic masculinity are becoming more and more globalized. To what extent does the portrayal of masculinity in a television broadcast reflect localized and/or globalized forms of hegemonic masculinity in a specific country? An examination of the ways men athletes are presented in an European country such as the Netherlands should give an indication as to the extent to which this globalization is occurring. Specifically, if the Dutch representation of male athletes differs from that of the American media, then the difference could be considered an illustration of the localized nature of hegemonic masculinity.   Similarities between the Dutch and the American media's representation of male athletes could support Connell's argument that the ideals of hegemonic masculinity are (becoming) increasingly globalized.

The representation of women athletes in the sport media has received more international (research) attention than that of male athletes, has been well documented for various Anglo-Saxon countries, and shows few cultural differences (see Kinkema & Harris, 1998 for a summary of this research). Although women athletes receive more television coverage during the Olympic Games than they do in regular sport programming, there are few, if any, qualitative differences between the way women are represented during regular and Olympic sports coverage. They, and their opponents, are often represented as physically strong, as somewhat unstable emotionally, and mentally and sometimes in a sexualized manner (Blom, 1997; Daddario, 1997; Kane & Lenskyj, 1998). Men's and women's events also tend to be presented differently.

Duncan & Messner (1998), in a study of television coverage of women's and men's basketball for example, found that the success of the women athletes was usually attributed to their talent, to luck and to support from coach and family; failure/losing was often attributed to psychological weaknesses and lack of skill. In other words, representation of the event (audience building) and of the athletes is a gendered dynamic.

Representation of black and white athletes

Mediated sport not only constructs meanings given to 'male' and 'female' but also to 'black athlete' and 'white athlete.' Research that focuses on the representation of black women athletes is relatively rare perhaps because these athletes have been almost invisible in the media (Hilliard, 1995; Lumpkin & Williams; 1991). Harris (cited in Davis & Harris, 1998) reports that African American women athletes tend to be presented in ways similar to African American men who are represented in contradictory ways. Sabo & Jansen (1992) argue that all male athletes in national sports wear a coat of hegemonic masculinity but that this coat has contradictions for black men. Research that compares ways in which white and black, usually African American, male athletes are described, shows that the accomplishments of black athletes are more frequently ascribed to physical aspects, while those of white male athletes are more often ascribed to mental aspects (Dufur, 1997; Sabo & Jansen, 1992; 1998). The implicit message is that black male athletes are 'natural' athletes who rely less on cognitive skills than do white athletes.

There is evidence, however, that this difference in type of descriptors is decreasing and/or has disappeared in American and British television broadcasts (McCarthy & Jones, 1997; McCarthy, Jones & Armour, 1998; Sabo, Jansen, Tate, Duncan & Leggett, 1996). McCarthy, Jones & Armour (1998), for example, after studying more than 100 hours of comments made during British televised football matches, found that the number of negative comments about mental aspects of the performance of blacks and whites did not differ significantly. They did find however, that blacks received many more positive physical descriptors (94%) than did white players (75%). They conclude that although these black football players were portrayed as mentally and physically strong, they were still marked as physically stronger than their white counterparts. Their portrayal confirms and simultaneously challenges stereotypes about black male athletes.

Genres

Sport broadcasts, including those of women's sports, are usually constructed as a male genre, that is, in a manner so that men can identify with and be involved with them (Kinkema & Harris, 1998; Rose & Friedman, 1997). Ironically this does not mean that women's sport broadcasts are presented like men's sports to attract more (male) viewers. The assumption of heterosexuality embedded in sport (see chapter 9 in this book) means that women athletes and their sports have to be constructed to appeal to the predominantly male audience. This catering to a male audience results in part, in the sexualization of women athletes in the broadcasting of women's sports such as using cleavage shots and emphasizing appearance (Duncan, 1990). The sexualization of female athletes is not the only dynamic incorporated in the broadcast of women's sports. Duncan & Messner (1998) show that more effort was put into 'audience building', that is, building excitement and suspense for men's than for women's basketball championship games. The production quality of women's games was inferior to that of the men's. Men's games featured more details on players, statistics and frequent slow motion replays that increased their appeal. These gender differences in 'audience building' suggest that women's sports are less important than men's sports. Consequently, women's sports stay in a secondary or supporting role in a male genre.

There have, however, been attempts to attract more female viewers for Olympic broadcasts of women's and men's sports. Daddario (1997), in a study of genres and broadcasting of the Olympic Games by American television producers, shows that a female subgenre was added to the male genre to attract female viewers (and keep the male viewers). This was done by adding more background/human interest stories. Research shows that 42% and 58% of the Dutch viewers of the 1996 Olympics were women and men respectively; the corresponding percentages are 35% and 65% for regular sport broadcasts (Verspeek, 1998). The reason for the change in the gender ratio of the audience between regular and Olympic viewing has not been explored, so it is unclear whether Dutch television producers followed a similar genre strategy as NBC did. Nationality and/or media hype may play a large role since the European and World Championships of men's soccer show similar gender viewer percentages as the Olympics (NOS/KLO, 1999; Peeters, Meijs, & Van Den Brug, 1999). There is no available research that examines what has been done, if anything, to attract more black viewers.

There is little available research on genres and race and the intersection between genres, race and gender. Fiske (1987) and Hall (1995) have suggested that most of what has been defined as 'black' genre consists of comedy; this definition of a black genre is congruent with the dominant stereotype of blacks as entertainers. Possibly producers may do little to frame sport broadcasts for black audiences. This means that black viewers see many broadcasts intended for a white audience. The purpose of this chapter then is to examine , with the use of three case studies, the way in which Dutch television constructed white and black women athletes and engaged in audience building (presentation of an event) during their coverage of the 1996 Olympic games.

14.2 Methodology

We used the results of a time analysis across gender and race of the 180 hours of 1996 Dutch Olympic broadcasts to select the case studies used in this chapter (Blom, 1997). Selection of the events to be used for the case studies was complex because we wanted to use comparative events with respect to 1) the amount of coverage (finals tend to be covered in their entirety), 2) the extent of nationalism (number of Dutch athletes competing), 3) the proportion of black and white, male and female athletes in the event. In addition, the type of coverage selected for this study had to reflect the findings of the entire media research project (Blom, 1997; Knoppers & Elling, 1999a; Van der Ven, 1997). Since the Dutch Olympic team consisted of only ten blacks who were minimally visible in the television broadcasts Dutch blacks were literally not in the picture.[2] Consequently we chose finals in which either both (white) Dutch women and men played/competed for a medal, or in which no Dutch were involved at all. To keep the effects of nationalism to a minimum we explored how Dutch television covered white Dutch men and women and non-Dutch white and black men and women. Dutch coverage of black athletes was primarily confined to women's and men's athletics, men's basketball, men's football and men's boxing, events in which no Dutch teams participated. Men's and women's athletics and field hockey received the most coverage during the entire Olympic period. Dutch teams/athletes did not qualify for the finals in athletics. Consequently, we chose three case studies: two comparable live events from athletics, featuring primarily non Dutch black male and female athletes, two comparable live events from field hockey involving white male and female Dutch and non Dutch teams; and, a non-live program 'Highlights of the Olympics' shown on the last day.

We chose the two 200 meter finals in athletics for the first case study. These were comparable events because there were no Dutch athletes in these finals, thus reducing the effects nationalism might have on the broadcasts. Also, one white athlete and seven black athletes competed in each of the two finals. In addition, the favorites, Michael Johnson and Marie Jose Perec had already won a gold in the 400 meters. The total time devoted to the women's event was 9.20 minutes and the men's 200 meter consisted of 18.20 minutes.

The second case study involved the women's and men's Dutch field hockey teams. The women played for the bronze medal against

---

[2] The 'black' delegation consisted of seven male baseball players, a male volleyball player, a male judoka and a female athlete competing in track and field. The Dutch baseball team received little attention as did the women's softball team.

England and the men for the gold against Spain. These were comparable matches with respect to length of coverage and to importance. We do realize that the difference in importance between a 'bronze' or 'gold' medal match might have influenced the results especially with respect to audience building but these were the most similar cases possible. In both hockey finals all the participants were white.

In these two case studies we focused primarily on the remarks/phrases/attributions made by the commentator. All the commentators were white males.

The third case study is of a different type and consists of an analysis of the contents of the program 'Highlights of the Olympics' presented by Dutch television on the last day of the Olympics. The program took 77 minutes and was delivered with little or no commentary. The 'Highlights' program included a replay of all the 17 medal victories of Dutch athletes[3] and interviews with Dutch male officials. Summaries/segments of six other sports (that is, sports without Dutch athletes) were featured in the program: men's and women's athletics, women's gymnastics, men's basketball, men's boxing and men's football. 'Highlights' also featured five different compilations or segments each with a separate title and set to music but without commentary or subtitles: 1) 'Failures of the Olympics' (1.30 minutes), 2) 'Tears /disappointments' (1.20 minutes), 3) 'Exhaustion' (1.00 minute), 4) 'Fighting/anger' (1.10 minutes), 5) 'Winners' (2.10 minutes). This program was not live but a compilation produced by Dutch television. Consequently it gives a good example of what the producers of this program think is important in Olympic coverage, how they frame these events/athletes and how they construct race and gender.[4]

---

[3] The Dutch men and women athletes won eight and nine medals respectively.
[4] Possibly the material used to produce 'Highlights' was obtained via an international feed such as NBC. Our focus, however, was on what was selected and how it was presented.

14.3 Results and discussion

In general the commentary made during the live events of the 200 m finals and the hockey medal matches was sparse. Often minutes went by in the hockey matches without a comment by the commentator. Nonetheless there were some differences between the men's and women's events with respect to the comments made and the total broadcasting.

Although the chosen events seemed to be similar according to importance, there was an extra, unforeseen, difference which might have affected the results. In the 200 meter men's final a world record was broken[5] which obviously partly influenced the commentary at the end of the race and post event comments. In the following section we give a summary of the results.

Representation of gender and race: Descriptors/attributions

The Dutch sport media presented the women athletes in the case studies in an ambivalent manner. Winning/losing was primarily attributed to (physical or technical) skill and to (weak) mentality. For example, Perec's win in the 200meter was attributed to her long stride and to Ottey (second) giving up. The white women hockey players were primarily described as technically strong and as mentally unsure of themselves. This pattern of representation of women athletes was also followed in the 'Highlights'. The physical achievements (the winning of medals) and negative psychological aspects of the performance of women athletes (tears/exhaustion) were accentuated.[6]

---

[5] From 19.66 to 19.32 seconds.

[6] 'Failures of the Olympics' showed more men (9) than women (3) and white athletes only;'Tears /disappointments' depicted primarily white women (11) who cry because they lost; the three white men who were shown, cry because they won; 'Exhaustion' showed only white women (9); 'Fighting/anger' showed two shots of white women, two black men and five white men of whom two are coaches of women's teams. 'Winners' showed four white women (with the male coach included for three of the shots) and 16 shots of men athletes and coaches.

White and black women athletes were presented in a similar positive (physical) and negative (psychological) fashion in all three case studies. The casting of women athletes as being dependent on men (coaches, father) for their success introduced a pervasive element of heterosexuality. The emphasis on emotions, nervousness and their dependence on male figures dilutes the image of strength, high level of performance and ability (Creedon, 1998; Kane & Greendorfer, 1994).

Compared to the presentation of women athletes, the re presentation of males was remarkably unambivalent in all three case studies and is congruent with the structure of Western hegemonic masculinity (Connell, 1998). Black and white men were presented as independent, strong and stable athletes. There were a few shots of men crying but these always pertained to winning. The men participants in the 200 meters, and in the hockey finals, were cast as serious and respected athletes/ opponents and as rivals who respected each other's achievements. None of the black and white men who lost or made mistakes were described as having failed. There was little criticism of the Spanish and the Dutch hockey teams or of the sprinters. Johnson was described as too strong for his (strong) opponents who were also very strong and fast. The Dutch hockey team was described as too determined and skilled for the (highly skilled) opponents who had a dangerous center half-back and extraordinary stick technique. The four errors made by men in hockey were quickly 'erased', that is, they were followed with a positive comment 'good, 'beautiful move.' Similarly, more men than women were shown as 'failures' and also as 'winners' in the Highlights. This echoed Duncan & Messner'S (1998) finding that when men fail/err they always seem to make up for it by winning of by making the next shot a good one.

There were two differences in emphasis between the men's hockey and the 200 meter final, however. In the men's 200 meter final, which involved primarily black athletes, the strength and power of the athletes were highlighted; mental and physical strategies were rarely mentioned. In the men's hockey final, which involved white athletes, the emphasis was on technical skill; strength and power were rarely mentioned. Also, the coach was given much credit for the achievements of the hockey team. In contrast, no mention was made of coaches in the 200 meter men's final. The black sprinters were presented as strong and independent men who knew what they had to do. Nothing was said about their concentration, mental preparation, strategies or techniques except that Johnson has a stiff running style.

Differences in the representation of gender and race during a sprint and a hockey final can of course in part be attributed to the type of sport/event. Do strength and power form the defining characteristic of the 200 meter or any sprint, while the use of teamwork, strategy and skills defines hockey, and do the commentators simply reflect those definitions? Or are these constructions? The construction of any sprint as an event requiring primarily muscle power may for example do injustice to all the athletes who work on start and sprint techniques, on concentration, on mental training, on strategies, etc.. Although there have been many discussions about the essentialism in describing males as 'naturally' stronger than females, there is no available research that explores the extent to which each sport has its own defining characteristics and to which such characterizations might be related to gender and race. To what extent does the preponderance of black athletes in the sprints result in a representation of the sprints as requiring more 'natural' strength/ power than well-developed strategies and techniques? Such representation may strengthen the stereotype that black male athletes are 'natural' athletes and automatically do what is required to perform well.

Although these were case studies comparing different events, and little research has been done on the construction of hegemonic and marginalized masculinities in Dutch television, there is some evidence that the representation of the gold medal match of the Olympic hockey final may typify how white male Dutch athletes are represented in 'important' team sports. In a case-study on the television broadcasts of men's football during 'regular' competition, we found that the emphasis is on technical skills, individualism and cool headedness (Knoppers & Elling, 1999a). Similar to the presentation of the gold medal hockey final, there was little mention in the football broadcasts of teamwork, strength and power. Possibly Dutch public television broadcasts of 'important' men's team events celebrate a (white) masculinity based more on rationality, skills and individualism than on muscular strength, power and teamwork. It is also possible that an emphasis on technical skills pre-supposes the necessary strength. There is some available research that suggests that the dominant Dutch discourse about football assumes that strength is a prerequisite to playing well (Knoppers & Bouman, 1996; Knoppers & Elling, 1999b). Women, it is assumed, will never be able to play as well as the men because they [women] are physically weaker. Thus, an emphasis on technical skills in Dutch broadcasts may have a gendered strength/power subtext (Knoppers & Anthonissen, 2001).

The foregrounding of technical skills and individualism at the expense of strength and power may also be related to the type of media studied. In a study of Dutch newspaper coverage of the 1996 Olympics (Knoppers & Elling, 1999a) we found that 31% of the comments in the men's hockey gold medal match pertained to power and physical effort. In other words, the print media constructed the male athletes and their actions differently than did the visual media. Further (comparative) research is needed to determine to what extent re-presentations of 'important' men's team sport events vary across the types of media, sport as well as across race and gender.

Although in two of the case studies the comparisons involved a team sport and an individual sport, the manner in which gender and race were constructed in the third case study (Highlights) seems to confirm that the manner of representation goes beyond the specific sport. In the 'Highlights', black men were not only show-cased as spectacular athletes but also as entertainers in the basketball and football segments. These two sports received relatively little attention in the 16 days of Olympic coverage, perhaps because no Dutch basketball and football teams competed in the Olympics. The manner in which the black athletes were portrayed (with accompanying music and selected shots woven together) in the 'Highlights' indicates that these were carefully choreographed 'stories.' This musicalized performance of black male athletes is congruent with other research exploring race and ethnicity in television's portrayals of World Cup football (Tudor, 1998). Scheerder (1998) and

Tudor (1998) argue that such portrayals are rooted in stereotypical views of black Africans as having a 'natural sense of rhythm', as super strong men and as 'care free'. The images produced for the 'Highlights' section are part of and contribute to this stereotyping.

Genres

Although there was relative little commentary in both women's and men's events in the case studies, the audience building for hockey, two 'all- white' events, and the 200 meter, two primarily 'black' events, was developed in similar ways across gender. The men's events were each presented as 'the' event and as 'thrillers.' The 200 meter men's final began with a picture of the 'golden shoes' and was presented as a melodrama for a peak performance with a male hero. The men's hockey match was presented as a great and exciting melodrama ('the' final!) and was prefaced with the suggestion that it would be a real fight. This 'thriller' approach fits the manner in which male media sport is often presented on television. In addition the coverage of the 200 meter and hockey games after the actual events took longer for men than women (e.g. twenty minutes after the men's and eight minutes after the women's hockey game). The entire victory lap (200m) and the medal ceremony (hockey) of only the men were shown.

Duncan & Messner (1998) have shown how men's basketball championships were constructed as melodramas with a historic impact, while the women's championships were presented as a neighborhood game. Similarly in our study the women athletes and teams were not cast as strong rivals; their competitive history was glossed over. During and after the women's 200 meter race little was said about individual results; it was as if the athletes had nothing to do with each other, although the time between first and second place was smaller than that in the men's race. The fact that the women's hockey team had been seeded as eighth and was now playing for the bronze was not presented as noteworthy but was trivialized.

The men's events were clearly a male genre but drawing a conclusion about the women's events is more difficult. Women's events were framed in a way suggesting relative little importance, were assigned to black and white female athletes, and their events compared to the men's events. As we have mentioned before, part of the difference in audience building may have been influenced by the greater importance that was assigned to the men's events because of the difference of a gold vs bronze (hockey) match, and a world record vs Olympic record (200m). Yet as indicated earlier, we selected the specific case studies because their results reflected those of the entire research study. We conclude that the producers of Dutch public television did very little to attract (women) viewers in these three case studies since there were no human interest stories, and little was done to build an audience of men and women for the women's finals.

In addition, although the scholarly literature suggests that women athletes are often sexualized to attract male viewers, the only shots in the case studies that might be considered sexualization occurred at the end of each women's final with buttocks/briefs shots of Perec and of the women's hockey team. In other words, little or no sexualization occurred to attract (more) male viewers. Also, the only women presented in the 'Highlights' were Dutch (white) medal winners, not-Dutch black and white women in athletics, and not-Dutch white 'women' gymnasts; women dominated the segments depicting 'Tears/disappointment' and 'Exhaustion.' The increase in the percentage of Dutch women and men who watched the Olympic broadcasts as compared to regular sports programming may be more attributable to the nature of the event (world wide) rather than to programming efforts. Possibly these women's events were presented only because they were there, because of possible national interests (a medal), and/or the (in)availability of broadcasting feeds from other events. Possibly also, women's events were framed as secondary so as not to challenge the structure of hegemonic masculinity. These are of course speculations. To provide a more concrete answer we are currently exploring the discourse journalists use to explain their selection criteria (Knoppers & Elling, 2001).

Conclusion

Chandler (1988, p. 187) contends that a telecast reflects the 'producer's belief, examined and unexamined, about what a sport contest is and what it represents'. Taken as a whole, these cases studies meet the criteria for a (white) male genre. They emphasized success/achievement, physical and mental power and individualism. When women athletes were visible, their portrayal can best be characterized as 'ambivalent.' Their events were framed as secondary to the men's events. The presentation of men's and women's events and the 'Highlights' are not simply the result of ad hoc practices but are embedded in producers' discourses about the nature of sport, gender and race, and the relationship between sport and (public) television.

Although these broadcasts were constructed for a Dutch audience, the underlying assumption seems to be that Dutch viewers celebrate similar constructions of masculinity as do Americans. By constructing white and black women athletes as strong but also mentally unsure, and women's events as relatively unimportant even when a medal is involved, the challenge the presence of women athletes might pose to the structure of hegemonic masculinity is diluted. The way black male athletes were visible and presented fit the characteristics associated with hegemonic masculinity, but at the same time confirmed Sabo & Jansen'S (1992) conclusions that this masculinity has contradictions for black men athletes. The Dutch television's representation of the selected case studies of the 1996 Olympic Games seems primarily to have strengthened and/or sustained a globalization of a Western hegemonic masculinity.

References

Andrews, D.L. (1996). The fact(s) of Michael Jordan's Blackness: Excavating a floating racial signifier. *Sociology of Sport Journal*, 13, pp. 125-158.

Blom, M. (1997). *Gender and ethnicity in the sport media: A quantitative and qualitative analysis of the 1996 Olympic Games in Atlanta.* Unpublished Master's thesis, Center for Policy and Management, University of Utrecht, the Netherlands. (in Dutch).

Connell, R. W. (1998). Masculinities and globalization. *Men and Masculinities*, 1, pp. 3-23.

Creedon, P. (1998). Women, sport, and media institutions: Issues in sports journalism and marketing. In: L. Wenner (Ed.), *Media Sport* (pp. 88-99). London: Routledge.

Daddario, G. (1997). Gendered sports programming: 1992 Summer Olympic coverage and the feminine narrative form. *Sociology of Sport Journal*, 14, pp. 103-120.

Davis, L. & Harris, O. (1998). Race and ethnicity in the US sports media. In: L. Wenner (Ed.), *Media Sport* (pp. 154-169). London: Routledge.

Dijk, T. van (1993). *Elite discourse and racism.* Sage: Newbury Park, CA.

Dufur, M. (1997). Race logic and 'being like Mike': Representations of athletes in advertising, 1985 - 1994. *Sociological Focus*, 30, pp. 345-356.

Duncan, M. (1990). Sports photographs and sexual difference: Images of women and men in the 1984 and 1988 Olympic Games. *Sociology of Sport Journal*, 10, pp. 353- 372.

Duncan, M.C. & Messner, M. (1998). The media image of sport and gender. In: L. Wenner (Ed.), *Media Sport* (pp. 170-185). London: Routledge.

Duncan, M.C., Messner, M., Williams, L. & Jensen, K. (1990). *Gender stereotyping in televised sports.* Los Angeles, CA.: Amateur Athletic Foundation.

Fiske, J. (1987). *Television culture*. London: Methuen.

Hall, S. (1995). The whites in their eyes: Racist ideologies and the media. In: G. Dines & J. Humez (Eds.), *Gender, race and class in the media* (pp. 18-22). Thousend Oaks, California: Sage publications.

Higgs, C. T. & Weiler, K.H. (1994). Gender bias and the 1992 summer Olympic Games: An analysis of television coverage. *Journal of Sport and Social Issues*, 18, pp. 234-246.

Hilliard, D. (1995). *Race, gender, and the televisual representation of Olympic athletes*. Paper presented at the annual meeting of the North American Society for the Sociology of Sport, Sacramento, California.

Kane, M.J. & Greendorfer, S. (1994). The media's role in accommodating and resisting stereotyped images of women in sport. In: P. Creedon, (Ed.), *Women, media and sport: Challenging gender values* (pp. 28-44). Thousand Oaks, CA: Sage Publications.

Kane, M.J. & Lenskyj, H. (1998). Media treatment of female athletes: Issues of gender and sexualities. In: L. Wenner (Ed.) *Media Sport* (pp. 186-201) London: Routledge.

Kinkema, K. & Harris, J. (1998). MediaSport studies: Key research and emerging issues. In: L. Wenner (Ed.), *Media Sport* (pp. 27-54). London: Routledge.

Knoppers, A. & Anthonissen, A. (2001/in press). Meanings given to performance in Dutch sport organizations: Gender and racial/ethnic subtexts. *Sociology of Sport Journal*.

Knoppers, A. & Bouman, Y. (1996). *Trainers/coaches: A question of quality?* Papendal, Arnhem: NOC*NSF (in Dutch).

Knoppers, A. & Elling, A. (1999a). *Gender, ethnicity and the sport media: An inventory*. Utrecht/Tilburg: Center for Policy and Management, University of Utrecht/Leisure Studies, Tilburg University, the Netherlands. (in Dutch).

Knoppers, A. & Elling, A. (1999b). *It is more fun to play than to coach: Images of football coaches*. Zeist: Royal Dutch Football Association (in Dutch).

Knoppers, A. & Elling, A. (2001/in press). *Gender, ethnicity and the sport media: Selection and interpretation* Arnhem: NOC*NSF (in Dutch).

Lumpkin, A. & Williams, L. (1991). An analysis of Sports Illustrated feature articles, 1954- 1987, *Sociology of Sport Journal*, 8, pp. 16-32.

McCarthy, D. & Jones, R.L. (1997). Speed, aggression, strength, and tactical naïveté: The portrayal of the black soccer player on television, Journal of *Sport and Social Issues*, 21, pp. 348-362.

McCarthy, D. Jones, R.L. & Armour, K. (1998). *Constructing images and interpreting realities: The case of the black soccer player on television.* Paper presented at the British Sociological Association Annual Conference, April, 1998.

NOS/KLO (1999). *Year view television 1998.* Hilversum: NOS.

Peeters, A., Meijs, J, & Brug, H. Van den (1999). *Sport in the picture: Viewing preferences of men and women.* Hilversum, NL: Look and Listen Research. (in Dutch).

Rose, A. & Friedman, J. (1997). Television sports as mas(s)culine cult of distraction. In: A. Baker & T. Boyd (Eds.), *Out of bounds: Sports, media, and the politics of identity* (pp. 1-15). Bloomington, IN: Indiana University Press.

Rowe, D., McKay, J. & Miller, T. (1998). Come together: Sport, nationalism and the media image. In: L. Wenner (Ed.), *Media Sport* (pp. 119-133). London: Routledge.

Sabo, D., Curry, T., Jansen, S., Tate, D., Duncan, M.C., & Leggett, S. (1996). Televising international sport: Race, ethnicity, and international bias. *Journal of Sport and Social Issues*, 20, pp. 7-21.

Sabo, D. & Jansen, S.C. (1992). Images of men in sport media. In: S. Craig, (Ed.), *Men, masculinity and the media* (pp. 169-184). Newbury Park, CA: Sage Publications.

Sabo, D. & Jansen, S.C. (1998). Prometheus unbound: Constructions of masculinity in the sports media. In: L. Wenner (Ed.), *Media Sport* (pp. 203-217). London: Routledge.

Scheerder, J. (1998). The myth of the black super athlete. *Lichamelijke Opvoeding*, 14, 616-620. (in Dutch).

Spears, G. & Seydegart, K. (1996). *Gender portrayal in English television coverage of the 1994 Olympic Games*. Ottawa, Canada: Department of Canadian Heritage, Ministry of Supply and Services.

Stokvis, R. (2000). *The continually changing nature of sport journalism. Paper presentation at the congress 'The culture of journalism in the twentieth century'*, June 26-28, Amsterdam.

Toohey, K. (1997). Australian television, gender and the Olympic Games. *International Review of the Sociology of Sport*, 32, pp. 19-29.

Tudor, A. (1998). Sports reporting: Race, difference and identity. In C. Brants, J. Hermes & L. van Zoonen (Eds.), *The media in question: Popular cultures and public interests* (pp. 147-156). London: Sage Publications.

Ven, M. van der (1998). *An inventory and analysis of the portrayal of gender and ethnicity in 'regular' sport broadcasting*. Unpublished Master's thesis, Faculty of Social Sciences, University of Utrecht, the Netherlands (in Dutch).

Verspeek, J. (1998). *Gender and ratings of sport programs*. Hilversum, NL: Look and Listen Research. (in Dutch).

PART FOUR

VALUES IN YOUTH SPORT

15 CHILD-ORIENTED SPORT

Kristine De Martelaer, Paul De Knop & Albert Buisman

"The marriage between child and sport is not necessarily always happy" (Telama, 1999, p.13).

Introduction

In the research program 'Values & norms in sport' a considerable part was dedicated to youth sport. The chapter of which this paragraph is an introduction has the aim to take a look at the typical values and norms in sport for children. Telama (1999) points out the possibility of negative influences of sport on children. Though we must underline that the marriage between child and sport is also often a happy marriage.

This introduction has two basic functions: first of all it gives the state of the art of what can be considered as child-oriented sport, and second it offers a thread in the different youth sport contributions. The first paragraph is about the meaning of the term 'child-oriented sport', while the second paragraph will explain the link between child-orientation and values and norms. In the next paragraph we will focus on the different studies in this field, to end up with the introduction of the following chapters, providing the results of two research projects, i.e. "Organized sport programs for children: Do they meet the interests of the children effectively" and "Martial arts and children".

15.1 Description of child-oriented sport

This introduction deals with child-oriented sport, which can be interpreted as a synonym of child-friendliness of sport. In contributions about child-oriented sport the emphasis is usually on organized sport because of the impact of adults in comparison with the non-committal sport of children. In the literature both terms 'children' and 'youth' is used, referring to the broad category of young people.

In this book we opted for the first one, similarly with the definition of a child (all persons under 18) used in the United Nations Declaration on the Rights of the Child (Verhellen, 1994).

A child-oriented approach implies that adults, for example in a sports club, provide sport activities attuned to the wishes and capabilities of children. This involves sports technical, organizational, structural and supervisory adaptation (De Knop, Wylleman, Theeboom, De Martelaer, Van Puymbroeck & Wittock, 1994, p.15). Another definition of child-oriented organized sport is to optimize the pedagogical climate by taking into account:
- the development of children (physical, psycho-social and cognitive),
- the experiences of children and,
- general human principles, and herewith prepare the children to the future, adult life (De Martelaer, 1997).

These definitions contain two areas of tension:
(a)   the actual experiences of the children,
(b)   the future orientation towards adulthood,
characterized by the developmental stages, the individual meaning of the children themselves, and the social and cultural background. In a pedagogical relationship adults have to handle, in the interest(s) of children, more by way of security and the inner urge to explore and to be unique (Langeveld, 1972). Meijer (1995) underlines the child as a 'subject' in a pedagogical relationship and not an object that can be moulded by adults. Children have to be introduced to different meanings in order to realize the possibilities, ideas, interpretations, values etc. in society (Meijer, 1992). The process of growing into adulthood is influenced, by the guidance and policy of adults, as individuals and/or authorities and this is also true for youth sport. This implies the important task for adults to filter and watch the quality of sport on offer. Buisman, De Knop and Theeboom (1998) have worked out some quality criteria, typical for youth sport, formulated in questions:
1. To what extent is youth sport in harmony with the development and environment of children?
2. To what extent is an atmosphere of safety and care created in which the supervisory staff acts as if they have the best interests of children at heart?
3. To what extent are children encouraged to be self-reliant?

4. Is performing in sport more a matter of what one is allowed to do or what one is obliged to do?
5. Does the selection processes in youth sport affect the idea of participation, giving everyone equal opportunity to learn and play?
6. Is the participation of parents in the organization linked to the development of their children?
7. Do boys and girls get the same opportunities in sport?
8. Is there a broad offer for children or are they pushed in a specialization at early age?

While these topics are typical for the young sport participants, there are still some other more general aspects to check if a youth program is of good quality or not:
1. satisfaction / enjoyment of the participants,
2. reciprocity in personal relationships,
3. involvement of the participants in the process of learning skills (Buisman et al., 1998).

Such a pedagogical framework for youth sport is also developed elsewhere. A good example is the 'National Standards for Youth Sports' of the National Youth Sports Coaches Association (NYSCA, 1988) in the USA. Their central position is "Youth sports programs should be based on maximum participation. The program should focus on organizing meaningful play. Coaches should let children experience a variety of positions, and encourage children to be involved in making decisions. The level and length of athletic competition should be commensurate with the physical and emotional development of the child" (ibid., p.7). They offer several programs according to the age and development of children. Their aim group consists of parents, coaches and members of the board of sport clubs.

Quality criteria are also reflected in the rights of children in sport, where 'the best interest of the child' is the primary consideration (the UN Convention on the rights of the Child). Children have their own rights and it is a good exercise to answer the question if adults take into account these rights in sport (Andrews, 1999; De Martelaer, De Knop, Theeboom, & Van Heddegem, 1999, 2000a; Telama, 1999). The aim in organized youth sport is to keep the balance between: (a) what is important to fulfill the enjoyment and satisfaction of the children on the one hand, and (b) the more future oriented perspective on the other hand. Children have the right to play as a child, looking for their own meanings, and at the same time grow up as future adults with social desirable norms and values.

During childhood and puberty there are a lot of changes that have to be taken into account when studying the experiences of children in sport (Buisman & Baar, 1995). Creating a decent pedagogical climate in sport, developmental characteristics have to be considered, physically as well as psycho-social and cognitive development. Because the age groups usually described in the literature are quite large to specify characteristics in sport, in this text three sub-categories will be used.[1] For more details and references about developmental characteristics and didactical approaches in youth sport we refer to the literature (De Knop et al., 1994; De Knop & De Martelaer, 1998a; De Knop, Buisman & De Martelaer, 1998). Child-oriented sport means for **6-10 year-olds**:

- a broad general basic training, multi-faceted movement,
- aerobic exercises,
- capitalizing on their own creativity, fantasy,
- capitalizing on their desire to keep their knowledge up to date,
- capitalizing on their great curiosity,
- keeping teamwork within limits, given that this is still quite difficult at this stage,
- encouraging them to take pleasure in what they are doing, setting feasible assignments (this relates to the degree of difficulty of the assignments, the provision of facilitating materials, etc.),
- teaching coping skills.

The program and guidance for the **10-13 year-olds** should take into account the following developmental aspects:

- making allowance for the 'growth spurt',
- aerobic exercises,
- getting them to practice physical elasticity and suppleness,
- fostering self-reliance,
- teaching them to appreciate that talent/competence is decisive for performance,
- encouraging teamwork, group activities.

---

[1] For example Seifert & Hoffnung (1994) describe the 'middle years' (between 6 and 12 years of age or 'school age') and adolescence between 12 and about 20 years of age. Because in the beginning of puberty (the phase of the growth spurt) a child changes so much and so fast we described the phase 10-13 years separately.

Taking into account the development of **13-18 year-olds**, one has to consider the following in youth sport:
- making allowance for physical changes and individual differences,
- anaerobic as well as aerobic exercises,
- developing strength-training progressively,
- fostering self-reliance,
- helping youngsters in their search for an individual identity,
- getting youngsters involved in supervision and policy-making

These didactical tips provide general information for the 'average' youngster. Of course everyone develops in a specific way with his/her own characteristics and at his/her own speed.
Adult attitudes and actions towards children, as individuals and as a group, will influence the children and their development. Therefore 'the best interest of the child' as a primary consideration has to be seen in the broader context of norms and values in society in general, and in sport in particular. In the next paragraph we will take a look to the link between child-oriented sport and values and norms in sport.

15.2 Child-oriented sport in relationship with values and norms

"The question 'how could children benefit sports' is of value rather than 'how sports could benefit children'" (David, 1999).

The research program of values and norms in sport contains as the central issue the way values and norms are manifested in sport, and thus the different meanings existing in sport practise. The central task of the WNS-program was to clarify values from various perspectives, to stimulate a more balanced thinking and debate in sport (Buisman & Van Rossum, 1998). This chapter is focussing on the perspectives of the children themselves in order to illustrate what they value as to be important in their sport participation.

The quality criteria for youth sport have to be interpreted taking into account the 'typical characteristics of sport' (Steenbergen & Tamboer, 1998). These authors emphasize that competition, or exceeding the performance of others, is typical for sport. In order to achieve this goal uniform rules have to be respected, and a selection of the best is inevitable. This implicates a huge local, national, and international organization. In competitive sport the value of winning is usually one of the most important orientations. However talking about youth sport the 'progression-orientation' is even as important as the 'win-orientation' (Buisman et al., 1998). A progression-orientation refers for example to the challenge to run a better individual time or to learn a new skill (Buisman, 1995; Van Rossum, 1996), which is essential for children.

Modern sport cannot be identified with competitive sport alone, but with a wide range of new sports called 'sports modi' such as fitness, adventure and health sports (Crum, 1991; see also chapter 2 of this book). Central values here, within these non-competitive based sports, are health, sensation, and beauty of the body. The discussion about these values is also relevant in the context of youth sport. In gymnastic clubs for example, activities such as acro-gym, jazz-ballet, and fitness, offer a possibility to accentuate the values of fitness and health. The fitness culture among adults is evolving and the question is if the (individual) way of being active in a health club has a future for children (Buisman et al., 1998). Another example given by these authors is about the implications for the quality of the guidance when a young boy wants to climb the French mountains. Adventure and sensation can be offered with the prerequisite of a safety environment. Children need, more than adults, strict help and guidelines in order to assess what is safe and what is not.

Rinehart (2000) describes how alternative and extreme sports are becoming formal sports. This author brings up for discussion does the process of the actual organization and institutionalization of these activities meets the expectations of what can be understood as user-friendly sport? Youngsters in particular are looking for alternatives such as snowboarding, sky-surfing, in-line skating, in their quest to become or maintain active without the interference of undue authority. For example the core members of in-line and other sports claimed that they initiated their participation because it was something they could do by themselves, because it didn't require adult supervision, and because it was challenging. When 'fun' has somehow been made into 'work' for these athletes (organized competitions) there were more and more complaints (Rinehart, 2000). According to alternative sports practitioners 'authority' is represented by coaches, managers, organizing committees, corporate sponsors, media, rules enforcers, among many others. Due to the impact of adults, with a strong priority on competition (and thus winning), the very nature of the original activity will disappear. Young participants are looking for alternative sports activities with central values such as freedom, experiences of excellent movements, and creating an own youth culture. New members adopt the attitudes, style of dress, speech patterns and behaviours of the established members of the sub-culture (Donnely & Young, 1988). The question is how creative youngsters will be in time to find new trends in order to be free of adult interference.

Adults make rules in order to realize the organization of sport practice, offering a framework to try out own and others actions. Written and unwritten rules and norms refer to certain values or value-orientations. It is important to realise that these values differ according to the type of sport and the individuals. In some sports (for example soccer, basketball) adaptations are made concerning a smaller playing field, a smaller ball and fewer players. Concrete measures, for example, relating to a minimum age or to adapt the competition system and game rules, are different from one country to another and from one sport to another (Clearing House, 1999). Notwithstanding the various adaptations, sometimes norms and values in sport stipulated by adults are contradictory to the values of children.

During the last decades more children have applied for organized sport all over the world (De Knop, Engström, Skirstad & Weiss, 1996). More in particular the sport club is a popular organizational context in youth sport. Sport as a social institution and social practice is discussed in great detail in sociological handbooks and journals. Whether organized youth sport transmits values or not leaves researchers in a state of suspense. According to Eitzen (2000) this is an empirical question. What actually can be analyzed is the value-orientation of young sport participants, as the starting point of a discussion about child-oriented sport.

15.3 Illustration of the quality criteria for youth sport

In this paragraph an illustration will be given of value-orientations in youth sport, described from the perspective of child-oriented sport, more in particular from the eleven quality criteria in youth sport of Buisman et al. (1998). Before going to the specific criteria for children, illustrations are given of the three more general principles of good practice in sport.

15.3.1 Satisfaction / enjoyment of participants

Because athletes may be considered the prime beneficiaries of (amateur) athletic programs (Chelladurai, 1987) the effective athletic organization is the one that meets the needs of its athletes. From this point of view an understanding of the athletes' satisfaction level is crucial (Riemer & Chelladurai, 1998). Athlete satisfaction can be defined as "a positive affective state resulting from a complex evaluation of the structures, processes, and outcomes associated with the athletic experience" (Chelladurai & Riemer, 1997, p.35) These authors developed a classification of facets of the athletes' satisfaction and came to the 'Athlete Satisfaction Questionnaire'. The 15 sub-scales of this questionnaire address the most salient aspects of athletic participation: (a) performance (individual and team), (b) leadership, (c) the team, (d) the organization, and (e) the individual (Riemer & Chelladurai, 1998).

In the past much attention has been paid to the objective (measurable) data of sport participation. However, participation data is no indication of the quality of the experiences (Brettschneider & Bräutigam, 1990). Recently, there is a tendency to look more at the subjective approach to leisure and sport activities. Improving one's self is an important goal that children have in their sports activities. They are usually most motivated by intrinsic rewards, such as a stronger feeling of self-worth, a greater feeling of competence, being together with friends, and having fun by doing certain activities. Especially among young children satisfaction in sport has often a relational aspect, feeling safe, being accepted by the coach etc..

15.3.2 The reciprocity in the relationships

The coaches play an essential role in child-centred sports clubs, especially because of the increasingly younger age of children in sport. Studying the youth coach is often limited to the perspectives of adults. However it is assumed that the ultimate effects of coaching behaviours are mediated by the meaning that athletes attribute to them. General agreement exists that an important determinant of the effects of participation lies in the relationship between coach and athlete (De Knop et al., 1994; Martens, 1987; Seefeldt & Gould, 1980; Smith & Smoll, 1996). For youth members of sport clubs the coach is a figure of vital importance (De Knop, Laporte, Vanden Auweele, De

Martelaer, Heite, Rzewnicki, Verhoeven, & Wylleman, 1996b). The way they experience the activities depends on the person who is guiding. Most of the children indicated being satisfied with their coach, whereas an analysis of more detailed data reports children expecting their coach to react less angrily and a little more leniently. According to the youth coaches they are more caring than is experienced by the children. While a coach is convinced that he/she listens to youth members, children give significant lower scores on this item (De Knop et al., 1996b). The youth members have clear ideas about what a good coach should be. According to a young respondent a coach should not be angry when the child is performing less than expected, because as an athlete you do not perform badly intentionally. Children hate yelling or complaining coaches. They expect a coach to be strict but also to react in a friendly manner sometimes being a joker.

The coach should give attention to all children (talented or not), has to understand each child as an individual and is responsible for a good atmosphere in the group. The interest for the children should go further than the sport technical progress; listening to the life of the children outside of the sports club (school, other leisure activities, etc.) is essential. A youth coach is like a father figure, having a good judge of human/child nature and being on the same wavelength as the children.

In the quantitative research of De Knop et al. (1996b) differences were found in the perception of the coach according to the sport children do practise. While swimmers assess their coach as more angry, tennis players and gymnasts have more positive experiences of a caring and lenient coach. Boys have the experience of a caring but rather angry coach, while female athletes experience their coach as more lenient than boys do. The coach is experienced as less caring by older children and as more caring by those who train more intensively. A possible explanation for age differences is that adolescents sometimes feel misunderstood by adults and thus also by their coach. The fact that children who are more engaged in their sport have better experiences with the caring attitude of their coach can be a natural reaction of the coach, who will put more effort into those athletes who train often and intensively. Yet the coach is also seen as angry and reproachful by young athletes who display a great sports involvement, which ties in with the image of the 'benevolent autocrat' (Chelladurai, 1993).

15.3.3 The involvement of the participants

Sport organizers have the responsibility to search for values, experiences and needs of children (De Martelaer, De Knop, Van Heddegem, & Theeboom, 2000b). This can be done in an informal way (daily contacts) or in a structured way (surveys, youth council). Good communication with children is the core element of youth sport guidance and starts with listening carefully. One of the quality criteria in youth sport, the 'user quality', is taking into account what children and youngsters themselves value as important (De Knop & Buisman, 1998; De Knop, Van Hoecke, De Martelaer, Theeboom, Van Heddegem & Wylleman, 2000a). Though sports clubs seldom take the views of young people seriously (Buisman, 1983; De Martelaer, 1997; Duijvestijn, 1998), children participating in sport have the right to have a voice in planning and evaluating sport activities. Research has shown that, when children do not feel they can have a say in deciding to take part in sport, there is a greater chance they will drop out (Baar, 1996; Gould & Petlichkoff, 1988).

15.3.4 Development and experiences of children and youngsters

Children (up to 12 years of age) are busy with their present experiences, here and now in the immediate surrounding. They want to play, have fun and learn new skills. It is not yet relevant to focus on future aims in their sport career. Adolescents, focusing on their own role in the group, are more future-oriented looking for the place of sport in their daily life.

A remarkable trend is the increasing seriousness because norms and values of adult sport have influenced youth sport to a large extent (De Knop, et al., 1996a). Converting children into mini-adults at a younger and younger age can deny them opportunities for spontaneous play, which is also a worthwhile learning experience. Converting play into work can expose young athletes to stress, so they become dissatisfied and give up sport (Burton & Martens, 1986; Coakley, 1992; De Knop & De Martelaer, 1998a/b; Rotella, Hanson & Coop, 1991). Drop out of youth sport is in many cases a direct consequence of a disappointing experience in the sports club (Vanreusel, De Knop, De Martelaer, Impens, Roelandt, Teirlynck & Wylleman, 1992). Some sports, for example athletics and swimming are too much a copy of the adult approach to competition. Children complain about the competitions and training sessions because they are monotonous (De Martelaer & De Knop, 1998; Vloet & Buisman, 1998).

15.3.5 Atmosphere of safety and care

The sports club is responsible for the 'physical safety' of the accommodation, the program and the guidance, in order to avoid injuries. Moreover there is the important role of the coach to be as a 'father figure' for the children. For the youngest participants (up till about 8 years of age) there is the continuous concern to create conditions so that they feel safe in the group. Towards older children the coaches have the role to stimulate them in their autonomy, creating challenging but safe situations (Buisman et al., 1998).

15.3.6 Independence of children and youngsters

In order to help promote the decision-making skills and autonomy, coaches should give children as much responsibility as possible (Martens, 1988). According to this author, even at the youngest ages, there are possibilities to promote a sense of belonging, responsibility, and accountability. Examples are: having a task in keeping the score, organizing equipment, etc. Older children can share responsibility for organizing games and practices. To realize independency the coach has to reach plural movement ability, which means that children learn: (a) motor skills together with social and cognitive skills, (b) skills to act in different roles (Timmers, 1993). There are the different gradation or phases to arrive at independency: (1) independent, alone or together, fulfilling a task, (2) independent, alone or together, organizing tasks, rules, etc., (3) independent observing and giving someone instructions, (4) independent, alone or together creating and changing movement situations, a game, and (5) independent drawing up a training- and exercise program (Timmers, 1993).

15.3.7 Pressure to perform

The hierarchical ordering that people give to playing well, playing fairly, and winning has been labelled 'game orientation' (Knoppers, 1985). According to Shields & Bredemeier (1995) several researchers have found that age is a significant predictor of game orientation, with the professional orientation (outcome is stressed most, fairness least) increasingly embraced with advancing age. When the internal aim of competition, winning, is not the exclusive aim, competition can be mutually enjoyable and a satisfying means of improving abilities, challenging boundaries, and expressing one's affective need for joy, and community (Shields & Bredemeier, 1995). It is only from the age of 10 or 12 years that children are able to interpret competition in the same terms as adults. Therefore, it is advisable to encourage young people to engage in real sports competition only after they reach this age (De Knop et al., 1994).

15.3.8 Equal opportunity for everyone

An important issue is the field of tension between offering every child equal opportunity to learn, to play and to compete on the one hand, and the demands of competitive sport selecting and accentuating talented children on the other hand. This is a subject under discussion at local and higher level. Until recently only a few Flemish sport federations had a sport policy favouring young members at all levels (De Knop, Laporte, Van Meerbeek, De Martelaer, Impens & Roelandt, 1991). The majority of the sport federations did not take much effort to write down a decent policy and concrete program for youngsters. The new Flemish decree on the recognition and subsidy of sport federations (1999) is actually a stimulus to change this situation. According to this decree, federations have to implement 'basic tasks' such as managers and coaches training, guiding their sport clubs in sport technical aspects, management and sport promotion. The decree covers also some 'facultative tasks' that can be subsidized, for example for a specific youth sport policy. This decree, which has made a start in 2000, is an impulse for sport federations and indirectly also for sport clubs to ameliorate their youth sport policy and guidance. For the moment it is too early to assess the effect of this decree.

15.3.9 Participation of parents in the organization

In the literature (Hellstadt, 1987) a parental involvement continuum is suggested, ranging form under-involvement through moderate involvement to over-involvement. They call the moderate involvement 'the comfort zone'. In the case of young children, clubs need the commitment of the parents; they bring them to the training sessions and the competitions. This gives the opportunity for a good relationship between those responsible in the sports club and the parents with their child(ren). Once children grow up and come to puberty it is reasonable that parents withdraw gradually. This implies they want direct communication between the club and the youngsters but does not mean that parents are not interested anymore. Few sports clubs are aware of and active in building up a good relationship with parents (De Haan, Van Iersel, Horvers, Vloet, De Knop, & Buisman, 1997). This research indicated that parents are often willing to engage, but clubs fail to give the necessary information about tasks, commissions, etc..

15.3.10 Chances for boys and girls to play together

Popularity of sports according to sex depends on the culture of each specific sport. In hippic sports for example girls and boys can compete together, while hockey is a typical example where participants are separated at an early age. A remarkable phenomenon is the actual policy of the soccer federation where girls and boys of primary school age compete together and against each other (Buisman, 1998).

15.3.11 Broad offer versus specialization at early age

Taking into account the developmental stages of children, it is advisable for young children (up to 10 years) to introduce them to a general and broad basic training for all sports (De Knop et al., 1994). Early specialization in one sports discipline, and even in specific functions, for example training only as a goalkeeper, has to be avoided. On the other hand there is an increasing freedom that causes, in combination with the large amount of leisure possibilities, problems for youngsters to make a (good) choice. Today consumers can select from an increasing offer of programs, events, and facilities within the cultural, sport, recreational, and tourist domains. As a youngster you need to have strong legs to be able to carry the increasing freedom and the growing number of alternatives (De Knop et al., 1996a). The aim was to give concrete form to the concept 'child-oriented sport'. This is done based on information about eleven criteria, three general principles of good practice in sport and eight specific principles for youth sport. We can conclude there is no general answer, there are age differences as well as individual preferences.

15.4 Introduction to the following chapters

Young participants have a clear view of the quality of youth sport, based on their daily experiences in sport. Adults should never forget to listen and especially observe children during their leisure time in order to understand what they appreciate when they are master of themselves and of the (sport) situation. The tendency of looking for the subjective approach to leisure and sport is in accordance with the evolution from a 'top-down' determinism toward a 'bottom-up' understanding of social life (Eitzen, 2000). A bottom-up understanding of youth sport requires that we do fieldwork, immersing ourselves in the social world that can be observed among organized youth sport.

The two chapters, following this introduction, deal with such a bottom-up understanding by describing results of phenomenological research in youth sport. In the contribution of Baar (chapter 16) research will be described about the experiences of children in four branches of sports, namely soccer, tennis, gymnastics and volleyball. This research focuses specifically on the transition from "Little League Sports" to sports for children who are slightly older. Based on questionnaires about their opinions on sports, in-depth information is gathered and inductively content analyzed. The second contribution of Theeboom (chapter 17) is about the experiences of children in martial arts. Children engaged in eight different martial arts were interviewed and the data was also analyzed through qualitative research methodology. The conceptual framework 'double character of sport' will be used to describe the results.

References

Andrews, J. (1999). Synthèse finale. In : Institut International des droits de l'enfant. *Un champion à tout prix? Les droit de l'enfant et le sport* (pp. 147-152). Institut International des droits de l'enfant & Institut Universitaire Kurt Bösch.

Baar, P. (1996). Drop out in gymnastics for boys, a phenomenological study of the causes and backgrounds. In: A. Buisman (Ed.), *Jeugdsport en Beleid* (pp.128-147). Houten/Diegem: Bohn Stafleu van Loghum. (in Dutch).

Brettschneider, W.-D. & Bräutigam, M. (1990). *Sport in the daily life of youngsters – Research Report*. Materialen zum Sport in Nordrhein-Westfalen, Düsseldorf Kultusministerium Nordrhein-Westfalen. (in German).

Buisman, A.J. (1983). How child-friendly is a sports club? In: *NKS. Congresverslag "Jeugd-Sport-Beleid"*. 's-Hertogenbosch: NKS. (in Dutch).

Buisman, A.J (1998). Youth Sport, a particular story. *Tijdschrift over jeugd en samenleving,* 2, pp. 67-77. (in Dutch).

Buisman, A.J. (1995). Achievement in sport: a pedagogical analysis of meanings. In: A.J Buisman (Ed.), *Jongeren over sport* (pp. 41-63), Houten/Diegem: Bohn Stafleu van Loghum. (in Dutch).

Buisman, A.J., Knop, P. De & Theeboom, M. (1998). Quality of youth sport; towards a pedagogical framework. In: P. De Knop & A.J. Buisman (Eds.), *Kwaliteit van Jeugdsport*. (pp. 29-61), Brussel: VUBpress. (in Dutch).

Buisman, A.J. & Baar, P. (1995). The meaning of a youth perspective in sport. In: A.J Buisman (Ed.), *Jongeren over sport* (pp.7-27), Houten/Diegem: Bohn Stafleu van Loghum. (in Dutch).

Buisman, A.J. & Rossum, J van (1998). Values and value clarification in sport. In: J. Steenbergen, A.J. Buisman, P. De Knop, & J.M.H. Lucassen (Eds.), *Waarden en normen in de sport*. (pp. 13-43). Houten/Diegem: Bohn Stafleu van Loghum. (in Dutch).

Burton, D. & Martens, R. (1986). Pinned by their own goals: An exploratory investigation into why kids drop out of wrestling. *Journal of Sport Psychology*, 8, pp. 183-197.

Chelladurai, P. (1987). Multidimensionality and multiple perspectives of organizational effectiveness. *Journal of Sport management*, 1, pp. 37-47.

Chelladurai, P. (1993). Leadership. In: R.N. Singer, M. Murpy & L.K. Tennant (Eds.), *Handbook of research on sport psychology* (pp. 647-671). New York, NJ: Macmillan.

Chelladurai, P. & Riemer, H.A. (1997). A classification of the facets of athlete satisfaction. *Journal of Sport Management*, 11, pp. 133-159.

Clearing House (1999). The Rights of the Child in Sport. *Sports Information Bulletin*, 2, (51), pp. 7-44.

Coakley, J. (1992). Burnout among adolescent athletes: A personal failure or social problem? *Sociology of Sport Journal*, 33, pp. 231-244.

Crum, B. (1991). *About the sportification of society*. Haarlem: De Vrieseborch. (in Dutch).

David, P. (1999). Children's rights and sports. *The International Journal of Children's Rights*, 7, pp. 53-81.

Donnely, P. & Young, K. (1988). The construction and confirmation of identity in sport subcultures. *Sociology of Sport Journal*, 5 (3), pp. 223-40

Duijvestijn, P. (1998). *Participation of youngsters in the sports club*. Gouda: Assist (in Dutch).

Eitzen, D.S. (2000). Social control and sport, In: J. Coakley & E. Dunning (Eds), *Handbook of Sport Studies* (pp. 370-381). London: Sage.

Gould, D. & Petlichkoff, L. (1988). Psychological stress and the age-group wrestler. In: E.W. Brown & C.F. Branta (Eds.), *Competitive sports for children and youth* (pp. 63-73). Champaign, ILL: Human Kinetics.

Haan, M., de, Iersel, B. van, Horvers, C., Vloet, L., Knop, P De & Buisman, A.J. (1997). Family and sports clubs – About the relationship of parents with the sports club of their children. *Lichamelijke opvoeding*, 19, pp. 63-69. (in Dutch).

Hellstadt, J.C. (1987). The coach/parent/athlete relationships. *Sports Psychologist*, 1(2), pp. 151-160.

Knop, P. De, Laporte, W., Meerbeek, R. van, Martelaer, K. De, Impens, G. & Roelandt, F. (1991). *Physical fitness and sport participation of the Flamish youth: analysis of organized sport in Flanders*. Brussel: BLOSO/IOS. (in Dutch).

Knop, P. De, Wylleman, P., Theeboom, M., Martelaer, K. De, Puymbroek, L. van & Wittock, H. (1994). *Youth-friendly sport clubs. Developing an effective youth sport policy*, Brussel: VUBPress. (in Dutch).

Knop, P. De, Engström, L.M., Skirstad, B. & Weiss, M.R. (1996a). *Worldwide trends in youth sport*. Champaign, ILL: Human Kinetics.

Knop, P. De, Laporte, W. Auweele, Y., Vanden, Martelaer, K. De, Heite, S., Rzewnicki, R., Verhoeven, M., & Wylleman, P. (1996a). *Youth-friendliness in organized sport*. Brussel: BLOSO/IOS. (In Dutch).

Knop, P. De & Martelaer, K. De (1998a). Youth sport: a developmental, psychological and pedagogical perspective. *Lichamelijke Opvoeding*, 86, 4, pp. 152-157. (in Dutch).

Knop, P. De & Martelaer, K. De (1998a). Quality requirements in youth sport from a developmental and pedagogical perspective. In: P. De Knop & A.J. Buisman (Eds.), *Kwaliteit van Jeugdsport* (pp. 63-77), Brussel: VUBpress. (in Dutch).

Knop, P. De & Buisman, A.J. (1998). *Quality of youth sport*. Brussel: VUBpress. (in Dutch).

Knop, P. De, Buisman, A.J. & Martelaer, K. De (1998). *Quality and quality improvement in youth sport: The ideal image approach, the customer-centered approach and the approach from the perspective of the service provider,* 6th Congress of the European Association for Sport Management, "Service Quality in Sport" Conference Proceedings, Madeira (Portugal), October 4, 1998.

Knop, P. De, Hoecke, J. Van, Martelaer, K. De, Theeboom, M., Heddegem, L. Van & Wylleman, P. (2000A). *Quality Management in the Sport Clubs: Youth Functioning.* Gent: Publicatiefonds voor Lichamelijke Opvoeding. (in Dutch).

Knoppers, (A. (1985). Professionalization of attitudes: A review and critique. *Quest,* 37, pp. 92-102.

Langeveld, M.J. (1972). *Developemental psychology.* Groningen, Nederland: Wolters-Noordhoff. (in Dutch).

Martelaer, K. De (1997). *Study of the youth-orientation of organized swimming in Flanders.* Unpublished doctoral dissertation. Brussel: Free University of Brussels. (in Dutch).

Martelaer, K. De & Knop, P. De (1998). Youth-friendliness of organized swimming : growing toward independency. In: P. De Knop & A.J. Buisman (Eds.), *Kwaliteit van Jeugdsport* (pp. 311-336) Brussel: VUBPRESS. (In Dutch).

Martelaer, K. De, Knop, P. De, Theeboom, M. & Heddegem L. van (1999). L'intérêt supérieur de l'enfant dans le sport et la situation actuelle en Flandre. In : Institut International des droits de l'enfant. *Un champion à tout prix? Les droits de l'enfant et le sport* (pp. 65-84). Institut International des droits de l'enfant & Institut Universitaire Kurt Bösch.

Martelaer, K. De, Knop, P. De, Theeboom, M. & Heddegem, L. van (2000a). The UN Convention as a basis for elaborating rights of children in sport. *Journal of Leisurability,* 2, pp. 3-10.

Martelaer, K. De, Knop, P. De, Heddegem, L. van & Theeboom, M. (2000b). *Organised sport: participation and experiences of children, 2000,* International Conference for Physical Educators (ICPE 2000), Hong Kong, 7-8 July 2000.

Martens, R. (1987). *Coaches guide to sports psychology*. Champaign, ILL: Human Kinetics.

Martens, R. (1988). Helping children become independent, responsible adults through sports. In: E.W. Brown & C.F. Branta (Eds.), *Competitive sports for children and youth: An overview of research and issues* (pp.297-307). Champaign, ILL: Human Kinetics.

Meijer, W.A.J. (1992). *General pedagogy and cultural diversity*. Nijkerk: Intro. (in Dutch).

Meijer, W.A.J. (1995). *Perspectives on human beings and education*. Nijkerk: Intro. (in Dutch).

National Youth Sports Coaches Association, (NYSCA) (1988). *National Standards for Youth Sports*. West Palm Beach (Fl.), USA: NYSCA.

Riemer, H.A., & Chelladurai, P. (1998). Development of the Athlete Satisfaction Questionnaire (ASQ). *Journal of Sport & Exercise Psychology*, 20, pp. 127-156.

Rinehart, R.E. (2000). Arriving sport: alternatives to formal sport, In J. Coakley & E. Dunning (Eds.), *Handbook of Sport studies* (pp. 504-519), London: Sage.

Rossum, J.H.A. van (1996). I want to be the first. Empirical comments on the primacy of willing to win in sport and games. In: A.J. Buisman (Ed.), *Jeugdsport en Beleid* (pp. 109-128), Houten/Diegem: Bohn Stafleu van Loghum. (in Dutch).

Rotella, Hanson & Coop (1991). Burnout in youth sports. *The Elementary School Journal*, 91, pp. 421-428.

Seefeldt, V. & Gould, D. (1980). *Physical and psychological effects of athletic competition on children and youth*. Washington, CD: ERIC Clearinghouse on Teacher Education.

Seifert, K.L. & Hoffnung, R.J. (1994). *Child and Adolescent Development*. Boston/Toronto: Houghton Mifflin Company.

Shields, D.L.L. & Bredemeier, B.J.L. (1995). *Character Development and Physical Activity*. Champaign, ILL: Human Kinetics.

Smith, R.E. & Smoll, F.L. (1996). The coach as a focus of research and intervention in youth sports. In: F.L. Smoll, & R.E. Smith (Eds.), *Children and Youth Sport. A biopsychosocial perspective* (pp.125-141). Madison: Brown & Benchmark.

Steenbergen, J. & Tamboer, J.W.I. (1998). The double character of sport: conceptual dynamics. In: J. Steenbergen, A.J. Buisman, P. De Knop, & J.M.H. Lucassen (Eds.), *Waarden en normen in de sport* (pp. 69-95). Houten/Diegem: Bohn Stafleu van Loghum. (in Dutch).

Telama, R. (1999). Le sport et l'enfant: un marriage heureux. In : Institut International des droits de l'enfant. *Un champion à tout prix? Les droit de l'enfant et le sport* (pp. 11-24). Institut International des droits de l'enfant & Institut Universitaire Kurt Bösch.

Timmers, E. (1993). Working independent. Getting more out of our lessons. *Lichamelijke Opvoeding*, 2, pp. 52-57. (in Dutch).

Vanreusel, B., Knop, P. De, Martelaer, K. De, Impens, G., Roelandt, F., Teirlynck, P., & Wylleman, P. (1992). *Physical Fitness and Sport Participation of the Flemish Youth*. (Volume 4. Participation and Dropout). Brussel: IOS. (in Dutch).

Verhellen, E. (1994). *Convention on the rights of the child. Background, motivation, strategies, main themes*. Leuven/Apeldoorn: Garant.

Vloet, L. & Buisman, A. (1998). Youth athletics for everyone ... Differentiation as quality criterion. In: P. De Knop & A.J. Buisman (Eds.), *Kwaliteit van Jeugdsport* (pp. 289-310). Brussel: VUBPRESS. (in Dutch).

16 ORGANIZED SPORT PROGRAMS FOR CHILDREN: DO THEY MEET THE INTERESTS OF THE CHILDREN EFFECTIVELY?

Paul Baar

Introduction

There are many theories about what sport really is, why children play sports and how sports can be classified. In the Netherlands, however, relatively little research has hitherto been done to find out how children themselves experience organized sports programs and what they like about the various sports. To fill this lacuna, a research has now been conducted to find out to what extent four particular sports, namely soccer, tennis, gymnastics and volleyball (as offered by sports clubs as a voluntary leisure activity in the Netherlands), appeal to children.

The research, a project of the program "Values and Standards in the Field of Sport" (Buisman, De Knop, Lucassen & Tamboer, 1994), is focused specifically on the transition at the age of 10 to 13 from junior level with "soft" rules to intermediate or senior level with "strict" or adult rules. There may be a mismatch between the sports as offered by sports clubs and the rules of the game on the one hand, and children's interests and capabilities on the other. This may largely account for the widely fluctuating and often temporary pursuit of such sports by children in this age bracket in the Netherlands, and also for the drop-out rate. This "problem" calls for the actual significance children attribute to their sports to be re-assessed. Do the organized youth sport programs meet the interests of the children effectively? The objective of this project is to take stock of the ideas children have about sport, in order to initiate discussion between educationalists about the content of organized youth sport programs. Certain points of interest are examined that have been revealed by the research project, initiated in 1994, into how children in the 10 to 13 age bracket experience competitive sports. This age group is of particular interest because it is between these ages that children tend to drop out of sport (Baar, 1991). It is also a period of transition from childhood to the start of adulthood, with the onset of adolescence and accelerating cognitive, physical and psycho-social development. This in turn has consequences for the way in which juvenile sports are organized. The general question posed by the project is, therefore, how children experience competitive sports and to what extent four offered disciplines – football (soccer), volleyball, gymnastics and tennis – satisfy children's capabilities and interests.

This chapter will be mainly limited to a discussion of children's sports interests. To what extent are young players satisfied with the way their respective sports are played and practised? Also studied is how far one should go in adapting sports to suit children's levels of development, and what those adaptations could be in the various disciplines, in the views of the children themselves.

16.1 Method

The method used for this research is interpretative, and is based on the Grounded Theory developed by Glaser & Strauss (Symbolic Interactionism). Researchers use a grounded theory approach when they want to take a fresh look at phenomena. This theory focuses on describing the experiences children have with sports, based on the children's points of view. In the project, comprising a number of partial studies, boys and girls were asked for their opinions on sports (Baar 1996a/b; Bossema, 1997; Van den Berg, 1997; Van de Brand & Twerda, 1996; Van Schip, 1998, 1999; Van Zweden, 1998). This chapter is concentrated on one of these partial studies.

An open-ended questionnaire, particularly amenable to soliciting the experiences children have with their sport, was designed to elicit preferences as to how the various sports are or should be practised and adapted. The questionnaire was submitted to 277 children: 64 soccer players: 38 boys and 26 girls (Van den Berg, 1997); 103 volleyball players: 42 boys and 61 girls (Van de Brand & Twerda, 1996); 59 gymnasts: 12 boys and 47 girls (Bossema, 1997); 51 tennis players: 23 boys and 28 girls (Van Zweden, 1998). The study was carried out in several districts in the Netherlands. The athletes came from different sports clubs per sport. The majority of them were sporting on a recreational, competitive level: from children who had just entered sport to sub-top athletes who belonged to the "elite" in their district. This sample is assumed to be representative of the heterogeneous youth sport in the Netherlands, aged 10 – 13 years.

The open questionnaire comprises several topics. The topic related to the theme in this chapter, had 3 open-ended questions:

-"If you could change the way (sport) is played or practised, would you do so?"

-"If your answer is YES, what would you change and why?"

-"If your answer is NO, why not?

The data was subsequently processed and analysed in qualitative terms. In summary, all possibly relevant topics were distinguished, coded and identified with key words and later reduced, by constant and systematic comparison, to a list with concepts that encompassed the central themes in the questionnaires. The findings of a qualitative analysis are more idiographic than nomothetic. They are focused on describing individual experiences and meanings, and testing to see whether findings can illuminate and be relevant to other children, coaches and trainers in the practice of sport.

16.2 Results

In analogue with the above mentioned questions, the results to be presented will illuminate the following issues: the general opinion about their respective sports, the proposed changes per sport to make the sport even more attractive for them, and the (possible) underlying motives for children not to change their sport.

No structural gaps in the sports programs on offer

Arguably the sports offering for children is still sufficiently attractive and challenging. To the question: "If you could change the way (sport) is played or practised, would you do so?", 53 per cent responded in the first instance that they did not wish to do so, 46 per cent proposed one of more changes and 1 per cent did not answer the question.

Further study of the respondents proposing changes reveals that 14 children answered "no" in the first instance, but then went on to propose a change. Moreover, 23 children proposed changes but said at the same time they were satisfied with the way their sport was now played or practised and wanted no further changes. If we include these two groups with the above-mentioned 53 per cent, we can conclude that 67 per cent of the children expressed an explicitly positive opinion about the way their sport was played or practised. The other children who proposed changes did not express explicitly negative opinions about their respective sports.

The young sports participants questioned in this survey do not perceive any structural gaps or insuperable difficulties in the offered sports programs. This finding is supported by other sports drop-out surveys in the Netherlands (Baar, 1991; Bassa & Naafs, 1986; Hofstede & Hümmels, 1994) which reveal that the great majority of those dropping out of sport still have a positive attitude to the sport they have abandoned. So the sport itself is evidently an almost negligible factor in children's decisions to discontinue a particular sport. Rather, such decisions are prompted by personal considerations and factors relating to the sports club in question.

Changes per sport

Although the majority of the children were satisfied with the way their sport is practised at present, they did give some useful tips as to how the playing of these sports could be made even more attractive. The children's proposals were generally made with a view to keeping the game going (continuity) with as few dead moments and as many exciting action moments as possible. In addition, children want to practise a sport in their own way as far as possible, in which process a great deal of intensive movement and varied training exercises would make the sport even more attractive for them (Baar, 1996a). Some of the proposed changes per sport will now be briefly reviewed.

Volleyball
In volleyball (Van de Brand & Twerda, 1996) children are taught to play the game differently when they move up from junior level. For example, they have to serve a heavier and larger ball over a higher net and a longer distance (preferably overarm). Evidently many children find this difficult to begin with. It was therefore proposed that the

court should be made larger so that the ball can be successfully played more frequently. Children in the age bracket in question are still growing and still have to learn how to handle their physical strength, for example how hard the ball must be struck. Thus, as a child gains better control of his physical strength, he will develop the ability to make soft serves.

Another proposal was that a game should last longer. Respondents preferred a fixed duration of play, or the old scoring system effective prior to 1st January 1995. At the time this research was done (1996), a game was won by the team that first scores 17 points. Another expressed preference was that a two-point lead should be needed to win, to create greater tension and prolong the game.

Children like to score as much as possible. Scoring a point forms the reward for an act of movement. Tips were provided to that end, e.g. the non-scoring team should be able to score as well – as in the rally points system, which, in 1996, normally was only played on a higher level in the fifth set. It was also proposed that the net be lowered so that serving and spiking have a greater chance of success. In competitive play any error or foul committed counts. Children prefer to correct errors, to be given the chance to do it properly, and several of them considered that net faults that do not affect rallies should be abolished - or abolished altogether in the junior game.

Net faults can also be committed during the serve, whereupon service passes over to the opponents (note: this rule has been changed in September 2000; now it is allowed to make net faults). Some children proposed that the serving team be given another chance, as in tennis and table tennis. And why not? If service passes to the opponents after three good serves anyway, why should the serving team not be given another chance if it commits a net serve? Comparing the rules of one sport with those of another can be quite illuminating, and this proposal makes it clear that sports can learn a lot from one another.

Another suggestion with regard to fouls and errors was that the ball should then be played over again. Another one was that the same player should be allowed to play the ball twice in succession. It is not always feasible to return the ball over the net after just three touches, particularly after a brilliant save at the back of the court.

The children's suggestions are not only intended to reduce the likelihood of fouls and errors, but are also good ideas for sustaining rallies during play to give the game greater continuity.

Soccer

Just as volleyball players spurn the idea of being able to kick the ball, so some football players would explicitly prefer the ball to be kicked into play instead of thrown in (van den Berg, 1997). If the aim of the throw-in is to resume play as quickly as possible, the ball could just as well be kicked into play (as in indoor football); after all, football "ought" to be played with the feet. Some respondents said they would like to be allowed to jump when the ball is thrown in. Young children often do so automatically, and are upset when the referee blows his whistle for that reason. Play then has to be resumed, and in the worst case the ball is passed to the opponents.

Some children also wanted to be able to pass the ball back to the goalkeeper. In the view of young children in particular, the passing-back rule (intended to thwart time-wasting in adult matches) adds little to the game. The offside rule was regarded as a nuisance by some children, and was unclear to many of them (young children in particular). In practice, this rule tends to interrupt play too often, although children did understand its purpose. Boys in particular inventively devised all kinds of ways to supervise play as effectively as possible. Having more referees and linesmen was proposed, as well as referees unaffiliated to the competing clubs, allowing linesmen to give cards, transmitters in the goal, replacing a player after five personal fouls (as in basketball).

As regards blowing the whistle on fouls, the general view was that referees should not be too strict on minor infringements. Football still has a macho image, and a certain amount of rough-and-tumble and knock-for-knock may be generally acceptable. Stern action was, however, advocated against "professional" fouls entailing a high risk of injury. The interesting thing is that controls and sanctions of this kind seem to evaporate when children play football informally (on the street or rough grass). Children want to be constantly active when playing sport. If the game is interrupted too often or has too many dead moments, they lose interest. A study by Coakley (1998) reveals that children playing sport in an informal setting prefer flexible rules under which a great deal is allowed – up to and including ignoring the rules altogether – as long as this does not disturb or interrupt the action. This does not mean that children clearly prefer unorganized sports. On the contrary, they derive great enjoyment from competitive sports. But the game is then played in a setting largely governed by rules, where many parameters are fixed. Not because this is necessary for the children but it is just how the game should be played.

Tennis

Tennis players were the most satisfied with the way their sport is played (Van Zweden, 1998). Whereas the change ratio was about fifty-fifty in the other sports, 63 per cent of tennis players said they did not want their sport to be changed in any way. This percentage may be partly attributable to the fact that many of the tennis-playing respondents had only been playing for a short while and so had had less time to form an opinion.

Incidentally, most of the tennis players questioned in this survey tended to play "recreationally", which may go to explain why they made relatively few proposals for modifying or adapting the rules of the game. In football and volleyball it is more usual for children to play in competitive leagues or tournaments, or at least regular matches.

As in volleyball it was proposed that the court should be enlarged and the net lowered, and even that the net and service court lines be eliminated altogether. Here too, the impression was gained that children want to be active as much as possible and disdain any aspects that entail deferral or interruption of the essential movement activity, e.g. warming up, picking up the balls and halting play after a net serve. The most frequent comment amongst tennis players was that the scoring system could be made 'normal': 1, 2, 3 etc. instead of 15, 30, 40 etc. and preferably in their own language (Dutch) instead of English.

Gymnastics

Apart from making proposals as to how this sport should be modified or adapted, the gymnasts questioned in this survey, unlike the other sports practitioners, mainly commented on aspects relating to the content of the training sessions and to individual preferences for particular parts or exercises. Thus, some children mentioned the "boring" long mat on which little variation is possible. It was proposed that this be made more resilient so that better bouncing and higher jumps could be achieved (Bossema, 1997). Children have a tremendous urge to keep moving, and so the gymnasts were keen to practise dynamic and optimum forms of movement. One of the conclusions of a sports drop-out survey amongst former gymnasts (Baar, 1991) was that boys discontinue gymnastics because they cannot work off their energy and miss the running element in gymnastics (they then tend to change over to football). Gymnastic exercises are of brief duration, between which there are many moments of inactivity. Vaulting and trampolining are favourite exercises because they best satisfy children's urge to move their bodies: the high degree of running, jumping and somersaulting make these activities more lively than other gymnastic disciplines.

Children want continuity in their sport, with many action moments. Their preferences for longer training sessions with smaller training groups and more (adult) coaching make this clear. One hour of gym is too short to really get going. If the group is large, the children often have to cope with differences of standard, as a result of which participants are held back and have to wait a long time for their turn. The findings of this survey reveals that fear and daring are particular features of gymnastics. During training children are frequently confronted with certain movements that they initially do not dare to undertake. Besides the fact that balancing at the limits of one's capabilities can be exciting, the awareness of risks becomes greater as children grow older. Girls in particular frequently reported their fear of falls, injuries, pain, heights, disorientation etc. So it is not so surprising that participants want to make this sport "safer" by taking all kinds of protective measures. For example, soft-padding and widening the parallel bars, providing them with a pit or simply lowering them to just above the floor. Apart from protective measures of this kind, a good working relationship with the trainer is important. Several children wanted more support and attention from their trainer when performing exercises liable to result in injuries (parallel bars and long horse). Trainers and helpers are not always fully attentive, or cannot always give individual assistance due to the size of the group.

Moreover, the underlying idea in gymnastics is that the children must get used to "scary" exercises as quickly as possible, otherwise they will never learn them. But how are children to deal with this approach? It is all very well for the trainer to say you can cope with a particular exercise, but the problem in such cases is that children blame themselves for not being able or not daring to tackle it. It is not usual to mention pain and fear at the gym club and so children are more or less forced to suppress such feelings. Incidentally, it is worth reporting that the girls questioned in this survey appreciated trainers not so much for their professional expertise as for their positive social skills.

16.3 Why children do not want to change their sport

The majority of the children reported that they felt no urge to change their sporting discipline in a structural way. 67 per cent of the children expressed an explicitly positive opinion about the way their sport was played or practised. How can we interpret this?

Many children find it difficult to devise new rules of the game themselves or modifications of the prevailing ones. This is partly because many of them have been pursuing their respective sports for less than one year. Such children are still exploring their capabilities and are not yet ready to contemplate possible changes. It may be that not all children have yet developed the cognitive ability of devising rules of the game themselves. Many of them said they could not imagine what should be changed in the way their sport is played or practised. One comment should be made about the data-collection method used: a disadvantage of a written questionnaire is that writing skills are required of children that not all of them master. A verbal interview may well have uncovered more and different information, as follow-up questions can then be asked.

While young children were quite inventive in devising rules of the game, older children were far less so. This has to do with children's yearning to grow up. The desire to conform with the rules in force for the older age groups and adults, and to play "just like" and "together with" their seniors is a central aspect of the way children experience sports. Respect for the (traditional) rules as they are is so great that many children are reluctant to contemplate departing from them or changing them. This idea of "that's how it should be" is reflected in statements like "otherwise it's not football any more". In particular, volleyball players changing over from junior to intermediate level feel that only then are they really playing volleyball. They then join "the other group" and no longer have to play the "little kids' games". Not every change or adaptation is necessarily an improvement. In volleyball, some rules were changed in January 1995, like serving from the yellow end line and being able to touch the ball with the whole body.

The serving rule did not come in for any criticism, but the rule allowing the ball to be played with the whole body - including the feet - met with a lot of opposition by the children:

> Since first January 1995, there's a rule that you can also kick. I find that a stupid rule. It turns the game into football. (Girl, 11 years old).

It is possible that volleyball players feel "kicking" to be diametrically opposed to "hand-batting", just as footballers are not allowed to touch the ball with their hands (which is why the footballers questioned preferred to kick in the ball rather than throw it in). One reason why children opt for a particular sport is the specific movements that typify that sport. Another explanation for the "violent" rejection of this rule could be that volleyball players want to distance themselves from football. In the Netherlands football is clearly the number one sport in the popularity stakes and attracts by far the most media coverage. Distancing oneself from a "big brother" creates an individual identity, and this is clearly reflected in volleyball practice. For example, if the ball is kicked in the course of a training session, the immediate reaction is often "this isn't a football club!" The fact that girls are so negative about volleyball "being turned into football" may be because they tend to regard football as a boys' sport.

Children's reluctance to change the rules of the game may also be explained in that children already find the sport challenging enough and/or difficult enough, or in that they have (just) got used to it. We see this in the gymnasts in particular, who regret constantly having to learn new exercises. Such gymnasts have often been members of a gymnastics club for several years and have devoted a lot of effort and energy to their sport. So they are afraid that, if changes are introduced, they will have to invest even more effort and energy in order to master new proficiencies, which may in turn induce feelings of uncertainty and incompetence.

Conclusion

The question that now can be asked, in view of the survey results, is how far can one go with adapting sports to cater for the capabilities and interests of children, and what those adaptations could be in the various disciplines? The children's message is clear: they are generally satisfied with the way sports are currently played and practised, and all kinds of specific tips were given for making those sports even more attractive than they already are. In such a way, children can help to give form and content to the sports they pursue, provided the organizing bodies are prepared to make appropriate changes to the way they are played in the light of the points raised by the children themselves. Some suggestions even crossed the boundaries of a particular sport: the various sports can learn from one another. Sometimes the children considered that changes went too far, such as the above-mentioned "football rule" in volleyball, but in any case there is no question of a "gulf" between sports as currently structured and sports clubs' offerings on the one hand, and what children themselves can and want to do on the other.

What tasks remain for those offering these four sports, assuming the survey findings are also true for the large numbers of children pursuing competitive sport on a weekly basis? Can it then be assumed that all is well with the sports programs on offer? In my view, making competitive sport suitable for children is not just a question of how the sport itself is organized. The way in which children pursuing those sports are handled by coaches, trainers and referees, and introduced by them into the parameters of the game is at least an equally important factor in catering for children or making sports "child-friendly". Moreover, the attitudes and wishes of children with regard to the game should be properly considered, so that adapted criteria can be formulated to govern the way the sport is pursued. This would enable sports associations and clubs to pursue juvenile sport policies fully catering for the particular significances that children attribute to organized competitive sport.

References

Baar, P. (1991). *Sport withdrawal of male youth gymnasts – A qualitative research on the backgrounds of sport withdrawal of young male gymnasts of the Royal Dutch Gymnastics Association.* Pedagogic master thesis. Utrecht: Utrecht University. (in Dutch).

Baar, P. (1996a). *Children writing about sport – A report on the experiences of children at the age of 10-13 with organized sport programs.* Arnhem: NOC*NSF. (in Dutch).

Baar, P. (1996b). Experiences in Volleyball – Research on the experiences in organized youth sports among volleyball players at the age of 10-13. *Volley Techno*, pp. 4-13. (in Dutch).

Bassa, P. & Naafs, A. (1986). *Research on sport activity patterns among members in the Dutch Handball Association.* Zaltbommel: NHV. (in Dutch).

Berg, G. van den (1997). *How do children experience soccer – A research on the experiences of children at the age of 10-13 with youth soccer programs.* Pedagogic master thesis. Utrecht: Utrecht University. (in Dutch).

Bossema, C. (1997). *The world of gymnastics through children's eyes a sport pedagogical study.* Pedagogic master thesis. Utrecht: Utrecht University. (in Dutch).

Brand, B. van de & Twerda, R. (1996). *How do children experience volleyball – A research on the play experiences of children at the age of 10–13 with youth volleyball programs.* Pedagogic master thesis. Utrecht: Utrecht University. (in Dutch).

Buisman, A., De Knop, P., Lucassen & J.W.I. Tamboer, J. (1994). *Values and Standards in the Field of Sport.* Arnhem: NOC*NSF. (in Dutch).

Coakley, J. (1998). *Sport in Society - Issues and Controversies.* Boston e.a: Mc Graw-Hill.

Hofstede, A. & Hümmels, M. (1994). *Soccer players without a club. Motives for youths to give up their soccer.* Enschede: Informatie & Onderzoek. (in Dutch).

Schip, B. van (1998). *The internal goods of gymnastics: A theoretical framework. Pedagogic literature study.* Utrecht: Utrecht University (in Dutch).

Schip, B. van (1999). *'Dancing it goes the easy way ....' A qualitative research on children's experience (aged 10–13 years) with the internal goods of gymnastics.* Pedagogic master thesis. Utrecht: Utrecht University. (in Dutch).

Zweden, J. van (1998). *Children writing about tennis – A report on the experiences of children at the age 10-13 with youth tennis programs.* Pedagogic master thesis. Utrecht: Utrecht University. (in Dutch).

17 MARTIAL ARTS AND CHILDREN

Marc Theeboom

Introduction

Today, Asian martial arts are popular among youth all over the world. International comparative studies have indicated that in most countries martial arts are among the most popular extracurricular sports that are practised by children between 10 and 15 years (Clearing House, 1997; De Knop, Engström, Skirstad, & Weiss, 1996). Furthermore, findings showed that Asian martial arts were among the top 10 most practised sports in general. With regard to organized sport in particular, they came in second place after soccer and were regarded as one of the most important new trends in sports participation.

According to Van Bottenburg (1994), the popularity of Asian martial arts in the West has resulted from a number of factors, such as the growing economic power and international prestige of Japan and, to a lesser extent, other Eastern-Asian countries. Also, the post war stationing of American and European troops in Japan and South Korea, as well as the emigration of Asians to the United States and Europe, have contributed to the spread of Asian martial arts in the West.

Other factors may also be accountable for the popularity of Asian martial arts. According to Harman (1986), there is a new appreciation for traditional and holistic approaches in culture at large, which is reflected in the fascination for psychic phenomena, astrology, reincarnation, extraterrestrial being, etc. More specifically, Harman stated that this has resulted in the health area in an appreciation, among other things, for acupuncture, native herbal medicine, faith healing, while in physical education Eastern movement disciplines (e.g. martial arts and yoga) have become popular. This evolution, which is primarily concerned with defining values, meanings and goals, can partly be explained as a reaction to the confusion about values that exists in modern Western society. Harman indicated that this confusion, which can be examplified by the substitution of pseudo-values such as economic indicators to guide our societal decision making, emerged since the 'debunking' of religion by science. This has resulted in the new appreciation for holistic approaches that not too long ago were dismissed as 'pre-scientific'. This trend can partly explain the increasing international popularity of taijiquan, a traditional Chinese martial art which emphasizes concentration and relaxation while slowly performing a variety of fighting techniques (Moegling, 1986; Sagot, 1992).

A number of studies have reported the popularity of (Asian) martial arts among children. This chapter discusses the most important findings of a study that has analysed views and experiences among young martial artists and instructors. Prior to this discussion, a description of the evolution, as well as of the main characteristics of the martial arts and their practice will be provided. Finally, the results of the study will be situated within the 'double character of sport' which is the conceptual framework of the 'Values and Norms in Sport' program.

17.1 Evolution of Asian Martial Arts

Although many Asian countries have their own martial arts, it is well-documented that most of these sports originated in China (Maliszewski, 1992). The first signs of a structured fighting system date back to the Shang dynasty (1,600-1,066 B.C., Li & Du, 1991). During the 'Autumn and Spring Period' (770-476 B.C.), martial arts contests were held regularly (Xu, 1991). Through the centuries, these fighting skills became more varied and refined. Gradually this knowledge spread to other parts of Asia, where specific local variations were developed. This resulted in a myriad of other Asian fighting styles, in addition to the existing varied system of Chinese martial arts (Draeger & Smith, 1975).

17.2 Characteristics of Asian Martial Arts

All martial arts can be distinguished by their specific characteristics. For example, some types focus primarily on leg techniques (e.g. kicks and sweeps), while others emphasize the use of head-locks, throws and joint-locks or armed skills (e.g. using traditional swords or sticks). In general, Asian martial arts practice consists of three forms: (a) individual routines, (b) partner routines, and (c) free fights.

17.2.1 Individual Routines

A routine (or kata) is an individual exercise that consists of several armed or unarmed techniques that are performed consecutively according to a pre-arranged set of movements and stances. Routines can also be performed simultaneously in a group. Most Asian martial arts have individual routine practice.

Partner Routines

These routines are performed with a partner. Similar to the individual routines, they include a pre-arranged set of armed or unarmed techniques.

Free Fights

In this kind of form, two opponents can freely use their techniques according to a specific set of rules. Most Asian martial arts include free fights. In contrast to the Chinese martial arts, some Japanese martial arts include free fights with weapons. An example is the Japanese art of kendo (or sword fighting), in which participants use (bamboo) swords and wear protective gear.

17.3 Approaches of Martial Arts Practice

Variations over time have altered the characteristics of the Asian martial arts. Due to cultural and situational differences between Eastern and Western societies, the introduction of Asian martial arts in the West has had a distinct influence on their specific characteristics (Förster, 1986; Fuller, 1988; Guttmann, 1991). As a result, even Asian martial arts that are practiced in the West cannot be characterized by a clear and uniform concept. Three different approaches to Asian martial arts practice in the West have been described: (a) traditional, (b) efficiency, and (c) sporting (Theeboom, De Knop & Wylleman, 1995).

Traditional Approach

In this approach, participants strive for unity and coordination between internal (e.g. spiritual and mental) and external (e.g. physical) elements. According to this view, physical excellence in martial arts will not go without spiritual or mental cultivation (Kleinman, 1986). Back & Kim (1984) described four criteria that need to be fulfilled to keep the status of a traditional Asian martial art: (a) recognition of national or cultural origin, (b) development of fighting skills, (c) presence of artistic aspects, and (d) spiritual development.

Efficiency Approach

The efficiency approach emphasizes effectiveness and application of the techniques in a fight. Martial arts in this approach are mainly practised for self-defense reasons. Although one might argue that this approach actually goes back to the origin of the martial arts, that is, to know how to protect oneself, in Asia this function has lost a great deal of its importance, as other functions became more important (e.g., aestheticism, health and fitness). For example, distinct changes in form, content and function have characterized the development of the Chinese martial arts (Theeboom & De Knop, 1997). In the West however, the efficiency approach is very popular. According to Van Bottenburg (1994), this is the result of a growing commercialization among martial arts schools. Often the value of these schools is measured by the degree to which fighting skills are used efficiently by their students. As a result many martial arts schools are constantly looking for harder and more efficient fighting techniques to offer. Van Bottenburg (1994) has described this evolution as the 'hardening' of martial arts.

Sporting Approach

The sporting approach does not focus primarily on the acquisition of fighting competence, but rather regards martial arts as sports with positive effects on the physical, mental and social state of its participants. Unlike the efficiency approach where 'anything goes', in this third view the variety of fighting skills is restricted to what is allowed according to specific competition rules. Although it is important to mention that recent evolutions in martial arts competitions, such as the introduction of so-called 'ultimate or cage fighting' where only a very limited set of rules is used, raise doubts about whether these activities can still be referred to as sport. Consequently, some have described this trend as a 'desportification' of the martial arts (van Bottenburg & Heilbron, 1996), as these extreme fighting systems have a very limited set of rules and consequently show more resemblance to actual (street)fighting than to sport. One can refer here to the definition of sport as described by Steenbergen & Tamboer (1998), who defined sports as 'physical games' in which players are confronted with movement problems (e.g. running faster or jumping higher than others). These problems can only be solved by overcoming a number of 'unnecessary obstacles' (limitations or rules). With hardly any of these obstacles (forbidden techniques), most of these extreme fighting forms cannot be regarded as sports. Förster (1986) even described this trend as the 'brutalization' of the Asian martial arts.

The concept that three different approaches of martial arts practice exist shows similarity with recent findings of Columbus & Rice's (1998) phenomenological analysis of everyday life experiences of martial artists, in which they distinguished either 'compensatory' or 'emancipatory' adaptive functions contingent on context. According to their study, for some participants martial arts training compensated for felt lack of safety or lack of order and self-discipline, while others experienced martial arts in an emancipatory mode which would help them to use their skills to overcome challenges in everyday life and expanded their psychological life. While the former function of compensation shows some resemblance with the efficiency approach, the latter function can be compared to the traditional approach. Furthermore, Columbus & Rice (ibid.) pointed out that other contexts are possible as well. They referred here to martial arts as competitive sports, which clearly shows similarity with a sporting approach of martial arts practice.

17.4 Martial Arts and Children

However, despite the growing popularity of the martial arts among youth in the West, and the different approaches that exist, little is known about the way children experience the martial arts. For example, it remains unclear how children deal with harder martial arts. Will the practice of this kind of martial arts have an influence on the way they deal with violence? As indicated by Mitchell (1992), it is important to take the mental immaturity of children that are involved in martial arts into account. He referred to the fact that a nine-year-old black belt is not a martial artist, but "… at best he is a nine-year-old child who has been trained to use potentially dangerous techniques" (p.105). Consequently, various questions can be asked, such as "Why do youngsters practise martial arts?"; "How do they deal with the potentially dangerous fighting skills they learn?"; "How do they handle conflicts?"; "Do they experience any behavioral or psychological effects of martial arts practice?"; "Do they consider the martial arts as a sport or a way of life?"; etc.

Therefore, a study was set up to analyse experiences of *young* martial artists and youth trainers. The results of these two analyses will now be described separately in the next two sections.

17.5 Young martial artists

Method
Experiences of youngsters were analysed through qualitative research methodology (in-depth interviews). Forty children between the age of 8 and 12 years were interviewed (23 boys and 17 girls). All of them were at least one year involved in martial arts training. Children were randomly selected from clubs that had a specific youth section. Eight different martial arts were included (i.e., judo, karate, taekwondo, aikido, wrestling, kickboxing, wushu and boxing). From each sport 5 children were interviewed. The main purpose was to collect data with regard to children's experiences and ideas of their own martial arts involvement (e.g., participation motives, training and competition experiences, effects on behaviour). Semi-structured interviews were audiotaped and inductively content analysed.

Results

Findings revealed that most of the children in this study considered the ability to defend oneself an important motive to become involved in martial arts. This ability was not primarily directed towards physical assaults on the streets, but appears to be more regarded as a way to be able to deal with situations at school in which children are harassed by their peers.

However, learning to defend oneself seems not to be children's main motive. It was often regarded as an 'additional advantage'. The most important reasons for participation that were mentioned included enjoyment in the sport, being together with friends and perceiving physical competence. According to the children in this study, martial arts teachers play an important role in experiencing practices in a positive way. Also, a number of the children indicated that their parents encouraged them to start martial arts practice as a safety precaution. Other children were motivated by parents or friends that were involved in the martial arts themselves.

It is also noteworthy that no explicit choices appeared to be made for a particular martial art. Findings seemed to indicate that most children choose a specific martial art based on mere practical reasons (e.g. popularity of a club; personal contacts with members; distance from home). Also, most of them indicated that before they started practising, they did not have a clear view of the characteristics of the particular martial art they became involved in. Only a few of them (or their parents) deliberately selected a 'non-violent' martial art. Other motives were less mentioned, such as improvement of physical condition and flexibility, or the influence of the media.

Most children in this study were critical with regard to the violence that is showed in martial arts movies. They made a clear difference between the skills that are showed in films and the techniques they learn. These children indicated that, in contrast to what is shown in films, there is no pain involved during their own practice.

Children also indicated that they will not defend themselves if they have other alternatives, even if they realise that they might have an advantage through their martial arts background. It is interesting to note that, with regard to this, most children said that they experience a number of positive effects of martial arts practice on their behavior and personality. Here, reference was made to an increase in self confidence as a result of improved physical strength. Other effects that were reported related to better self-control and social skills as well as to the use of a non-violent attitude with regard to conflict resolution.

It is also interesting to indicate that several children said that they do not often talk about their sport to their friends. They prefer to discuss the martial arts and their experiences only with other martial artists.

Finally, it is important to mention that no distinct differences in the answers were found between boys and girls.

17.6 Youth trainers

Method

Similar to the first part of this study, a variety of martial arts was included (i.e. karate, aikido, judo, taekwondo, kickboxing, thaiboxing, wushu, boxing and wrestling). In total, 14 teachers and 12 assistant-teachers were involved. All of them were males. Except for boxing, all other teachers were active in regular clubs. Teachers were randomly selected from clubs that work with youth. The boxing teachers take part in a project which aims at the social integration of underprivileged youth. The assistant-teachers in this project were mainly older youth who originally came from the target group themselves.

The majority of the teachers from this study have a long experience in martial arts (between 25 and 50 years!). Consequently, most of them became involved in martial arts at a young age (one teacher was even only 5 years old when he started). The teachers from the boxing project were considerably younger (mean age 25.5 yrs.). Only the project leader had 19 years of boxing experience. Here too, a qualitative research methodology, with semi-structured interview, was used. Trainers were asked about their own experiences, motives and views on martial arts practice for children.

Results

Almost all teachers from this study have positive experiences with regard to the time they were students themselves. However, there is a distinct difference among the interviewees in the way they look back at their own teacher. Some were very positive, while others made critical remarks with regard to the pedagogical approach their own teachers used. Despite this difference in opinion, most teachers indicated that, compared to their own teachers, they use a less traditional approach.

Respondents clearly referred to pedagogically oriented goals they want to achieve in working with children. Among other things, these goals included increased responsibility, self-worth, discipline, assertivity, learning to deal with one another, showing respect, getting used to physical contact, knowing how to abreact, enjoyment and recreation. Most teachers indicated that they try to achieve these goals through regular communication with the children themselves. Through this way, they feel they can evaluate to what extent they reach their goals. It is also interesting to note that several teachers indicated that they feel they have to (partially) take over the educating role of parents and school teachers.

For most teachers the effects of practice are not a result of the type of martial art, but are primarily caused by the kind of approach that is used. Often they indicated that especially the government especially should closely monitor that martial arts practice is well guided.

All teachers indicated to have changed their approach with children through the years. The emphasis has moved from teaching and correcting techniques to striving for more pedagogical goals. According to the teachers this is the result of a changed situation in which they feel they have to deal with children that have changed themselves, and with parents who raise their children with a lack of discipline.

Teachers were also asked if they see a difference between martial arts and other sports. A number of them indicated they saw a difference with regard to Asian martial arts as they show a clear connection with Asian culture. They further stated that martial arts are based on specific philosophical traditions, which make it easier to also use these sports as a means of education. According to them, this is not the case with most other (Western) martial arts.

Also, a number of teachers indicated that children often do not know what to expect when they first come to a martial arts school. This means that they do not choose explicitly for a martial art. In many cases children come with a friend or are sent by their parents.

The majority of the teachers said that children do not come to learn how to fight, but regard this more as a recreational activity. Furthermore, most of them indicated that they do not consider it important that children learn to defend themselves. According to them, self-defense does not make sense as children will almost always lose when they are confronted with adults. However as some teachers underlined, children are often sent by their parents explicitly for that reason.

There is no consensus among the teachers that were interviewed with regard to participation of children in competition. Not all teachers are in favour of competition for children, although this sometimes depends on the kind of competition (routines or combat). There is also a difference in the way teachers deal with the misuse of the techniques outside the club. Some teachers are in favour of a hard approach where they use punishment or even expel children. Others on the other hand, like to use a more communicative (prevention) approach.

17.7 Discussion and Conclusions

As the 'double character of sport' has been used as the conceptual framework of the 'Values and Norms in Sport' research program (see chapter 2 of this book), the findings of this study will also be situated within this concept.

Firstly, the matter of specific 'character' of the martial arts will be considered. In fact this involves the extent to which martial arts can be distinguished from ordinary fighting. One might say that martial arts can be differentiated from fighting by the fact they are subjected to a number of rules ('obstacles'). The fewer rules that exist in a martial art, the lesser it can be regarded as a sport, and the more it resembles ordinary fighting. This means that the character of martial arts is also related to the extent that there are rules with regard to the way techniques are allowed to be used. It will, however, be difficult to make a clear distinction between a martial art and fighting solely based on the number of forbidden techniques that exist.

The character of martial arts also depends on a number of other characteristics. For example, there is a 'moral code of behaviour' that martial artists seem to follow. The most important aspects of this code are the respect for the own style, teacher and opponent (Theeboom & Van Stiphout, 1993). The existence of such a code is probably the reason why it is often believed that martial arts have a socializing effect. Based on the data from the present study, it appears that most children that were interviewed follow a similar code which will, according to them, lead them how to respond in a non-violent way to conflicts. It is also interesting to refer here to the fact that most children in this study seem to be reluctant to talk about their martial arts practice to outsiders. Perhaps this might be explained by the fact that they feel more linked to a 'tradition of modesty', which exists within Asian martial arts, or because they rather want to avoid being 'tested' by others on their fighting skills. Another possible explanation might be that they simply try to prevent their being described as being 'aggressive'.

Although at first sight it appears that the character of martial arts can easily be determined, one cannot conclude that martial arts practice can be described in a unambiguous way, as it is characterized by three different approaches. Therefore, one should always take into account the kind of approach that is used when the character of martial arts is defined.

Secondly, next to an essentialistic definition (with an emphasis on the character of sport), the double character of sport is also described by a operationalistic definition, where martial arts are considered as a means of reaching extrinsic goals. This instrumental aspect is regarded by many as the most important argument in the legitimation of martial arts practice. This aspect is even considered to be more important than the actual participation and the processes that are linked to it. Here, emphasis is primarily put on the moral educational value of martial arts. Findings of this study seem to support the fact that participants experience this value. However, one should not forget that this data was collected through self-report. Also, it is difficult to determine the effects objectively as various factors will play a role. Whether it should be concluded therefore that the instrumental function of martial arts is an exaggeration, is probably not correct as well. Based on the literature and the findings of the present study, underprivileged youth are often attracted to martial arts. This fact alone will enable teachers in general to work successfully and regularly with this group. Possibly, it is in this context that one might find a clear instrumental function of the martial arts.

The martial arts are also often under discussion in a general social context. This refers to the problematic relationship that exists between the character of some rules and actions that are typical for the martial arts and general norms and values in society at large. This is a result of the fact that the activity here (i.e. fighting) can also be looked at outside the sport context. Furthermore, as indicated by Parry (1998), the discussion on the social acceptability of (some) martial arts is not situated on a medical level, but on a moral one. Moreover one can ask to what extent this discussion has to be aimed at the martial arts themselves or should it be focused on a number of norms and values in a Western society, as they appear to have a distinct influence on the way martial arts are practised? However, it is probably more important to consider the acceptability of martial arts in view of the approach of practice that is used. Therefore, one should always take into account the principles and goals that are set in martial arts practice. From such a perspective the practice of a sport, where its major aim is to increase the efficiency of fighting skills that can (primarily) be used outside a sport context (e.g. as a means of self-defense), is highly questionable. In their definition of sport, Steenbergen & Tamboer (1998) did not consider a similar physical activity as being part of the hard core of the 'sports family'.

Consequently, this approach is less to be recommended when used with children. Besides, in an efficiency approach, the typical cultural, spiritual and artistic characteristics of Asian martial arts are largely neglected. Both in the literature and in this study these typical characteristics are highly valued. Therefore, it is reasonable to be in favour of a traditional approach to martial arts practice. However, it became clear that it is necessary to make some changes in this approach within a Western context because of cultural differences. These changes will be mostly situated on a pedagogical level (e.g. Theeboom, De Knop, & Weiss, 1995). Finally, a sporting approach can probably also be acceptable if restrictions with regard to the rules and organization of combat competitions are included.

17.8 Recommendations

A number of recommendations can be formulated with regard to a government policy towards martial arts practice for children. These recommendations are based on the assumption that the prohibition, or no official recognition, for some harder martial arts will not necessarily lead to the disappearance of these disciplines. It is therefore probably better to consider a more positive approach of recognition, in which the martial arts world itself also has a say. The involvement of martial artists themselves in this discussion is very important. Too often however, their experiences and views are not heard, but only interpreted and judged from a general perspective by outsiders. To date only a limited number of authors have stressed the importance to also consider the views and experiences of martial artists themselves (e.g. Burke, 1998; Wacquant, 1992). It is clear that this will add a very different dimension to the discussion of the social acceptability of some martial arts and, consequently, to the role of the government. For example, an involvement of the martial arts community might be organized through a kind of self-regulation, but under government control. Recognizing martial arts will, however, always be linked to a number of conditions. Next is a description of some of these conditions.

17.8.1 Expertise of Teachers

Because of the importance of guidance, attention needs to be paid to the training of teachers. Although a certain specificity for each discipline is required, the training will be situated on a general level as it primarily has to be focused on a pedagogically sound approach. This means that it is to be recommended that courses for martial arts teachers have a general character that exceeds the specificity of individual disciplines. It is important that a certain protection for participants can be provided with regard to the expertise of the teachers. This protection does not only relate to the sport-pedagogical level and the general basic knowledge on training and coaching aspects, as this is a requirement for most sports. However, because of the unfamiliarity of some specific disciplines among the general public, it is also necessary to look after the real sport-technical level of the teachers. One has to avoid the misuse of trust of the participants by some 'pseudo' or 'self-made' teachers. It is only logical that this kind of control of the sport-technical expertise will be organized in consultation with the martial arts associations themselves.

17.8.2 Approaches of Martial Arts Practice

It is important to always take into account the kind of approach to martial arts practice. The efficiency approach of martial arts participation can be regarded as the least suitable for young martial artists. In this context one can refer to the organization of martial arts for youngsters with the sole purpose of improving their self-defense skills. Because of its onesidedness such an approach needs to be avoided. Moreover, a mere technical initiation appears not to be really effective for children. It is necessary always to consider other aspects as well (such as the improvement of assertiveness, conflict resolution). It is particularly recommended that Western children strive for a combination of a traditional and a sporting approach.

17.8.3 Organization and Regulation of Martial Arts Competitions

Because of the reservations among a number of teachers with regard to combat competitions, it is necessary that the organization and regulation of this kind of competition for children is medically and pedagogically sound. Because of the specificity of each individual discipline, it is difficult to formulate a number of specific organizational guidelines. Based on the reactions of the teachers, a number of general recommendations with regard to combat competitions for children can be formulated:
- children must never be obliged to take part;
- there needs to be minimum requirements with regard to the technical level before one can enter a competition;
- full-contact competitions need to be avoided;
- specific protective equipment for children is required;
- a strict application of the rules is needed;
- there needs to be enough guarantees that participants have an equal technical level;
- punching and kicking to the head are preferably forbidden;
- each child must be guided during competitions;
- before being allowed to take part, children should be able to understand what competition participation really means.

References

Back, A. & Kim, D. (1984). The future course of the Eastern martial arts. *Quest*, 36, pp.7-14.

Bottenburg, M. van (1994). *Hidden competition: About the different popularity of sports*. Amsterdam: Bert Bakker. (in Dutch).

Bottenburg, M. van & Heilbron, J. (1996). *The hardening of competitive fighting*. Amsterdam: Diopter. (in Dutch).

Burke, M. (1998). Is boxing violent? Let's ask some boxers. D. Hemphill (Ed.), *All part of the game. Violence and Australian sport* (pp. 111-132). Melbourne: Walla Walla Press.

Clearing House. (1997). Sports participation in Europe. *Sport Information Bulletin*, 10 (44), pp. 5-56.

Columbus, P.J. & Rice, D. (1998). Phenomenological meanings of martial arts participation. *Journal of Sport Behavior*, 21, pp. 16-28.

Draeger, D. F. & Smith, R.W. (1975). *Asian Martial Arts*. Den Haag: Bert Bakker. (in Dutch).

Förster, A. (1986). The nature of martial arts and their change in the West. S. Kleinman (Ed.), *Mind and body. East meets West* (pp. 83-88). Champaign, ILL.: Human Kinetics.

Fuller, J.R. (1988). Martial arts and psychological health. *British Journal of Medical Psychology*, 61, pp. 317-328.

Guttmann, A. (1991). Sports Diffusion. A Response to Maguire and the Americanization Commentaries. *Sociology of Sport Journal*, 8, pp. 185-190.

Harman, W.W. (1986). The changing image of man/woman: signs of a second Copernican revolution. S. Kleinman (Ed.), *Mind and body: East meets West* (pp. 3-6). Champaign, ILL.: Human Kinetics.

Kleinman, S. (Ed./1986). *Mind and body: East meets West.*, Champaign, ILL.: Human Kinetics.

Knop, P. De, Engström, L. M., Skirstad, B., & Weiss, M. R. (Eds.) (1996). *Worldwide trends in youth sport*. Champaign, ILL.: Human Kinetics.

Li, T., & Du, X. (1991). *A guide to Chinese martial arts*. Beijing, People's Republic of China: Foreign Languages Press.

Maliszewski, M. (1992). Meditative-religious traditions of fighting arts and martial ways. *Journal of Asian Martial Arts*, 1 (3), pp. 1-104.

Mitchell, D. (1992). *The young martial artist*. London: Pelham Books.

Moegling, K. (1986). Tai Chi Chuan. Ruhe in der Bewegung. *Sportpädagogik*, 10 (1), pp. 37-42.

Parry, S. J. (1998). Violence and aggression in contemporary sport. In: M.J. McNamee & S.J. Parry (Eds.), *Ethics and Sport* (pp. 205-224). London: E&FN Spon.

Sagot, J.J. (1992). Le T'ai Chi Ch'uan. *Education Physique et Sport*, (234), pp. 19-23.

Steenbergen, J. & Tamboer, J.W.I. (1998). The double character of sport: conceptual dynamics. In: J. Steenbergen, A.J. Buisman, P. De Knop, & J.M.H. Lucassen (Eds.), *Waarden en normen in de sport* (pp. 69-95). Houten/Diegem: Bohn Stafleu Van Loghum. (in Dutch).

Theeboom, M. & Knop, P. De (1997). An analysis of the development of Wushu. *International Review for the Sociology of Sport*, 32, pp. 267-282.

Theeboom, M., Knop, P. De & Weiss, M.R. (1995). Motivational climate, psychological responses, and motor skill development in children's sport: a field-based intervention study. *Journal of Sport and Exercise Psychology*, 17, pp. 294-311.

Theeboom, M., Knop, P. De & Wylleman, P. (1995). Traditional Asian martial arts and the West. *Journal of Comparative Physical Education and Sport*, 17, pp. 57-69.

Theeboom, M. & Stiphout, E. van (1993). The Eastern Martial Arts: Can you still follow?. *Tijdschrift voor Lichamelijke Opvoeding*, (3), pp. 7-11. (in Dutch).

Wacquant, L. (1992). The social logic of boxing in Black Chicago: Toward a sociology of pugilism. *Sociology of Sport Journal*, 9, pp. 221-254.

Xu, C. (1991). Discovering the secrets of martial arts. *China Today*, 9, pp. 8-11.

18 IN CONCLUSION

Paul De Knop, Paul Verweel & Anton Anthonissen

Introduction

In this final chapter the necessity of research for policy will be highlighted as well as the need for policy in research. The necessity of research lies in a number of sport-specific and social developments which are producing an increasing diversity of sports participants, sports and sports organisations, and which make the legitimacy of sport more fragmented (Coakley, 1998; Crum, 1991; Doherty & Chelladurai, 1999). Sports managers and policy-makers have a need, on the one hand, for organisational concepts for sports and, on the other, they require empirical research which is necessary in order to support policy.

Besides the fragmentation of sports there is also an increasing fragmentation in the development of scientific understanding. Research in the Netherlands and Flanders takes place on the basis of different paradigms: interpretative or functional. The value of differing scientific perspectives is to be found in the supplementary perspectives which they allow to be developed.

The seven-year research program "Values and Norms in Sport" deals with all these aspects, leading to a wealth of results. In this chapter we will look back again at this program. The results will be evaluated and some recommendations for further research and policy will be made.

18.1 Need for research in sports policy

Everyone knows that policy must be knowledge-driven. Whether one is determining the nature or severity of a policy problem, selecting a policy approach, implementing a policy or evaluating the effectiveness of an existing policy, one always needs reliable information to be able to increase the rationality and legitimacy (and by doing so the quality) of the policy actions (e.g. Hoogerwerf & Herwijer, 1998). The information is far from always available in sufficient quantity. This is also the case in the sport sector. Sports policy is therefore a non-starter without research. Sportspolicy without research can be compared with trying to navigate a ship without a compass.

However, as this book shows, the value of research goes beyond merely collecting information. It has to do with developing and testing new concepts which endow empirical observations with significance. It is only in connection with concepts and empirical observations that information for sports participants, managers and policy-makers is significant. In this context, Weick (1995) remarks: "Sense-making is connecting a frame with a cue". Conceptualising the values and norms of sports culture, social participation, working on the basis of demand and the (double) character of sport, are important frames which play a role in the present work.

Due to a number of recent developments (the necessarity of demand driven services, lack of fair play, failures to accept differences etc.), the need for an adequate supply of information and conceptualisation, knowledge accumulation, has actually increased. This increase has occurred in almost all policy sectors, but especially in rapidly growing areas and those that are gaining in social importance, such as the sports sector. First, social change is taking place more rapidly than formerly, which means that knowledge of the effects of social developments on sport becomes outdated more quickly. Second, the heterogeneity of society is increasing. Sports policy must therefore make allowance for the great variety of wishes and needs of individuals and groups. Customised work is becoming more important, and that makes greater demands on the information supply. Third, society is becoming more and more complex. Developments in society and developments in sport are increasingly interrelated, are bound more firmly together and are also assuming an increasingly international character (e.g. Ester, Geurt & Vermeulen, 1997). All this means an increasing need for research in the area of sports policy.

18.2 The need for policy in the area of sports policy research

The current need for research in sports policy is multifaceted and can be delineated in different ways:

- The different types of research must also be carried out in such a way as to meet different end-uses. There is a need for policy-directed research that has the aim of supporting the development of sports policy. There is also a need for practice-oriented research that is directly usable by and serviceable for field organisations and market parties in the sports sector. In addition there is a need for science-oriented research, which is more reflective in nature and which focuses on generalisation and theorising (Bos, 1993; Knoppers, 2000).
- Which type of research and end-use the policy requires depends very heavily on the various policy phases (Bressers & Hoogerwerf, 1995; Hoogerwerf & Herweijer, 1998). Monitoring and exploratory studies, for example, are primarily required for the identification of policy problems; case studies, comparative and experimental research are needed for policy preparation; action research is required for implementation; and an evaluation study is needed to assess the policy being pursued (e.g. Gorter, 1991; Kemper, 1991).
- The specific need for research in sports policy arises in respect of a large number of policy themes, such as sport-intrinsic and sport-extrinsic subjects (for example fair play and integration and multi-culturalism), developments in the field of recreational and top-level sport, the internal culture of sports organisations, the knowledge and skills of sports managers, and questions relating to the quality of the sports infrastructure and participation in sport (e.g. Anthonissen & Boessenkool, 1998; Van Bottenburg & Geesink, 2000).

A policy is also required to assemble all this information into a harmonious whole. In other words, we are not making a plea here in any way for 'research into research', but –much more– for a reciprocal process in which research stands at the service of sports policy and for a sports policy in which research has obtained a prominent place.

18.3 The need for research into values and norms in sport

Organised sport in the Netherlands and Belgium (and many other Western European countries) has taken the form of a broad, popular movement that is promoted as a powerful, valuable driving force in society. Sport has become the biggest voluntary organisation in these countries and therefore is increasingly regarded as the 'new binding agent for society' (Kearney, 1992; Van Bottenburg & Schuyt 1996). This argumentation gives rise to high expectations without it actually being clear what is concerned by 'new binding' and in which ways sport differentiates or even segregates between individuals and groups. It is recognised that, in order to be able to play this important role in society, sport had to meet certain norms. This feeling has become even more explicit because of some dark clouds that can be glimpsed at the sports horizon. An increasing number of signals hint that sport may be heading towards the beginning of a values crisis.

This is especially true of international elite sport. Doping is the most obvious symptom of the values crisis, but the struggle for money, power and fame also leads to increased cheating, violence, more serious sports injuries and corruption. It is also true at local level, however. As a result of the emphasis on sport as 'the new binding agent', the government is putting an ever-increasing amount of money into recreational and elite sport. This also means that sport is increasingly being called to account for its results –in both the qualitative and quantitative sense–, something which has long been the case in other sectors of society: 'value for money'. However, this gives rise to a kind of *radical instrumentalism* (Suits, 1989): sport is only legitimated if sports is functional and has its worth for society.

Sport is also confronted by increasing differences in the standards applied. The way funds are distributed across the different sectors of sport means that various different systems of values are struggling for primacy, increasingly leading to developing their own dynamism, thus causing conflicts of interest within the sports sector (for example between elite- and recreational sports).

These types of value problems are threatening the reputation and the credibility of sport. If they are allowed to develop and take root in (organised) sport, they could cause sport to lose its foundation as a potentially unifying, valuable popular movement in society.

Parents, public authorities, sponsors and the media will then be able to take a sceptical and negative view of sport. The recruitment of young sports participants and voluntary managers will decrease. The recruitment of volunteers, and thus the volunteer culture, will be affected, meaning that it will not be possible to effectively meet the changing demands expressed by sports participants (and potential participants).

Sport participation will get involved in a vicious circle. Consequently, the sports movement, sports policy and sports research must meet society's requirements in terms of value legitimisation. The 'Values and Norms in Sport' (WNS) program described in this book has tried to meet (some of) these needs.

18.4 The 'Values and Norms in Sport' research program

The WNS program has attempted to:

I   provide a conceptual clarification of different values and norms in sport and in sports organisations (e.g. by making a conceptual distinction between more 'intrinsically' related values, like fair play, and more 'extrinsically' related or instrumental values, like social integration, and by revealing the increased legitimization of sports by (often poorly defined) umbrella terms like health, socialisation and social integration along with empirical validation).

II   study the question of which are the values and norms are ascribed to and predominate in sport and sports organisations?

     a) Sport displays a certain resistance to concerning itself with social issues, man-women images, ethnicities, homosexuality/heterosexuality, young-old images etc. Organized and media sport especially in the Netherlands and in Flanders have a strong focus on an internally-oriented pyramidal framework, one which is male and heterosexual and focuses on top performance and adults.

     b) Sport gives clear significance to cohesion: organising identification is only understood from an integration perspective, although integration can also be brought about through the perspective of differentiation and fragmentation.

c) These predominant values and norms are reinforced by new dominant relationships caused by developments in the sports sector such as commercialisation, advent of professionals, policy circuit of authorities and value for (subsidised) money.

III describe how conflicting values and norms can be made visible in the practice of sport and sport organisations (e.g. within youth sport, the Olympic spirit, the sports media and supporting & sport organisations).

IV provide recommendations on how these values and norms can be influenced by policy:

a) Focus on values and norms

b) Give differences a place in sports policy

c) Organise differences in value orientations

d) Conceptualise changes in context and behaviour of sports participants

e) See threats as opportunities (as is happening in other sectors of society).

Several policy or promotional campaigns regarding values and norms in sport can be listed. Although it is impossible within the context of this final chapter to provide an all-embracing overview, we have made an analysis of program launched in Europe during the past 10 years as described in the Sports Information Bulletin (Council of Europe, 1994, 1995a/b, 1998, 1999a/b).

In Norway, for example, a campaign called 'Basic Values in Sport' was launched in February 1993 with a high priority for the period 1993 to 1998. The main aim for the Norwegian Confederation of Sports was to ensure that sport survived as a positive creator of values for individuals and for society (NIF, 1993). The campaign aimed to define a common set of values for sport in Norway and to stimulate the realization of these values in practical sporting behavior. This was necessary to try to counteract negative trends, such as drug abuse, increasing commercialization and violence in sport.

In June 1996 Sweden followed with a similar campaign on ethics in sport. Under the slogan 'Starting the wave', different projects aimed at some ethical problem areas – such as fair play and the fight against doping, sport for all and the meaningless violence in our society – were created.

Regarding the subject of violence in sport the United Kingdom and Spain have developed a large number of special laws and regulations in an attempt to control this phenomenon and in order to ensure the safety of spectators and players. In 1995 France founded the 'French Association for Sports without Violence and for Fair Play'. The two most important aims of this organization were:

-   To protect sport, both in practice and in its approach to the environment, against all forms of violence and cheating which may discredit it.
-   To defend sports ethics and promote the sporting spirit and the essential display of it, namely fair play.

Sport can also offer a common language and a platform for social democracy; which may lead to conditions for political democracy and for the development of democratic citizenship, with full cultural comprehension and a fight against prejudices. Sport may in this way contribute to limiting the social exclusion of minority groups, traditionally marginalized groups or groups with special needs. Over the past decade concrete projects with sport as a means of helping to improve social cohesion and integration have therefore been started in the member countries of the Council of Europe. These include the projects 'Sport against racism'(Finland), 'Sport on Wheels'(Denmark) and 'Re-socialization of prisoners through sport'(Czech Republic).

A similar project on values and norms in sport that is research-based, that comprises multi-objective target groups and topics and has a strategic plan for implementation, was not found in the literature. Another major difference is that in our research program sport is not only perceived as a means: the intrinsic values of sport are also considered and researched. In other words the values and norms in sport projects described in the previous chapters can be considered as being unique in this sense.

18.5 The level of the research

There is a need for different types of research, ranging from conceptual research, monitoring, strategic research, case studies, comparative and experimental research to intervention and evaluation research. The Values & Norms study was aimed at all these different levels of research. Critical research – both conceptual and empirical - has, however, had priority. The line of argumentation and results of social critical research provide the jumping-off point for examining a social question or policy problem in a different way, so as to then start thinking about it in different terms or in order to select a differently formulated solution strategy. In sports policy research, data is regularly used in an instrumental and legitimising fashion. Critical, conceptual and empirical research is not so common in this field. From this point of view the Values & Norms project has therefore been innovative and, in a conceptual sense, very influential as well.

In addition, the fact that for seven consecutive years fundamental social scientific sports research has been done with a diversity of themes in a broad umbrella framework (values and norms in sports) by different universities with different approaches is unique. The problems tackled by the various constituent research projects were primarily determined on the basis of scientific insights and not by the policy question. In the history of sports science research in the Netherlands (and, to a lesser extent, in Flanders as well) this is almost a unique situation. It should be noted, however, that there is a need for more fundamental and more longitudinal research in the area of values and norms in sport. A more fundamentally embedded research program based on values and norms in sport is therefore recommended.

18.6 Are the results of the WNS program valuable for sports practice/sports policy?

Several hints have been provided for sports practice as well as numerous recommendations for sports policy on how the values and norms in sport can be influenced. What needs to be done now is to draw up a long-term strategic plan to work on the values and norms in sport with the following overall aim: strengthen the position of sport as a plural popular movement and driving force in society and stimulate critical reflection on the meaning of specific values for the individual and for society. In this respect it is important to understand that change is not pre-destined by fate, futurists, computer forecasts or supernatural forces. It is created by the collective actions of human beings (cf Coakley, 1990). This means that the future of sport (and values and norms) will not just happen according to some predicted patterns. Instead it will be shaped by people making choices about what they want sport to be in the future. Those choices will be limited by existing social conditions and guided by people's perceptions and evaluations of what sport is today. Thus values and norms in sport, as they were identified, clarified and researched in this book, should be subjected to a real public debate, i.e. the whole sports movement should be stimulated to discuss the various issues related to the value benefits and the value problems of sport. Although this phase was more comprehensive, an in-depth debate should now take place which has already been started by means of several actions (see table 1).

The sports movement needs a framework for discussion because:
- There is a general, growing interest in, and awareness of, value issues in society, and therefore a more systematic way of thinking is available.
- Diversity in sport requires a more demand-driven approach to organising because the processes of multi-culturalism and individualism are leading to a further differentation of services.
- Sport, as the biggest voluntary movement, constitutes social-cultural capital of most Western European countries and this form of capital needs attention in times of economic growth.

- Continual reflection on existing dominant and marginal values is essential if sport wants to be able to maintain the large number of sports practitioners and sports volunteers. Stimulation of positive values is essential if sport still wants to be assured of funding from the public authorities, the business world and the customers themselves.
- Value fragmentation, and increasing value conflicts ask for clarification and reflection.
- Attention needs to be paid to non-dominant values in order to prevent some groups being socially disadvantaged.

Accordingly, an in–depth observation, discussion and theory are needed in order to understand the values of sport.

Table 1: The public debate on values and norms in sport stimulated by the WNS program

1. The publication of a (Dutch) book (Steenbergen, Buisman, De Knop & Lucassen, 1998)
2. Seminars in which researchers, policy makers and practioners discussed results in the light of policy recommendations and their practical use.
3. Several research reports on the project have been published and are available to sports organizations
4. A national symposium for sports federations
5. Several articles about and interviews of researchers in sports journals and newspapers.
6. Consultancy by researchers for several sports policy programs and organisations, including:
• Jeugd in Beweging (Youth on the Move)
• Sport, Tolerantie en Fair Play (Sport, Tolerance and Fair Play)
• Beleid ter Voorkoming van Seksuele Intimidatie (Policy for the prevention of sexual intimidation)
• Vrijwilligersbeleid in de Sportvereniging (Policy related to volunteers in the sports club)
• Kwaliteit in de sport (Quality in sport)
• Ontwikkeling van een beleidskader 'Respect en fair play' (development of a policy-framework regarding 'values, norms and fair play in sport')

Furthermore, we would like to provide some general recommendations (for more specific recommendations we refer to the chapters themselves):

1. Recommendations for sports administrators:
- Sports administrators should ensure that values and norms are not neglected in sports programs.
- Sports administrators should ensure that comprehensive training programs, including a reflection on values and norms, are provided for all those who work directly with athletes on a regular and intensive basis.
- Sports administrators should ensure that social issues are represented in their methods of organising.

2. Recommendations for coaches:
- Coaches should carefully reflect on their own coaching philosophy and objectives. Like Martens (1988) we recommend a simple philosophy grounded in the slogan 'Athletes first, winning second' (ibid., p. 299). The coach must be mindful that the rights of children must be respected (e.g. De Knop, De Martelaer, Theeboom & Van Heddegem, 1999).
- Coaches should encourage sports participants to reflect on the values and norms in sport.
- Coaches should expect players to treat opponents and officials with respect.
- Coaches need to provide information to athletes about their rights.

3. Recommendations for policy makers:
- For example: take greater account of the variety of demands expressed by individuals and different social groups, pay more attention to social issues and collaboration.
- Invest in both supporting functionalistic and social critical research.

18.7 New questions/challenges for practice and theory

Coming to the end of the book it is fruitful to look into the future and to explicate new questions and challenges as well for practice as for theory:

-   Changing environmental factors (multi-culturalism, individualisation, globalisation, technological developments etc.) pose new challenges and demand new changes in the form and content of sport-specific values. Conversely, it will be interesting to see to what extent the contribution to social cohesion envisaged as coming from sport-intrinsic values can actually be given shape.
-   How can social issues be given more explicit attention in the way the Dutch and Flemish sports sector is organised, not only in policy, recruitment and selection, but also in behaviour (for example, the emphasis on technosport does not necessarily lead to the destruction of spontaneity and expression – cf Coakley, 1998).
-   Another important point is how managers will be able to deal with internal and external differentiation in meanings in and around sport. How does a recreational sport country such as the Netherlands deal with the increasingly separate and independent nature of the content and function of elite sport in relation to recreational sport, and the increasing popularity of new types of sport and organisational possibilities?
-   An increasing effort to certify youth coaches as experts to satisfy parents' demands for more professional approaches to youth sport, and to minimise legal liability (e.g De Knop, 1998).
-   An important question is whether the organisation of science and the progress of (social critical) conceptual and empirical research will succeed in keeping up with these developments. The increasing fragmentation of research requires greater attention and co-ordination to continue to give form and content to mutual research programs.

In other words the debate on values and norms in sport does not end with this book. Much work has yet to be done theoretically, empirically, and educationally on this vital topic of values and norms in sport, in the present as well as in the future. We invite all researchers, policy makers, educators, managers, officials, parents and others who are participating in the sports world to join us in that rewarding task so that sport can embody its fullest capacity for pleasure, solidarity, health, compassion, fairness, sports personship and integrity.

References

Anthonissen, A & Boessenkool, J. (1998). *Meanings of Management: Diversity of Managerial Performances in Amateur Sport Organizations*. Utrecht: ISOR. (in Dutch).

Bos, B. (1993). *Public institutions between goal and market*. Zoetermeer: Economisch Instituut voor het midden- en kleinbedrijf. (in Dutch).

Bottenburg, M. van & Geesink, J. (2000). *Programming research in sport*. 's-Hertogenbosch: Diopter. (in Dutch).

Bottenburg, M. van & Schuyt, K. (1996). *The Social Meaning of Sport*. Arnhem: NOC*NSF. (in Dutch).

Bressers, J. & Hoogerwerf, A. (1995). *Policy evaluation*. Alphen a/d Rijn: Samson. (in Dutch).

Coakley, J. (1998). *Sport in Society: issues and controversies*. Boston: Mc Graw-Hill.

Council of Europe (1994). A Norwegian strategy for research and documentation in the field of doping. *Sports Information Bulletin*, 36, pp. 61/62.

Council of Europe (1995a). 'Starting the wave', a national campaign on ethics in sport in Sweden. *Sports Information Bulletin*, 43, p. 115.

Council of Europe (1995b). New 'Sport and Foreigners' scheme in the Netherlands. *Sports Information Bulletin*, 43, p. 123.

Council of Europe (1998). *A study of laws affecting sport in countries having acceded to the European Cultural Convention*. Nicosia: Council of Europe.

Council of Europe (1999a). *Social Cohesion and Sport*. Brussels: Council of
    Europe.

Council of Europe (1999b). The French Association for Sports without Violence
    and for Fair Play. *Sports Information Bulletin*, 54, p. 105.

Crum, B. (1991). *The sportification of Society*. Rijswijk: Ministerie van WVC.
    (in Dutch).

Doherty, A. & Chelladurai, P. (1999). Managing Cultural Diversity in Sport
    Organizations. A theoretical perspective. *Journal of Sport Management*,
    13, pp. 280-297.

Ester, P., Geurt, J. & Vermeulen, M. (1997). *The makers of future. Usefulness
    and necessity of forecasting for policy research*. Tilburg: TUP. (in Dutch).

Gorter, K.A. (1991). *The role of research for research policy*. The Hague:
    NIMAWO. (in Dutch).

Hoogerwerf, A. & Herweijer, N. (1998). *Public policy. An introduction to policy
    sciences*. Alphen a/d Rijn: Samson. (in Dutch).

Kemper, A.B.A. (1991). Policy researched? *Spel en Sport*, 2, pp. 2-7. (in Dutch).

Knop, P. De (1998). *Youth sports policy, quo vadis? The need for quality
    assurance*. Zeist: Jan Luiting Fonds. (in Dutch).

Knop, P. De, Martelaer, K. De, Theeboom, M. & Heddegem, L. van (1999). The
    rights of children in sport: the best interest of children in sport and the
    actual situation in Flanders. In: J. Zermatten (Ed.), *A champion against
    all: The rights of children in sport* (pp. 65-84). Sion: IDE.

Knoppers, A. (Ed./2000). *The Construction of Meaning in Sport Organisations*.
    Maastricht: Shaker.

Martens, R. (1988). Helping children become independent, responsible adults
    through sports. In: E.W. Brown & C.F. Branta (Eds.), *Competitive sports
    for children and youth: An overview of research and issues* (pp. 297-307).
    Champaign, Illinois: Human Kinetics.

NIF (1993). *Sport for a better society*. Oslo: Author.

Kearny, A.T. (1992). *Sport as a source of inspiration for our society.* Arnhem: NOC*NSF. (in Dutch).

Steenbergen, J., Buisman, A.J, Knop, P. De & Lucassen, J.M.H. (1998). *Values and Norms in Sport.* Houten/Diegem: Bohn Stafleu Van Loghum. (in Dutch).

Suits, B. (1989). The trick of the disappearing goal. *Journal of the Philosophy of Sport*, XVI, pp. 1-12.

Weick, K. (1995). *Sensemaking in Organizations.* London: Sage publications.

Index

Sport & Society

Volume 1
an Tomlinson/
cott Fleming (eds.)
**thics, Sport and
eisure**
rises and Critiques

d edition, 282 pages
perback, 14.8 x 21 cm
BN 1-84126-060-6
14.95 UK/$ 24.00 US/
34.95 CDN

Volume 2
Graham McFee/
Alan Tomlinson (eds.)
**Education, Sport and
Leisure**
Connections and Controversies

2nd edition, 222 pages
Paperback, 14.8 x 21 cm
ISBN 1-84126-061-4
£ 12.95 UK/$ 17.95 US/
$ 25.95 CDN

Volume 3
Alan Tomlinson (ed.)
**Gender, Sport and
Leisure**
Continuities and Challenges

2nd edition
264 pages
Paperback, 14.8 x 21 cm
ISBN 1-84126-062-2
£ 14.95 UK/$ 24.00 US/
$ 34.95 CDN

Volume 4
John Sugden/
Alain Bairner (eds.)
**Sport in Divided
Societies**

2nd edition
236 pages, 8 figures
Paperback, 14.8 x 21 cm
ISBN 1-84126-043-6
£ 12.95 UK/$ 17.95 US/
$ 25.95 CDN

lume 5
urice Roche (ed.)
**ort, Popular Culture
d Identity**

d edition
6 pages
igures
perback, 14.8 x 21 cm
N 1-84126-044-4
2.95 UK/$ 17.95 US/
25.95 CDN

Volume 6
Lincoln Allison (ed.)
Taking Sport Seriously

2nd edition
204 pages
Paperback, 14.8 x 21 cm
ISBN 1-84126-045-2
£ 14.95 UK/$ 17.95 US/
$ 25.95 CDN

Volume 7
Graham McFee (ed.)
**Dance, Education and
Philosophy**

198 pages
2 figures
Paperback, 14.8 x 21 cm
ISBN 1-84126-008-8
£ 12.95 UK/$ 17.95 US/
$ 25.95 CDN

Volume 9
Marc Keech/
Graham McFee (eds.)
**Issues and Values in
Sport and Leisure
Cultures**

286 pages
Paperback, 14.8 x 21 cm
ISBN 1-84126-055-X
£ 14.95 UK/$ 24.00 US/
$ 34.95 CDN

**MEYER
& MEYER
SPORT**

YER & MEYER Verlag | Von-Coels-Straße 390 | D-52080 Aachen, Germany | Fax ++49 (0)241-9 58 10 10